The Yoga Sutras of Patanjali

The Yoga Sutras of Patanjali

SWAMI VENKATESANANDA

Swami Venkatesananda with his guru
Swami Sivananda Maharaj

MOTILAL BANARSIDASS PUBLISHERS
PRIVATE LIMITED • DELHI

Third Revised Edition: Delhi, ***2008***
First Published in 1988 by The Divine Life Society,
Shivanandanagar, Uttarakhand (India);
Second Revised edition in 2001, Reprinted in 2005

ISBN : 978-81-208-3351-7

MOTILAL BANARSIDASS
41 U.A. Bungalow Road, Jawahar Nagar, Delhi 110 007
8 Mahalaxmi Chamber, 22 Bhulabhai Desai Road, Mumbai 400 026
203 Royapettah High Road, Mylapore, Chennai 600 004
236, 9th Main III Block, Jayanagar, Bangalore 560 011
Sanas Plaza, 1302 Baji Rao Road, Pune 411 002
8 Camac Street, Kolkata 700 017
Ashok Rajpath, Patna 800 004
Chowk, Varanasi 221 001

Cover Photo by Richard Woldendorp/Photo Index

PRINTED IN INDIA

By Jainendra Prakash Jain at Shri Jainendra Press,
A-45, Naraina, Phase-I, New Delhi 110 028
and Published by Narendra Prakash Jain for
Motilal Banarsidass Publishers Private Limited,
Bungalow Road, Delhi 110 007

CONTENTS

PREFACE

Swami Venkatesananda lived the spirit of the Yoga Sūtras of Patanjali, and the many series of talks he gave on this subject in Australia, South Africa, Germany, Canada, etc., have inspired many to take up the practice of Raja Yoga.

His New Interpretative Translation of the Yoga Sūtras, ENLIGHTENED LIVING (published by the Chiltern Yoga Trust of South Africa in 1975) is regarded as a springboard to the understanding of the Sūtras. It has been incorporated in this present publication.

Swami Venkatesananda spoke equally to both men and women, and his use of the masculine pronouns 'he' and 'him' does not exclude the feminine. It is, in fact, shorthand for 'human being'! He did not feel it necessary to distinguish between male and female, and the editor has continued the tradition in this publication.

In this book, 'yoga' has been recognised as a word in common usage, and as such has not been italicised.

INTRODUCTION TO 'ENLIGHTENED LIVING'

There are many spiritually elevated people in the world, but not many levitating yogis: and the Yoga Sūtras of Patanjali Maharṣi are meant to elevate the spirit of every man, not to teach him how to levitate. This is clearly the gospel of enlightened living, neither an escape from life nor a hallucinatory 'light'. The attempt in this little book has been to expose that gospel, to avoid technicalities, and to relate the whole yoga philosophy to the ordinary and simple daily life of everyone.

There are very many excellent translations of the Sūtras: this, however, is an interpretative translation. There are several scholarly and erudite commentaries, too: this is definitely not one of them. This book is not meant for the research scholar but for one who is in search of truth which shall free him from self-ignorance.

The incisive language of the Sūtras cannot be preserved in translation. An extraordinary feature of the Sūtras is the avoidance of direct commandments, dogmatic assertions and the use of active voice. Whereas every effort has been made to retain the structure of the text, in a few cases (for example, in Sūtra I. 49) slight changes have had to be made to sustain the easy flow of thought. (The words which represent the translation of the text are underlined.)

Anyone who translates a text which is in the Sanskrit

language is confronted by two difficulties: (a) not all languages have concise words or phrases which accurately convey the exact sense in which the Sanskrit word is used in the text; and (b) the Sanskrit word itself has a number of meanings, and it is easier to choose the correct meaning when the word is used in a structurally complete prose or verse, than when it occurs in the Sūtras. From a cursory glance at the very many available translations of the Sūtras it is easy to see that each one has translated some Sūtras differently, without being unfaithful to the text.

Some translators, eager to build a 'philosophical system' on the foundation of the Sūtras have treated some words in the text as proper names of specific philosophical categories. Such a treatment inevitably limits the understanding of the purport of the text. The text itself seems to use two or more words to refer to a single factor: for example, *samādhi* and *samāpattiḥ* are used synonymously. There is a danger of regarding words as names: for then they create forms or images that perpetuate ignorance while creating an illusion of knowledge. This pitfall has been avoided in this book, and the actual meaning of the words has been sought, regardless of how the 'philosophical system' has classified them. When this is done, it is discovered that there is a continuous and smooth flow in the sequence of the Sūtras. (Where the text clearly warrants another meaning, such an alternative meaning has also been given: examples are II. 30, II. 36 and IV. 31).

The gospel of yoga suggests not a withdrawal nor an escape from the world, but the abandonment of the mental conditioning which creates a division between the 'me' and 'the world' (including the world of psychological experiences). Meditation is the vigorous search for the true identity of the 'me', not a psychic jugglery nor a technique for deep relaxation. Seen from this angle, the fundamental categories of yoga (*citta*, and *nirodha*—vide I. 2), take on a character completely different to the one that prevails in the minds of most practitioners of yoga: it is hard to translate *citta* and *vṛtti,* and the student has to discover the meaning in himself as Patanjali's message saturates his whole being. *Nirodha* does not imply suppression, restraint or control, in the usual (and brutal) connotations of those words, but a vigilantly watchful understanding of the movements of thought in the mind—which is stillness of a different kind.

The reader will not fail to notice that the teachings of yoga are universal and that they do not interfere with one's religious faith or occupation or life-style. Everyone who lives is entitled to enlightenment that instantly transforms every-day life into enlightened living.

ACKNOWLEDGEMENTS

This book was compiled and edited from the many talks given by Swami Venkatesananda on the Yoga Sūtras of Patanjali. Both published talks and audio tapes were used. If any errors are found in the editing, the fault is the editor's!

The Chiltern Yoga Trust (Astralia) wishes to express its gratitude to all who made this publication possible, in particular to the following:

Rosemary Van and Val Pritchard who helped with the initial typing. Padma Pyner, Hamsa Hyder, Catherin Bull, Rasik Devia, Priya Hart, Shelah Perrot and Anita Ray who read and checked the manuscript at various stages.

Ray Byartt who typed the bulk of the manuscripts straight onto disc, hence saving the compiler years of work.

Shivanand Guness of Mauritius who designed the final page layout and prepared the disc for the press.

To Narasimhulu of Sivananda Press, who gave his most valuable advice.

To H.H. Swami Krishnananda Maharaj for graciously consenting to write the Foreword.

We pay homage to:

Patanjali Maharṣi who centuries ago propounded the magnificent science contained in his Yoga Sūtras.

Our beloved guru, Swami Venkatesananda, who

enlightened our lives with his love, humour and wisdom, and his brilliant and inspiring teaching of Raja Yoga.

Our humble and grateful thanks to all.

Swami Lakshmi Ananda

GENERAL INTRODUCTION

No-one knows anything about Patanjali, the author of the Yoga Sūtras. There is as much guesswork as evidence. Some say he was a grammarian, and some say he was a great yogi. In any case, the text ascribed to him is called Yoga Sūtras.

Sūtras are terse expressions that are almost totally unintelligible and allow for any number of interpretations. They are not well laid out, well planned essays on yoga, but ungrammatical expressions. Sometimes either the subject, object or predicate is missing. (Maybe they were the notes kept by the students, or which the master himself had prepared.) Therefore to understand the Sūtras it becomes necessary to have a commentator, otherwise the uninitiated will find them difficult to understand.

If you pick up any standard English-Sanskrit dictionary and look up the word yoga, you will find a whole page full of meanings. Therefore, when a great master gives brief notes, using words like yoga, *citta* and *vṛtti,* we are as far from understanding the meaning as any other student is, or was. However, I prefer to look at all these things without a commentary.

A commentary on any book is already polluted, because it passes through the brain of the author. So if one is a serious student of yoga, wanting to understand things without being prejudiced by what others have said or thought about it, one should go straight to the text of Yoga Sūtras, buy a Sanskrit-English dictionary and try out combinations and computations of words. (You might even discover extraordinary meanings to these Yoga Sūtras—which is a very nice thing to do, for a research scholar!)

If you are not prepared to do this you are dependent upon some commentary or other, and any commentary is as good or as bad as any other; all have been produced by well-meaning, well-intentioned people (like the current commentator!).

The yoga described in the Yoga Sūtras is called Raja Yoga in the sense that it is scientific, both rational and emotional together, and involves our total life without dissecting it. So whatever be your station in life you must be able to practise this yoga, otherwise it is not Raja Yoga.

Raja means royal, and there are two suggestions why this particular path or method could be called royal in comparison with others. One suggestion is that it is fit only for kings. We need a bold understanding, a courageous, adventurous spirit. If you do not have that spirit, but want to beg, "God please give me this, God please give me that," don't touch Raja Yoga. It is fit only for royal sages. Another suggestion is that it is the royal road; you go straight, you don't beat about the bush. Instead of analysing all the factors that may be related to the problem, instead of cutting down the branches and dealing with the trunk, you go straight to the root of the problem itself. All problems have a single source. Patanjali assures us that the bondage does not lie outside, it is in you; pain does not lie outside, but is in you; pleasure does not lie outside, but is in you.

The name Raja Yoga does not occur in the Yoga Sūtras, only the word 'yoga' does. In actual fact, there *is* no Raja Yoga—it is either yoga or no yoga. Because the word 'yoga' means harmony, union, coming together or meeting, if we create divisions in the name of yoga, none of these things *are* yoga. Yoga is where you and I meet. What does not bring about this harmony is not yoga. Therefore, even though we have prestigiously called it Rája Yoga, the author himself does not claim that.

The very nature of the Scripture is such that it is almost ridiculous to talk about it in an impersonal way; it has to be a dialogue between two people—only then is it useful. The enquiry has to arise in the heart of the seeker; and then in the dialogue the seeker ascends step by step, with the help of the guide. If it is commented on—either in writing or in a talk—it seems to lose a certain intimacy, a certain inspiring, heartwarming characteristic that the text possesses.

Sometimes this little book seems to have no meaning at all: and sometimes it hits me like a bolt from the blue. Patanjali says that when you are sick or when the mind is absolutely dull it has no meaning, it is just a piece of paper; but when the mind has been jolted out of its dullness and is awake and alert, every time you read this you will gain a new meaning, because there is something new happening within you. Only then has this any meaning at all.

The words themselves are just loosely strung. If you pick up half a dozen translations you will be shocked to see that all of them differ from one another. Even contradictory meanings have been derived from the same expressions. But that's not serious, because the

Sūtras allow (and are capable of) being twisted and turned like that of the famous Delphic Oracle, *"The Greeks the Romans shall conquer"*. Confusing, ambiguous: who is going to conquer whom? That is exactly the nature of the Sūtras, and depending on your own inner maturity you derive your own meaning from them.

The Scripture is a closed book, useless and probably dangerous, if one has not arrived at a clear understanding of the foundations. I mention the word dangerous (against my own better judgement). Danger arises from the fact that the Scripture gives a technique for concentration and meditation which can be practised by anyone at all, whether he is spiritually awake or not, stupid, dull, vicious or good. It also hints at the truth that if you are able to meditate deeply and become one with the object of your meditation you will come to know it in essence. My guru used to say that that is the principle used in great discoveries by scientists, and great achievements by artists. (A man who has painted a glorious portrait has actually entered into or become one with the object of the subject he has chosen, and therefore he has been able to produce such an enthralling painting.) The Scripture also says that in this manner you can acquire all sorts of psychic powers—thought reading, telepathy, E.S.P., etc. There is no harm, but one who enters into that by-way may never come back to the spiritual path again. He becomes so terribly involved with psychic phenomena that he is not interested in spiritual fruit at all. So, to the unqualified person taking up the practice or study of Raja Yoga there is this little danger.

What are the qualifications then? The qualified

student must have arrived at the fundamental cognition that there is this ignorance that makes him forget that everything in the world is changing and impermanent, that everything that is born must die, that everything that has been created must be destroyed. This ignorance is the root of sorrow—but the student must arrive at this himself, he cannot get it from somebody else.

The teaching points out that there is this Cosmic Being or Cosmic Consciousness, which has mysteriously been disrupted or fractured by an ego sense that says, "This is 'I' and therefore that is 'you'." From this division flows the interminable stream of worry, anxiety, fear and hate. How do you find an end to this interminable stream? By realising you *are* the stream. The moment you realise this, the menace has ceased.

Why is this yoga or doctrine expounded at all? To point out in utter simplicity that all our problems arise from non-understanding of the very simple truth that whatever there is, is an indivisible whole. If this understanding arises, all problems are dissolved immediately.

It has to be taken for granted in the beginning that there is a state of consciousness which is accessible to all of us, in which there is neither contradiction, confusion, conflict nor distress, but in which there is great joy, bliss and peace: and that state of consciousness is reached through meditation, through yoga—which is the understanding of the modifications of the mind. We need to mention this at this stage for two reasons:

1. You must have an idea of the door through which to run when there is a threat. You have to know that there *is* a possibility; and when a crisis arises in your life, instead of becoming frustrated you know how to go

deeper within yourself. If you learn the technique when there are no problems, it will stand you in good stead when the need arises.

2. Life is problems—without problems there is no life! Having come into this problematical existence, it is like trying to untie a tangle. When you try to untangle a knot you find you are making more knots, so you get fed up and leave it. We take our problems for granted Most people in day-to-day living do not notice them, because they are not aware that there is a thing called 'peace of mind', an existence called 'being unconditioned'.

So the object, or goal, of yoga (if it can be regarded as such) is to discover the absence of what we have misunderstood to be the individual personality. One has to discover for oneself that it is not there. If I sit here and think, "I do not exist," it seems that I am denying this truth—as for instance when somebody says, "I think God does not exist," he believes in God very much more than some people in the church do! Similarly, one may say, "I think there is an individual soul, a personality, an ego." Another might say, "The ego does not exist." Both of them assume something.

As long as you regard yourself as a personality that is more important than the totality, problems will continue to exist. When you think you are very important, then you are denying the existence of the one indivisible being of which we are all cells. That is the problem with our life.

If you are miserable it is only because you think you are only this body, this personality—which is not the truth. Swami Sivananda once remarked during a rather disappointing event when someone had cheated, "You feel unhappy only because you think you are Swami So-and-so and that the other person is totally different from you. If this division disappears, you realise that the cheater and the cheated are both limbs of the same being, and you don't feel unhappy about it." There is a beautiful saying in Tamil, *"If accidentally your own finger pokes your eye, will you cut your finger off?"* He represents the finger and you represent the eye. Both of you belong to the same organism.

It is because of this division or fragmentation that has arisen in us that we feel miserable, and it is from this fragmentation that all our problems arise. How can this be overcome or solved except by realising the indivisibility of the being?

It is no use denying the existence of the ego—we have to see its non-existence for ourselves. When that is seen, the quality of our life changes dramatically, totally, without our wishing for it or praying for it, and without the use of what we are accustomed to call 'will-power'. The moment you realise that the cup of milk you are holding in your hand only looks like milk, but is really poison, do you have to use your will-power to drop it? No! When somebody says, "Oh, look out, it is poison," the cup immediately drops from your hand!

With such spontaneity life will change if one is able to discover for oneself that what exists is the river of consciousness. In this, whirlpools dance around, come together and pass again and again; certain molecules stick together and they look like this or that figure; and some of these molecules dance themselves apart from one another, and don't form at all. This change is continually taking place—there is nothing static in this universe. We are all part of the cosmic drama that is going on, the cosmic river that is flowing. One who discovers this is free.

If the inner intelligence is wide awake, life flows smoothly, without any problems. This awakened intelligence fills and penetrates every aspect of our life—right from our physical postures, our breathing, our relationship with one another, our conduct in this world, our attitude to this world and to other beings, and to physiological and psychological experiences. If all these can provoke or trigger self-knowledge or self-understanding, then in the light of that, the arising of problems can be completely and totally avoided. Life becomes quite simple and smooth, however complex it might look in the eyes of others.

I am not saying, "And therefore you should lead a natural sort of life and walk about naked." Your life may appear to be complicated in the eyes of others, but within yourself you are so peaceful and so alert that in your own intelligence there is no problem. It is a terribly immature attitude to think that the practice of yoga is possible only if you alter your environment, shut yourself off, lose all family ties, renounce everything and live a life of poverty, etc. All that is just immature nonsense, because attachment is not *there,* it is in you. A person who professes to have no family ties may have cosmic worries! What is meant is Self-knowledge, self-awareness—not selfishness.

In the first three chapters of the Yoga Sūtras a number of methods are given to enable us to overcome the problem of fragmentation. If you have seen a mirage as a mirage, you've realised the truth. If you saw it as water, there is error. It is when you see it as water that you start running after it. If you saw it as a mirage you don't run after it. When the whole totality is immediately realised or understood to be the sole reality, then the fragment is restored to its place. Then everything exists except the problem. Nothing disappears except the error—the erroneous perception of water. The mirage, as such, does not disappear! That is precisely what happens to an enlightened person.

Communication

When you and I become one in a mystic way 'communication' happens. This happens very often between lovers, mother and child, or very close friends. We have all communicated like this with someone or other—but we think it is accidental. We are strangers to this communication, because we neglect those few occasions and they slip through our fingers. For instance, when a boy looks at a girl and smiles there is communication taking place, telepathy taking place—a fantastic thing going on there! We don't take any notice of it, we have codified and pigeon-holed all this. We are all looking for mental telepathy, but we have completely neglected the study of natural phenomena. We are running after something that *looks* like natural phenomena.

In this world counterfeit things sometimes have greater value than the original. Here is a nice story to illustrate this:

It is said that a wandering yogi and his disciple were having a discussion, during the course of which the master said, "In this world nobody cares for the genuine article—everybody runs after the imitation." The disciple said, "Sorry Master, for this once I don't agree with you." The Master didn't argue, because no one helps another by argument.

They continued their wandering and came to a village, outside of which there was a small hut with a banner in front: "Come and see a man grunt like a pig. Two rupee entrance fee." About a hundred people had paid the two rupees. As soon as the room was full a man entered through the back door, went onto the stage, and grunted like a pig. "Oh, marvellous!" Everybody clapped and then walked out. Two rupees gone! The Master and his disciple also saw the entertainment, and the Master made up his mind to teach his disciple in a very practical way.

When on their wanderings they came back again to the same village, he hired the hut and put up a little banner: "The grunting of a pig—the truth. Admission two rupees." Some young men gathered round the hut. The banner seemed to be mysterious! What does it mean? They thought, "We had lovely entertainment last week. There may be some more entertainment this time." A few of them bought the two rupee tickets and went in to see if they should all go in. The holy man entered through the back door, leading a real pig. He went onto the stage and twisted its tail—it grunted, as pigs alway grunt. The twelve people who were there said, "Oh, is that all! What is so great in it?" They walked away and told all the others, "Don't go in. It is only a pig."

So a man grunting like a pig is worth something; a pig grunting like itself is worth nothing! The truth is worth nothing; an imitation is worth a lot. Nobody wants to *be* a yogi, people want to *see* a yogi. But, here again, one can only *be*.

The truth only be communicated when you and I

drop our individual personalities and become one. Otherwise we are merely conveyors, just conveying junk—usually secondhand stuff. Communication takes place when we are both on the same level of consciousness. I am at the same level of consciousness as you are when *my* shoe pinches exactly where *yours* does. Then I will be able to understand what you are talking about, and then it is possible to communicate.

The great Masters communicated their teachings by waiting for the proper disciple to come in the proper spirit, approach the Master with the proper attitude and ask the right question in the right way. The disciples listened and then practised, listened and practised, to arrive at the same wavelength, the same experience where communication may happen. They had to live the life of a yogi, to be yogis all the time. Then the floodgate of knowledge or wisdom was opened—maybe by a look, a word or a smile. *Then* those words became meaningful, because communication was taking place. That is the reason why these terse Sūtras or aphorisms were meaningful to those first class students who were ready and looking for it. They didn't want to learn, they wanted to *be*. If you want to *be* a yogi, you can be taught yoga. But if you want to know what yoga is all about, no one can teach or communicate anything to you, they can only convey. (There is a famous saying in one of the Indian languages, *"A donkey may convey a load of sandalwood, but it doesn't know its fragrance."*)

Conveying

Conveying is useless and sometimes harmful, because when I convey an idea we are not on the same wave-length; but yet you hear those words and the words have different meanings to you. The original idea or object is completely lost. It is only then that problems arise.

We cannot solve a problem before it arises, in anticipation. For instance a little girl of ten cannot understand what labour pain means. You can explain with all your scientific knowledge, but it still means nothing. And therefore when yoga is explained thus, "Your ego will merge into Cosmic Consciousness," you are worried. You think, "I'll get lost, and who wants to get lost? I want to be my miserable self for all time to come. Oh, will my husband still be my husband?"

You are trapped in our own utter silliness, because there is no communication. You don't understand the meaning of these words, you only hear what they sound like.

The Sanskrit word for 'meaning' is *arṭha.* What is the meaning, the *arṭha,* of the word God? The dictionary says: "*Supreme Consciousness; Omnipresent, Omnipotent, Omniscient. God occurs in Genesis Chapter I, verse 2. In this context it means this, in that context it means something else.*" This is just words! Where is the meaning, the *arṭha*—not paraphrasing one word with another word, or finding more words for one word. What is the *arṭha,* and is it real to you? If it is not, all this is useless.

Can one convey the meaning? If I try to convey the meaning of the word 'yoga', you will take it in another sense. For instance, someone started telling me that the only difference between yoga and gymnastics is that in yoga there is breathing! Does it mean that in gymnastics you don't breathe? That is an example of conveying.

In communication this misunderstanding does not take place, because in communication the two become one. They are on the same wavelength and the meaning is transmitted from heart to heart. This is of course the best way to learn yoga and to study the Yoga Sūtras.

The next best way is to study as many commentaries as you can get hold of, but all the time watching within yourself, "Is this true, is this real? Does my whole being accept this, approve this, see this as a fact?" If not, then it is not true to you at that stage. You can read it again and again, but you must be honest enough to admit that it is not true to you *now*. You cannot accept it, nor reject it. You would be a hypocrite if you accepted it as true, you would be a fool if you rejected it as untrue. It is there, and you are studying it. It appears to be not quite real. Maybe you need more maturity, maybe the teacher is saying something which communicates nothing to you yet, because you have not risen to his state of consciousness. You must study again. Maybe you have missed some of the lessons that life is teaching you. You must watch life again a little more closely and carefully.

"All human relationships depend upon some gratification or other. This applies in the reverse too." When you hear this statement, first you think, "What is meant by this? Does it mean that there is no love between husband and wife? Is the person who said this so cruel, so cold and calculating?" It doesn't appeal to you—you think he is mad. But, keep it somewhere in your mind and begin to watch life a bit more closely. You have had a few experiences that seem to corroborate these statements more than your belief. This is interesting. You are firm in your beliefs—this is black and this is white—but *he* says that between black and

white there is a lot of grey. It doesn't appeal to you, it doesn't seem real or plausible, but you keep it there—either accepting, nor rejecting. Up till then it is merely conveying, it means nothing what-so-ever to you. All the yoga that we are talking about is utterly meaningless, until one day you come to the same experience that is described there.

That is the meaning, the stuff, the reality of the words, not the dictionary meaning. In an instant it occurs to you, "Hah, *that* is the truth." At that moment it is no longer a truth that has been conveyed to you by So-and-so, but a truth that you have discovered for yourself, within yourself, through your own experience.

It is only to that limited extent that a study of texts like the Yoga Sūtras may be of some relevance to us and to our lives. Depending on your own inner maturity, you derive your own meaning from it.

The Scripture is a closed book, useless and probably dangerous, if one has not arrived at a clear understanding of the foundations. Have you come face to face with the fundamental truth: that ignorance, egoity, likes, dislikes, clinging to life are the roots of sorrow? You must have arrived at this position by a very clear observation of life as it is, where you can quite clearly see that both attachment and aversion (love as opposed to hate) create misery in your life. This you cannot get from the book. If you think, "Patanjali says that attachment is bad, therefore I will not be attached," it is borrowed knowledge. You can be told for ten days that there is sorrow, disease and suffering in your life, that there is sorrow in birth and sorrow in death. If you say, "Is that so? But this chocolate cake is very good. Why does he say everything is sorrow?" Your own mind has not arrived at this position. It inwardly rebels. So, that there is sorrow, misery and suffering in your life, has to be seen by you; it cannot be infused into you by somebody else.

The state of perfection (if there is a state like that) or the culmination of yoga (if yoga has a goal) is said to be the state that is natural, something that *is* all the time. If it is regarded as a goal, please remember it is returning to the source, where the beginning and the end become one—360 degrees and 0 degrees. When these two become one, that is yoga, oneness. But these are merely words.

* * * * * * *

There is one more consideration before you go on to study the Sūtras. Is it a technique to be practised in your daily life? Does it demand exertion, effort? Or is it something (as the Zen practitioners might say) that spontaneously arises in you without effort, technique or trouble? Again, neither/nor.

It is neither a technique (a method involving effort) nor an accidental happening (where you lie down on your couch, and as you are about to fall asleep...!!). There is a middle way where you neither sleep, nor are you awake. You are neither exerting, nor are you totally relaxed. (Where wakefulness meets slumber, where day meets night and where night meets day are times regarded as auspicious for meditation and for prayers. Where the two meet, you cannot say it is either day or night.) But the beauty is that it is neither this nor that: neither exertion, nor total relaxation.

When it is a middle path between these two, it demands constant attention. Those of you who practise yoga postures might have discovered this already. If you are too strenuous in your exertion you are not able to pay attention to what is happening to the body. If you are like a jelly-fish, there is no posture at all. The intelligent practice of postures demands attention. Attention arises only when there is no tension, but where there is total inner awareness.

In yoga meditation, does this awareness follow a sequence of the practice of methods, or does it happen spontaneously? Is there a technique to it, or is there no technique to it? Neither of these positions is valid.

How do we solve this problem? Is the problem solved just like that, or do we have to strive? The question is: "Is enlightenment (the final solution of this problem) instantaneous or gradual?" If we ask this question: "Is death instantaneous or gradual?" what would be the answer? That death takes place just instantaneously (I'm not talking about death in a motor-car accident, but normal lying in bed and dying) or that it is a gradual process? It is probably both, or either, or neither—it depends on what you are looking for.

If we define the word 'death' as the cessation of life, it is again subject to all sorts of interpretations. Does the cessation of life mean cessation of the heart, or the breath, or some brain cells? If that is what is meant, then it does take place instantaneously, because till that moment, you are still alive, you are not dead, however deceptive that may be. You may be completely paralysed, or in a deep coma, but until the doctor comes and says, "This man is dead," you are not dead. You are alive till that last moment. Therefore we may say that death is instantaneous. But we also say, "Oh, he has been dying for the last two years." That means he has had one serious illness after another—first he lost his hearing, then his sight, then his teeth, then his mind, etc.—a long drawn out death; which is also true. Now you are whole, with all your senses in good shape and working order. If one of these things conks out, you are that much dead. If your arms are paralysed, that means you are that much dead. If we look at the whole thing in this manner, we can say that death is also a gradual process.

In the case of enlightenment too, one can look at this phenomenon (if one can categorise it as such) as an instantaneous process, or as a long drawn-out gradual process, or graded enlightenment. But it is good to realise that till the last step is taken the enlightenment is not complete and not certain. There is still a shadow of doubt. As long as this shadow of doubt lasts, it is not really enlightenment. There is a glimpse of this light shining through a veil—you may think that the veil may be thin, or dark, blue or white, but there is still the veil. Through that veil you are able to see a little of the truth.

If you have had this view, then it is possible for you to proceed towards enlightenment. There is no sense in foolishly asserting 'either or'—if *this* is true, that is wrong, if *that* is true, this is wrong. Once again you get into this conflict and difference of opinion, and lose sight of truth.

How do we come face to face with this realisation that this perpetual, beginningless and endless flow *alone* is Truth? Every second the ego is asserting itself.

Those people who would like a short-cut to enlightenment, are looking for trouble. When we look for a method or a practice that will firmly establish us in this enlightenment, so that we don't hereafter fall into error, that is trouble already. If in this fast-moving, eternally dynamic, ever-changing universe, you want to be rooted, firm, unmoving, you might as well be a statue—at least to human vision. There is nothing unmoving in this universe. If you are part of this cosmic stream, then you must expect to be met by an unexpected turn of events at every stage. You don't know what is coming.

The purpose of enlightenment is to enable you to flow along with every challenge as it comes, meet the most unexpected events and then not lose your head. When in the light of your own enlightenment you are able to see, it is not a problem; because when you are able to see there is no fear or confusion anymore. Day after day the light is still shining, and when a new problem crops up you will look at it and see the solution—because the problem carries its solution on its own shoulders!

Enlightenment enables us to flow along this stream of consciousness without experiencing grief, confusion or doubt, because the light removes only the doubt, grief and confusion. Life goes on exactly as it has been. Your most prosaic actions become yoga, and they create no problem at all.

The enlightened person is one who is never shocked. He has reached this stage of not being shocked by being constantly alert, vigilant, awake, and therefore constantly illumined, not because he is supposed to be rooted in some form of psychic power. That is what yoga demands of us. That is what yoga promises us.

So enlightenment is set up as the goal, and this goal has to be realised, not thought about. You cannot sit here and hypnotise yourself by repeatedly observing, "I am the immortal Consciousness." That is only thought! It was thought that created all this nuisance, and thinking about it only brings in one more thought!

There is a famous Zen doctrine: "First there was a tree. When I looked at it, it became the world. As I went on analysing it, I reached enlightenment. Then it became a tree again." When you take things for granted, you act and re-act mechanically, instinctively. When you understand its nature and truth, then the tree remains the tree and you remain you, but in the meantime a tremendous radical change has taken place. The husband remains a husband and the wife remains a wife, but suddenly there is no longer that guardedness, possessiveness and jealousy—the haunting problem-makers.

The Vedantins also give a beautiful and simple explanation. A man entered a house, something touched his foot and he jumped up, shouting, "Snake!" When the light was switched on he saw it was only some rubber. When the lights were switched off he saw the snake again, exactly as he saw it the first time; but this time he was not afraid. That is the whole thing in a nut shell.

It is not as if once you become a yogi some kind of light will come out of you. I have lived with Swami Sivananda, one of the greatest yogis, and I can say that all that I saw was a very beautiful human being! I have seen him shaken by some events, but in his case there is the recognition that it is rubber and not snake. It looks like a snake. That, no-one is going to alter.

So enlightenment is an inner awareness that suddenly transforms and transmutes your whole being, without interfering with the appearance. You still play your role in life and everything goes on normally. Perhaps only *then* it is normal, before it was subnormal! All these things are within reach of all of us at all times. But, unfortunately, we have never really been aware of the beautiful mystery of which we are made.

FOOTNOTE TO 'ENLIGHTENED LIVING'

To illustrate the translator's unique position., six important words that occur in the text are given below with a complete list of' their meanings as found in a medium-sized dictionary:

cittaṁ

1. Observing. attending. 2. (a) Thought, thinking, attention; (b) desire, intention, aim. 3. The mind. 4. The heart (considered as the seat of intellect). 5. Reason, intellect, reasoning faculty.

nirodha:

1. Confinement, locking up, imprisonment. 2. Enclosing, covering up. 3. Restraint, check, suppression, control. 4. Hindrance, obstruction, opposition. 5. Hurting, punishing, injuring. 6. Annihilation, complete destruction. 7. Aversion, dislike. 8. Disappointment, frustration of hopes (in dramatic language). 9. (With the Buddhists) Suppression of pain.

pranidhāna:

1: Applying, employing, application, use. 2. Great effort, energy. 3. Profound religious meditation, abstract contemplation. 4. Respectful behaviour towards. 5. Renunciation of the fruit of actions. 6. Entrance, access.7. (With Buddhists) A prayer, an entreaty.

pratyaya:

1. Conviction, settled belief. 2. Trust, reliance, faith,

confidence. 3. Conception, idea, notion, opinion. 4. Surety, certainty. 5. Knowledge, experience, cognition. 6. A cause, ground, means of action. 7. Celebrity, fame, renown. 8. A termination, an affix or suffix. 9. An oath. 10. A dependant. 11. A usage, practice. 12. A hole. 13. Intellect, understanding. 14. An assistant or associate. 15. An epithet of Viṣnu. 16. (With Buddhists) A co-operating cause. 17. An instrument, a means of agency. 18. Religious contemplation. 19. A householder who keeps a sacred fire.

samādhi:

1. Collecting, composing, concentrating. 2. Profound or abstract meditation, concentration of mind on one object, perfect absorption of thought into the one object of meditation, i.e., the Supreme Spirit (the 8th and last stage of Yoga). 3. Intentness, concentration (in general), fixing of thoughts. 4. Penance, religious obligation, devotion (to penance) 5. Bringing together, concentration, combination, collection. 6. Reconciliation, settling or composing differences. 7. Silence. 8. Agreement, assent, promise. 9. Requital. 10. Completion, accomplishment. 11. Perseverance in extreme difficulties. 12. Attempting impossibilities. 13. Laying up corn (in times of famine), storing grain. 14. A tomb. 15. The joint of the neck; a particular position of the neck. 16. (In rhetoric) A figure of speech. 17. One of the ten gunas or merits of style. 18. A religious vow or self-imposed restraint. 19. Support, upholding.

vṛtti:

1. Being, existence. 2. Abiding, remaining, attitude, being in a particular state. 3. State, condition. 4. Action, movement, function, operation. 5. Course, method. 6. Conduct, behaviour, course of conduct, mode of action.

7. Profession, occupation, business, employment, mode of leading life. 8. Livelihood, maintenance, means of subsistence or livelihood. 9. Wages, hire. 10. Cause of activity. 11. Respectful treatment. 12. Commentary Gloss, exposition. 13. Revolving, turning round. 14. The circumference of a wheel or circle. 15. A complex formation requiring resolution or explanation. 16. The power or force of a word by which it expresses, indicates or suggests a meaning; general character or force of a word. 17. Style in composition. 18. Customary allowance. 19. Manner of thinking.

SCHEME OF TRANSLITERATION

Vowels: a ā i ī u ū ṛ ṝ ḷ e

ai o au ṁ ḥ

Consonants:

gutturals	k	kh	g	gh	ṅ
palatals	c	ch	j	jh	ñ
cerebrals	ṭ	ṭh	ḍ	ḍh	ṇ
dentals	t	th	d	dh	n
labials	p	ph	b	bh	m
semi-vowels	y	r	l	v	
sibilants			s	as in sun	
			ś	palatal sibilant	
			ṣ	cerebral sibilant as in shun	
aspirate			h		

The above scheme does not facilitate the pronunciation of the syllable *jñā* that occurs often in the Sūtras as also in yoga literature (*jñāna* means knowledge). The *j* is not really pronounced as *j* but almost as *g*. It is followed by the *n* which partakes of the character of the guttural and the palatal *n*. Added to all this there is also a suggestion of *y* before the appropriate vowel completes the syllable.

FOREWORD

Sri Swami Venkatesanandaji was closely associated with Gurudev Sri Swami Sivanandaji Maharaj, and he was a veritable personal assistant to Sri Gurudev. Swami Venkatesananda turned out enormous work every day by attending to correspondence, by writing articles and commentaries, which were all a kind of masterpiece in themselves. Right from the beginning we both were intimate friends and we used to discuss common topics in a humorous way, of which method of speaking Swami Venkatesananda was a master. He would always be smiling and cut jokes even when we were discussing serious subjects like the famous Yoga Vasiṣṭha that we used to read together after the lunch hour every day. This is a sort of background of my intimacy with Swami Venkatesananda. He liked me very much and I too liked him equally.

He was a prolific writer and could write on any subject. The present occasion for me to write these few words is in connection with a series of lectures he delivered on the Yoga Sūtras of Patanjali, all of which were systematically edited by a devotee called Swami Lakshmi Ananda from Perth, Australia. I have gone through the manuscript of this book and find that it is excellent.

Here I would like to add that there is a much neglected sūtra of Patanjali to which commentators have been paying scant attention, and even when they were attempting to say something on this sūtra it was sketchy and lacked depth. This sūtra in the third chapter of the Yoga Aphorisms of Patanjali and begins with the words:

bahir akalpitā vṛttir mahā videhā

This is, in my opinion, the quintessence of the meditational technique described by Patanjali, by which we are introduced to the very heart of the matter so pithily and crisply. This sūtra makes out that there are two ways of the functioning of the mind, one in the form of a thought of an external object and another as a total and comprehensive operation in which the object in meditation becomes inseparable from its thought. Usually such an exercise is not humanly possible. Who can think in such a way that the object enters the mind itself and the object becomes the thought and the thought becomes the object. This is a staggering suggestion given by the sūtra that the entire world can enter into the process of thinking. If the universe enters the mind and the mind enters the universe, this exercise is said to lead to immediate liberation.

The sūtra beginning with vitarka etc. in the system of Patanjali refers actually to a series of meditations in an ascending order, first on the physical universe, then the subtle universe of potentials called tanmatras, the cosmic complex known as space and time and the cosmic Self sense leading to a bliss born of pure consciousness. Though the sūtra refers only to vitarka, vicāra, anandā and asmita, they are further capable of categorisation as involved in space-time consciousness or not involved in space-time consciousness. These stages are intricate and cannot be understood by merely a study of books.

Swami Venkatesananda has succeeded very commendably in expounding Sage Patanjali's Sūtras in a lucid manner, and I recommend this book to every seeker of Truth, who ardently pursues the Yoga System of Patanjali.

The Divine Life Society
Shivanandanagar,
Uttarakhand,
India.

Swami Krishanananda
April 22nd, 1998

CHAPTER ONE

I. 1 atha yogā 'nuśāsanaṃ

Now, when a sincere seeker approaches an enlightened teacher, with the right attitude of discipleship (viz., free of preconceived notions and prejudices, and full of intelligent faith and receptivity) and with the right spirit of inquiry, at the right time and the right place, communication of yoga takes place.

Here Patanjali says, "I am merely giving you instruction in yoga."

Yoga teaching cannot be applied. It has to grow out of you as flesh grows out of you and make you what you are, just as the bread and tomato you eat becomes assimilated. It is no longer bread and tomato, it becomes 'as similar' to you. The teaching must be assimilated so that it is no longer a foreign body, it has *become* you. This cannot be forced upon anyone.

Here the procedure is exactly the same as consuming food. The food for the stomach enters through the mouth, and the food for the *antaḥkaraṇa* (the subtle inner being) enters through the ears and the eyes. You can see the distinction between the ears and the eyes. Only sound waves can enter through the ears, only visual impressions can enter through the eyes, though both these may be coordinated and consumed by the spirit. In the same way, the mouth consumes one form of nourishment and the eyes and ears consume other forms of nourishment, but all of them have to be processed in a similar way. Food should not be swallowed without chewing. If you try to swallow something without chewing it, since the stomach doesn't have teeth it will throw it up or quickly eliminate it—either through the right channel or the wrong channel. Even so, unchewed spiritual food is a menace. If what you see, read or hear is gulped down without being chewed, it also comes out of your mouth or through the other ear. If you like to be a lecturer, you hear and you read, and as soon as the idea enters it immediately comes out through the mouth, and then its circuit is over. Even *you* don't remember later on what you read, heard or said.

Because of our anxiety to 'put things into practice', we hear something and we feel we must apply it to our lives. But applying the teaching doesn't work. The teaching has to be heard—*śravaṇa.* The next stage is *manana*—reflection. You reflect upon what you have heard. In order to reflect efficiently, the surface of the mirror should be clean and held steady so that the teaching you have heard is *reflected.* In order that the mind may reflect the teaching without distortion, it must be efficient, steady and free from distortion and dirt. All these are taught in yoga.

Listen to the teaching, and let it be reflected in you. Then it is assimilated—*nididhyāsana*—so that the teaching that you heard *becomes you,* and from there on the truth itself acts. If you try to act in accordance with the instruction—just as some people try to learn to cook from a cookery book—you make a mess of your life. For instance, if you want to make some coffee, the cookery book says, "Put a pot of milk on the stove". When it is coming to the boil, you must see what the book says. But before you can come back to the stove, there is no milk there! So that doesn't work. You must *become* the cookery book—which is what most Indian women do. They don't know how to give you a recipe in the manner of the cookery book, but say, "Take a little bit of salt and a little bit of ghee and keep it on the stove for some time..." How little is little, how much is much, how long is some time? Their cooking comes from their own sensitivity, not from the scales or the thermometer.

So here is instruction in yoga, listen to it. Let it be reflected in your heart and be assimilated by you. Later let this instruction *itself* act.

The author of the Yoga Sūtras does not claim to be the authority, nor does he impose the teaching upon anyone. It is only *anuśāsanaṃ*—a piece of wholesome advice. So here there is no compulsion or coercion, because when there is coercion there is no action at all. For instance, if you tell someone to speak the truth always, and they say they will, that is already the first lie! The mind immediately wants to find ways and means of satisfying itself without violating the letter of the commandment. So *anuśāsanaṃ* means 'optional' teaching. The choice is entirely yours. This must be very clearly understood, otherwise the whole Scripture is misunderstood.

Yoga is defined as:

I. 2 yogaś citta vṛtti nirodhaḥ

Yoga happens when there is stilling (in the sense of continual and vigilant watchfulness) of the movement of thought —without expression or suppression—in the indivisible intelligence in which there is no movement.

The words *citta vṛtti* and *nirodha* are almost impossible of direct translation. *Citta* has been translated into 'mind stuff'—unconscious mind, conscious mind, super–conscious mind, cosmic mind, individual mind and cosmic intelligence all put together. So *citta* is the consciousness that is indivisible, undivided. It is the totality of the mind, the mind–stuff, the totality of the intelligence which is indivisible, incapable of being partitioned—like space. Can it be known? Perhaps it can be experienced in the sense in which you and I experience the truth "I am alive."

Because this indivisible intelligence—which alone is the truth—is non–dual and expressible, all experiences concerning it, and all forms of expression that arise *in* it, are *vṛttis*. For instance, you utter the sentence, "I have an idea," in that there are four *vṛttis:* 'I' is the first, 'have' (or the sense of possession) is the second, 'an' (or one—or not many) is the third, and 'idea' is the fourth. So everything concerning anything that you wish to express, is a *vṛtti*. I hope it is vaguely clear (sorry for the contradictory expression); it should not be too vague and it should not be too clear. If it is too clear it is another *vṛtti*.

Vṛtti, has been rendered into thought wave, mental modification, or the ripples on the mind lake. (The more words you use, the more obscure the meaning becomes.)

If *vṛtti* is understood, the whole thing is understood. What *citta* is, is not for the intellect to understand, for the simple reason that the intellect can only produce *vṛttis*. So a *vṛtti* cannot understand what *citta* means. However much a limited, conditioned individual may try, he cannot grasp the infinite.

When the intellect begins to function it creates space, and beyond that space it creates an object for itself to know. With what can the subject be known? If the subject becomes the known, it becomes an object! Which is impossible. Therefore, when the intellect is forced to do it, the intellect creates an image (the object), calling it a subject! So when a person says, "I know God," that God becomes an object, not a subject. When a person says, "I have understood what the infinite means," he has only understood what the *word* infinite is. Can the infinite be known? What do you mean by that? You cannot deal with the infinite, the infinite deals with you! (There is only one way in which you can deal with the infinite, and that is to surrender yourself. See I. 23)

Vṛttis are the apparent modifications of the mind—thoughts, emotions, feelings, memories, etc. They are changing all the time. For instance, you meet a friend and in your heart there is happiness. You experience that happiness, and you become aware that that happiness is in you. Your mind itself has assumed the form of that happiness, there is nothing else. Then you go to town for an important appointment, and as you walk towards the railway platform you see the train pulling out. There is disappointment and anxiety. The anxiety is in you. Your mind itself has now assumed the form of that anxiety, and for the moment there is nothing else, you are swallowed up in it. (Luckily for you it is not the totality of the mind, because the mind was there before the anxiety arose and it will probably survive this anxiety. The yogi directly sees that this thing called anxiety is but a small, temporary fragment of the mind.)

Suddenly you realise that that which was happiness then, that *itself* is anxiety now. It has not changed. The apparent modification does not modify the mind, and therefore the mind (or the intelligence, awareness or consciousness) is forever indivisible. It does not undergo a permanent change either for the better or the worse—that is why it is possible for yoga to be practised! The same mind–stuff, which was happiness at one stage, has undergone a temporary change which now appears to be anxiety. This mind–stuff is *citta* and the apparent modifications—of happiness or anxiety—are the *vṛttis.*

Vṛttis are there, not because you created them, but because the potentiality of *vṛtti* formation is there in the mind. Why are they there? So that you may be vigilant. (Why has God created a thief? So that you may lock your door, not hate the thief. Swami Sivananda always exemplified this in his life. He didn't want his disciples to catch and kill the rats which came into their rooms and started to chew on their books and clothes. He said, "If you value your books, clothes and manuscripts, put them in a proper cupboard and lock them up. Why leave them carelessly around and then go catch all the rats that are nibbling at them and throw them in the Ganges? The rats are there to teach you caution." It's a beautiful way of looking at it. Every thing has a meaning, and it is up to this intelligence to discover that meaning.)

The relationship between what have been called the states of the mind (*vṛttis*) and the reality of the mind (*citta*) is like the relationship between the content of a wave and the ocean. (Right here it is good to remember that it is not necessary for the waves, whirlpools, ripples and the currents to cease in order that the ocean may continue to be ocean—ocean is always ocean, water is always water.) Just because two different words are used, it is dangerous to assume that these are two different existential facts. You use the words 'ocean' and 'wave'; these are not two different things. It does not mean that you take a big broom and sweep all the waves away and have only pure ocean—that is ridiculous. To be able to look there and see it is water, never mind what shape it is, that is yoga.

In Sanskrit there is a lovely word—*artha*—which is taken to mean 'meaning'. The dictionary meaning is quite different from what is meant by the word *artha*, because the dictionary gives synonyms or paraphrases which imply an explanation. In Sanskrit it implies the thing *itself*. For instance, if the word 'shirt' in Sanskrit is used and we are asked to give the *artha*, we are asked to give a shirt! So *artha* means the object itself.

When the words *citta* and *vṛtti* are used, what is the object they stand for? Here is a tape recorder—but what is the *citta*, what is the *vṛtti*? We don't want explanations. That is why Patanjali's Yoga Sūtras, a small little text, is almost like an atom bomb!

Vṛttis can be understood, can be known. Even to understand *vṛtti* it needs great steadiness of mind and concentration, because only that which is stable and unmoving can really and truly study that which is moving. It is important that *vṛttis* be understood and not turned into another concept. If it becomes another concept it is possible for you to think that you understand. You make an image of it and that destroys the whole meditation. Then we begin to project that image, and think about the state or stage when the *vṛtti* is not there.

Using modern psychological language, *vṛttis* can be approximately described as 'learned knowledge'. Any learned knowledge is *vṛtti*. To learned knowledge I might also add what is called instinct. It may be thought that instinct is not learned knowledge, but one can see again that it is a conditioning brought forward at birth.

Unlearned knowledge is what can be called natural knowledge, or intuitive knowledge. Intuitive knowledge is 'untutored knowledge'. A *vṛtti* cannot look at that untutored knowledge.

At one point all these *vṛttis* are seen by the observer as nothing other than intelligence, the same mind.

Can you observe the following within yourself? A memory, imagination or something else comes up—seeming to have its own independent existence. It seems to subside when you observe it; and it becomes nothing more and nothing less than the mind. That is called *nirodha.* While looking absolutely steadily within yourself, you see it as the *citta,* as the mind itself. Vāsiṣṭha describes this very beautifully in the **Yoga Vāsiṣṭha**: *"The indivisibility of the citta is realised as water mixing with water."* The *vṛtti* and the *citta,* being made of the same stuff, become one—as water becomes one with water.

The word *nirodha* is very difficult to translate. It has been rendered into suppression or restraint. This has given rise to all sorts of misunderstandings—people justifying suppression of thought, etc. How do you suppress thought? How do you suppress that which you don't even know and which you don't even see? Then you create something within yourself—'I am thinking of that ring now. I am going to suppress that thought.' What are you doing? You are not thinking. Which means you are thinking you are not thinking. What about the thought which says 'I am not thinking'? If you are not going to suppress the act of breathing and the pumping of your heart, why must you suppress another natural faculty called thought?

When you say that the content of the wave is water, what happens to the wave? Have you suppressed it, restrained it, abolished it? If you are still looking at the wave as a wave, you are not looking at the water. If you are looking at the whole thing as water, something has taken place within you, and that is called *nirodha.* So the word 'understanding' explains it better than the words 'suppression' or 'restraint'. The yogi is not interested in either expressing or suppressing, nor does he say that *this* alone is the truth or *that* alone is the truth.

Nirodha also means control, as in control of the car. Thought can be guided, attention can be focused—but that is not all. Unless you can come face to face with the thing called *vṛtti* and the thing called *citta,* your efforts at controlling or directing them are bound to be futile, if not dangerous.

Try to figure out the answer to this question: "What is the content of the wave?" and then transplant the whole process within yourself to your own psychological being—for instance by visualising the mind as the ocean. Just as a wave arises in the ocean, similarly the *vṛtti* of anxiety arises in the mind, the *citta.* Is this anxiety a completely different thing, or is it the same as your mind? What are these thoughts, feelings and emotions? They cannot be got rid of by either expressing them or suppressing them. Try just keeping them there. You blink and you see the ocean, you blink again and see the many waves. Which is real? This or that? *This* is one point of view, *that* is another point of view. But, what is the truth?

Nirodha is what happens to you when you sincerely, seriously and intelligently ask yourself this question. It is not control, elimination of anxiety or suppression of anxiety, because you are no longer anxious. When you are observing the mind and intelligently asking yourself this question, you are neither afraid of this anxiety, anxious about it nor eager to get rid of it. What is there to get rid of? And when you are intelligently studying this phenomenon called anxiety, then you are in a state of yoga.

When you look at the ocean you see the water and you see the waves. The content of the wave is water, the content of the ocean is water. If you can see merely water, that is the state of yoga. Something inexpressible but of tremendous importance takes place within you. It is not possible to make it an object of understanding, but it is something—and that is yoga. It is as if the totality called the ocean is looking at the wave. It is as if the totality of the mind, looking at this silly little anxiety, is not anxious about the anxiety any more. It is possible for the very simple reason that the mind is nothing but pure intelligence. That pure intelligence somehow confuses this small, temporary, insignificant fragment called a passing thought (or experience) with the whole of the mind. When this confusion somehow arises in the mind there is trouble; but when the totality of the mind—which is intelligence—observes this fragment called anxiety, what happens within you is called *nirodha*. It is controlled, but not controlled in the ordinary sense of the word; it is transcended, but not in the ordinary sense of the word; it is suppressed, but not in the ordinary sense of the word. A mysterious 'something' takes place within you which I might call understanding, knowledge or self–knowledge.

In that self–knowledge, sorrow, physical and psychological pain and suffering come to an end without seeking to alter the physical reality. Nothing is altered except the understanding, which undergoes a tremendous transformation. Sorrow is not looked upon as sorrow any more, whatever be the external condition in which we are placed.

When the *vṛttis* are controlled, it means that you are living with such intense awareness and care that in all these changes you are really unaffected. You are watching—intensely, immediately; and so here and now you are living with great alertness and vigilance. Suddenly, like a flash of lightning, you begin to understand that these changes happen, but there is an unchanging witness throughout. That which is aware of these changing moods is itself not changing. Waves roll on the surface of the ocean, but underneath the ground is still. But here the analogy is defective, because we are talking about two completely different things—the seabed and the water. In the case of the mind (or the consciousness or the intelligence) the whole thing takes place in one substance. It is the intelligence that in its unmodified state is able to watch all the modifications that take place on its own surface. The whole thing is *citta,* just as the waves, the currents, the streams and the unmoving substratum are the ocean. The movement takes place only in relation to an observer. The river flows only in relation to a person standing on its bank, but if you *are* the river, there is no motion, no change. You are the whole thing, you are the totality.

It is only when you separate yourself from any one of these experiences that it is seen as a movement; but when you *are* the total experience, the total intelligence, there is no movement. When you are the total consciousness, all changes that take place within the total consciousness are part of the total consciousness. For instance, when you look at the small fragments of your own physical body (your heart, etc.) you find tremendous activity going on in every department of your physical being, but when you view the whole thing it is one – steady, stable and peaceful. There are no changes at all. That is *citta vṛtti nirodha*. What *is* is what is, without distortion or limitation. That is the realisation of the truth.

Raja Yoga can be practised wherever you are, whatever you are doing. It does not interfere with your life style, your religious belief or disbelief, with whatever you are or your station in life. Therefore, it is possible for all of us; and it is meant for all of us. It is not something which can be practised for half an hour in the morning and ten minutes in the afternoon, but it is something which encompasses the whole of life.

Once this new vision is gained, then all division in life disappears—in exactly the same way as there seems to be a distance between two waves; but that wave, this wave and the space in between are all the one indivisible ocean. The distance has disappeared!

When you understand the content of these thoughts—fear, anxiety, etc.—you realise (not as a thought or object of psychological experience, but from within) that they are nothing but experiencing, and all words are but sounds. Language was not invented for the expression of this truth of divisionless oneness. When there is no division in one's vision (which is enlightenment), who are you going to talk to, and about what? Here is something which is not capable of being communicated, and need not be communicated. When you and I (two waves) somehow realise that we are both made of the same water, then there is heart to heart communication. It is beyond the realm of communication.

Can you understand the totality of the mind–stuff (the ocean), the intelligence, without particularising a concept and blessing that concept with the distinction of being a thing in itself? Can you become aware of the totality of existence, of the indivisibility of intelligence, without according a concept or an idea the distinction of being an independent entity in itself? That is the only thing that yoga asks of us.

[For more on *vṛttis,* see Appendix – *Vṛttis]*

I. 3 tadā draṣṭuḥ svarūpe 'vasthānaṃ

In the light of non–volitional, non–moving and therefore spontaneous and choice–less awareness, the undivided intelligence with its apparent and passing modifications or movements of thought within itself is not confused with nor confined to any of these. Then (when yoga thus happens), the see–er—or the homogenous intelligence which is ignorantly regarded as the separate experiencer of sensations and emotions, and the separate performer of actions—is not split up into one or the other of the states or modifications of the mind, and exists by itself and as itself.

When *yogaś citta vṛtti nirodhaḥ* has been achieved, then the see–er (or the experiencer) rests in himself in an unmodified state; he remains pure and unsullied, just as an experiencer.

(Here sight is given as a thing to cover perception by all the senses, as well as psychological perception. '*Draṣṭuḥ*' is one who sees, who experiences. [Please note that at this stage the first person singular 'I' is not used.])

There is nothing wrong with seeing or with sight, there is nothing wrong with things seen, and in the same way, there is absolutely nothing wrong with anything that happens to you—neither what is called pleasure nor what is called pain—as long as you don't call it anything and can just *be* that, without creating a division.

You go on seeing, and in the intensity of that vision suddenly there is an understanding that seeing alone is true, observation alone is true, pure experiencing alone is true. What is considered the ego is nothing but the pure experiencing, wanting (as it were) to experience its own experience. There is suddenly the awareness that consciousness *is* all the time and all experiencing is made possible *in* that consciousness *by* that consciousness. Consciousness rests, without a division, as the totality.

The see–er (or sight) remains as the pure experiencing, just as the ocean constantly remains the ocean. The waves may be breaking on the shore, but the ocean is not diminished thereby; the waves may be rolling back into the sea, but the ocean is not increased. In that pure experiencing there is no sorrow. Because this is unusual, the mind suggests that it is probably not true; but if you examine the state of sleep you see that there is no sorrow there, because there is not a division of the experience of sleep and the experienc*er* of sleep. You don't sleep; sleep sleeps you, or sleep sleeps itself and you are merely involved in it.

Any experience of a similar nature, in which there is no divided experience, is pure. In it there is no sin and no suffering. Such is the state of a yogi.

There the see–er, the observer of all this, the experiencer of all experiences, remains in his own state of perfection, unmodified by *vṛttis, saṃskaras,* ego–sense or mind. He neither undergoes modification nor creates a division between the object and the experience. So self–knowledge is not the absolute negation of any point of view, but the subtle transcendence of all individual points of view so that the totality may be realised. Therefore there is neither repression, suppression nor anything that we can discuss. There is nothing that the mind can grasp and hold. Because it is total, it is cosmic in its dimensions. It is the infinite. That infinite is the see–er, the experiencer of all experiences. That *is,* and therefore all else is. It is because *it* exists that everything else shines. And yet, strangely enough, even though that self continues to exist in all these states and continues to be the substratum of all these points of view, the observer remains forever unmodified. The self itself does not undergo modification. This state of yoga can be called deep meditation or superconscious state. When you are in that state of yoga it is there within you, and it is accessible.

In the state of yoga, intelligence functions naturally in its own natural form—or formlessness.

We do not suffer from our nature at all. I am a human being and it does not create any problem at all in my life, or cause me the least unhappiness. I am a man and it doesn't create any problem at all in my life. It doesn't bother me. That which is natural is free. The intelligence that is built into me sees the naturalness of it and therefore does not reject it; sees the naturalness of something passing and does not desire it. It is important to remember this.

That which is natural does not create any problem and is permanent, it doesn't change. If we talk of nature and the needlessness of the change in nature then somebody or other gets the wrong idea, "Oh, I am a man of vicious nature. I don't have to change my vicious nature." The viciousness is not part of your nature, it is a modification that comes in later, a change in the mood of the mind. If you say it is human nature to be violent sometimes, it cannot be sometimes; if you say there is violence in human nature, you must be violent from morning till night, and night till morning. You are a human being twenty four hours of the day. You were born a human being and will die as a human being.

I do not accept that violence is part of human nature –

it is not so. I have a rather unorthodox way of explaining it. You can't get angry at will. Try now! Anger is a change that takes place occasionally, so it is not part of your nature. It seems to possess you temporarily and then leave you.

So what is natural and therefore permanent does not cause any problem in our lives.

I. 4 vṛtti sārūpyam itaratra

At other times, when yoga does not happen and when the mind is busily occupied with the movement, there is a cloud of confusion in the undivided, homogeneous intelligence. In the shadow of that cloud, there arises false identification or cognition of the movement of the mind–fragment and hence distorted understanding. The single concept or idea or the single movement of thought is mistaken as the totality.

The definition is difficult to understand, the goal and the landmark are difficult to understand, but when it comes to this *Sūtra,* we can understand. If yoga does not happen then we recognise this landmark, because we are *in* that state. The mind is nothing but the prevailing *vṛtti.* My guru, Swami Sivananda, often used to ask, "Do you know what *vṛtti* is operating in your mind?"

We often use the expressions, "I think this is right, I think this is wrong". Do we ever know anything other than 'I think'? Whether it is explicitly said or implied, this 'I think' seems to form part of all our concepts, statements and experiences. That is interesting!

For instance, you think there is a pain in your stomach. What is this pain? It is a sensation. It is the manner in which the nerves behave and convey the message to your brain. When, how and why is it called pain? Because you think it is pain. At the time of experiencing this pain, the experience is real; but since you have conditioned yourself to thinking this is painful, you experience pain. In pleasure it is the same. Something that is painful according to you is pleasure to somebody else, or what is pleasure at one time is pain at another, depending upon what you think.

I will give you an example. A young lady is sitting in the audience. She feels somebody tickling her from behind. That is pure and simple experiencing—neither pleasurable nor painful. She looks back and sees her husband. She smiles—it is delightful. If it is not the husband but somebody else, she becomes angry. The experience—tickling—was the same, but in one case the mind says this is pleasure and enjoys it, and in the other case the mind says it is pain, and therefore it suffers pain. The purity of experiencing is lost and the prevailing thought becomes your experience. This is almost totally unrelated to the experiencing *itself,* which may be totally neutral.

Our whole life is made up of thinking it is pain and experiencing pain, thinking it is pleasure and experiencing pleasure. This is because we have not understood at all what *citta* is, what *vṛtti* is and what we do with the *citta* and *vṛtti.* When the understanding is not there we go round and round in circles, endlessly creating our own pain and our own pleasure, running away from self-created pain and running after self-created pleasure.

Yoga is a clear understanding of the relationship between mind and thought. If this understanding is not there, you mistake one single thought, feeling or emotion for the totality. This one little emotion becomes magnified to such an extent that it engulfs you. Thoughts and feelings that prevail in your mind determine the world around you and you are ruled by the prevailing mood of the mind.

You can see that successively changing moods of mind create problems in your life, causing a lot of sorrow, suffering and unhappiness. Then you begin to watch your mind and the problems that the mind creates in your life and to see them happen and how these changes take place.

You were asleep and when you woke up you realised that you slept like a log. You knew nothing. That is one state. That is not natural to you because you are not sleeping all the time. That mood passed away. Then you are in a new mood. You sit down to meditate. Your thoughts are all angelic, you are uplifted, elevated. Maybe you go to the celestial spheres and have a cup of tea with some of these celestial gods and goddesses! Then after forty-five minutes or so you leave the meditation seat. You are still in an exalted mood. You want to have a cup of coffee. You put the milk on the stove, and then the milk boils over. The exalted mood and the peace have gone. You are agitated. Just then your little baby comes in calling, "Mummy I want..." You shout, "Go away!"

How did this happen? A few minutes ago you were in the celestial spheres, and now you are so terribly agitated and anxious that you are slapping your own child!

When each one of these moods prevails you *are* that mood. You hardly remember what it was like to be peaceful, and when you are peaceful you hardly remember what it was like to be agitated. If you are able to remember you think you must be mad, "How could I ever do that?"

You try to tell yourself that next time the milk boils over you won't lose your temper or become nervous, but the next time the milk usually boils over when you are not looking. That is why it boils over! The next time it happens you are as mad, at least, as you were before, because this changed mood becomes you—there is no part of you left to control this. Is there a way in which you can modify this? It doesn't look like it, because every time the mood changes, the whole of you changes. You tend to identify yourself with each mood so thoroughly that nothing else seems to exist. Your consciousness clings to one little point of view, thinking that that is real. The yogi does not say that it is unreal, he merely says that that is not the totality, but a mere passing mood.

The self itself seems to undergo modification. You are what you think you are from moment to moment. Now you think you are a yogi; when you are dreaming that a tiger is about to attack you, you are a frightened man; when you are asleep you are stupid. It may be relevant to ask, "Which one is me?" Are you the stupid man, the frightened man or the yogi? How come you can be all three rolled into one? It doesn't seem to make any sense at all. In other words, experience seems to modify the self (or the experiencer). But does the experience that you are undergoing at the moment bring about a complete and irreversible transformation in the self? You thought you were somebody and that somebody was going to be that somebody until the body is dropped; but it is not so. When you go to sleep or when you dream there is not an irreversible change, because you wake up. So it seems as though these modifications are not irreversible—which means they are apparent. (That is what they mean when they call it illusion, *māyā*.)

The yogi is not motivated by happiness or unhappiness, because if there is a longing for happiness that is already unhappiness. He is merely interested in the knowledge, the pure experiencing, which is the same in all cases.

We may consider ourselves enlightened, clever and wise, but that only amounts to 'we think we are clever and wise.' All the time we only think. As long as this mental activity continues, we are still in confusion, we are fooling ourselves. When there is division in this vision there is self–limitation, and that limitation, whatever one may think oneself to be, is still limited.

I. 5 vṛttayaḥ pañcatayyaḥ kliṣṭā 'kliṣṭāḥ

These apparent movements or states or moods of the mind, which are concepts, ideas or images in it, can all be grouped under five categories, irrespective of whether they are experienced as painful or not–painful, and whether or not they are covertly or clearly tainted by the five–fold afflictions described later.

All *vṛttis*, regardless of whether they are painful or not–painful, can be grouped under five categories. They are the only basis for the changes that the mind undergoes.

These changes sometimes cause pleasant and sometimes unpleasant reactions. They are successive. You do not know of a state other than these, because as long as you are awake you are thinking, and you are a slave to these thoughts. You do not know if there is an 'I' apart from these changing moods of the mind. It is important for us to grasp this. At this stage there is not even a hope of overcoming this, you are merely studying it because you feel trapped in these changing moods of the mind and it doesn't feel good.

When you see that there is no possibility of you getting away from this, nor can you ever be reconciled to it, it is then that you are intensely and immediately caught up in this problem which is with you till it is finally solved. (Intensely to me means without a tense – without a past, present and a future, without separation in time; and immediately means without a mediator, without separation in space.) You cannot rebel against it because it is within you.

I. 6 pramāṇa viparyaya vikalpa nidrā smṛtayaḥ

These five categories of apparent movements of the mind are:

(1) proven theory, which is often assumed to have been reliably proved and therefore to constitute right knowledge; (or, rationalisation of the movement of thought),

(2) unsound thinking or wrong knowledge, assumptions, presumptions, beliefs (deductions and inference may be included here); (or verbal condemnation of the movement of thought as wrong),

(3) fancy or hallucination or imagination totally unrelated to any proven or assumed theories, which may also include the delusion that one is already out of the movement of thought;

(4) a state of dullness or sleep; or succumbing to the movement of thought, feeling it is impossible to go beyond it;

(5) memory, or the recollection of a teaching or an experience which gives rise to the notion that it is possible to go beyond the movement of thought; such a notion forms an image.

Whether you call them pleasant or unpleasant—right knowledge, wrong knowledge, imagination, sleep and memory are the five *vṛttis* or categories of mental and psychological limitation. All these *vṛttis* are fragments, and the fragment is not the total truth; but on account of our ignorance we take each one to be the total reality. For instance, you are happy at meeting a friend and there is nothing but happiness in you. Then you just miss the train you needed to catch and you are frustrated and ready to fight with anybody at that time. Since you are touching frustration and frustration is touching you, during that period you create frustration. When that has gone you become something else; and therefore this 'becoming' continues to change. You change from one to the other, imagining during that period that either the whole world is heaven or the whole world is hell. The mistaking of that partial experience for the totality or your whole being, is the error.

Raja Yoga is meant to enable us to understand the whole business of life—of experiencing and expression. When energy enters the personality it is the experience; and the same energy, when it leaves the personality, is the expression. It is the personality which interprets it as right knowledge, wrong knowledge, right action, indifferent action, wrong action, imagination, etc. Neither the flow of energy, nor the consciousness which is everywhere all the time, is affected by any of these. The energy that is constantly moving passes through you. It is not affected by anything that you do. Knowing that we are related to this life and to this world of experiencing and expression, a clear understanding of what a *vṛtti* is immediately enables us to understand the truth concerning the nature of both experience and expression.

The 'I am' is a *vṛtti,* and this *vṛtti* assumes from there on that what is happening everywhere is 'my' experience. For instance, when there is a cool breeze it flows everywhere, but you feel it on your back and so that becomes an experience to you. When you start to sneeze, that becomes an expression. At first it is an experience of cold and then it is an expression of sneezing.

If you know that even this 'I am' has not got an independent reality, but is one ripple in the totality, then there is no problem at all. It is not *you* experiencing any more, it is not *you* doing. 'I' is not the doer any more. Consciousness is there everywhere. That cannot be destroyed. It knows what to do because it is intelligent. It is only as long as the I feels itself to be the doer, when the action springs from the *vṛtti*, that there is the need for it to classify its action as right action, wrong action, etc.

Right knowledge

Even in what we have agreed to call the truth there is a lot of frustration, which is dreadfully obvious in the case of religion. You are quite definite that this is the truth, but someone else does not accept it as the truth. How is it that you cannot make him understand? So even in what is called right knowledge— if you assume responsibility for that and if your attitude and relationship towards him are based on what you are convinced is right knowledge— there is sorrow and the area around you is miserable.

Wrong knowledge

At other times the expression as it passes through the 'I am' is interpreted by the 'I am' in a wrong manner. If your actions and behaviour spring from wrong know-ledge they can lead into all sorts of difficulties, and are fraught with danger.

Imagination

Then there is imagination, where the same energy is flowing through the 'I am'. It is just thoughts flowing through. These thoughts have nothing whatsoever to do with the 'I am', which is itself a movement of energy in consciousness. If this 'I am' says a certain young lady is not a human being at all, but a goddess, that is imagination. Imagination gets a rude shock sooner or later. Here your actions and behaviour spring from that imagination, and any action that springs from imagination is foolish, stupid and is bound to (hopefully) bring some trouble or difficulty.

Memory

The flow of energy through this personality naturally leaves some trace, which is called the memory—*vāsanā* or *saṃskāra*. Action springing from that is fraught with danger. Any action which is based on memory is defective or inappropriate action. The world has been changing, but your action is based upon something which does not exist now, in the present. First of all the memory itself is a bit tricky, and if you assume the memory to be correct, it can already lead you astray. Even if the memory does not play tricks with you, any action that springs from that memory is defective and inappropriate, because the action is in the now but it springs from the past. The memory being a thing of the past, the past had better bury it. It has no relevance now at all, it is a distracting force.

Sleep

Sleep is not a complete non-existence of the self—if it is so, then it is *mokṣa*, liberation. Sleep is probably the best part of our life. If you add up all the hours that a person sleeps from birth till death it is at least half! In sleep the self thinks, "I don't think." (It can also be shutting one's mind away.)

Sleep also includes dreaming, and a lot of imagination and probably revival of memory also, so these five are not completely watertight and separate activities, but one interferes with the other and involves the other. There are permutations and combinations.

These five can also be interpreted in another way. For example, you see that your whole life is ruined by these *vṛtti,* and you must find out what they are. Who it is that finds out, is another *vṛtti.* The 'I know' is just as disastrous as the 'I don't know'. What you have read in Indian scriptures or some of Buddha's teachings is not *your* knowledge, but what you *think* is right knowledge; and all dogmas are made up of what you think. That is totally wrong knowledge. If you believe in this, once again you are caught—there is no freedom. You get reconciled to it, until the next blow comes along. As soon as the next blow strikes, you are awakened, disillusioned and you imagine that you are out of it. Who is thinking? The *vṛtti.* The *vṛtti* is not outside all this.

Sometimes you are granted an experience of having transcended the *vṛtti*—and you say, "That's it!" That is *not* it. It is not a thing which can be caught and stored in memory, but somehow you think you can recall that experience in memory. So, if in retrospect you remember having transcended the *vṛtti,* that is of no use to you *now,* and you cannot go back to that. When a remembered experience makes you feel, in the present, that you have transcended the *vṛtti,* this is considered the most subtle and intractable obstacle in Raja Yoga and meditation too.

So right knowledge, wrong knowledge, imagination, sleep and memory are the five forms of the *vṛtti* state within us, and all of them suffer from one universal characteristic—limitation. The enlightened person is able to look into that experience (or concept) and see the reality—which is intelligence. When that pure intelligence is ignored and these begin to rule you, there is no state of yoga.

These five cover our entire life. It is possible for us, if we are some sort of specialists, to take one of these and go to the root; but then unless your concentration is extremely strong, there is a risk of the self's activity being carried on in other spheres. If the concentration is strong you can dispel the idea of the self, but if it is not strong then it is possible that while you are working on one aspect, the other aspects are flourishing.

The self can go on thinking, creating thoughts and concepts, and of course think they are right and logical. (It might even think absurd thoughts and think that they are also right.) It can register impressions or experiences as memory and occasionally revive that memory. It can indulge in imagination; and when it doesn't want to do any of these it can go to sleep. This is the endless activity of the self. The self or the understander cannot be understood; but when these five activities are observed, through them one can go right up to this understander, find the understander. When the understander is understood in awakened intelligence, then the psychological disturbance—which is pain or sorrow in life—is removed.

Must the *vṛtti* disappear in a state of yoga? Perhaps yes, perhaps no. One has to approach that a bit cautiously. What was regarded as the object (whether the knowledge concerning it was valid or not valid, right or wrong) will continue to exist. You may have good or bad thoughts about a certain person; when you are spiritually awakened something happens within you, but he does not disappear.

It is a very tricky game from there. It is not right to say that when there is enlightenment these *vṛtti* will subside. They will not subside, as such—just as the waves, as such, do not subside—but your perception of the waves as something different, distinct and separate from the ocean has gone. What it is is inexpressible: a vision of the totality without the particulars being destroyed, and yet a vision in which there is no division. That is the state of yoga.

I. 7 pratyakṣā 'numānā 'gamāḥ pramāṇāni

What are proven theories?

Theories are said to derive their proof from one or the other of the following sources:

(1) direct perception, sense experience, or intuition,

(2) deduction or extension of direct perception and sense–experience or beliefs; in the absence of direct proof or experience, indirect proof is deduced from the right or wrong application of principles of logic chosen by oneself, which often lead to vague generalisations or presumptions that 'since the theory comes from a usually reliable source, it must be correct.'

(3) scriptural or other trustworthy testimony or authority—where, again, one accepts as proof the statements of those whom one has accepted as the authority, such acceptance being blind and fanatic.

Pramāṇa (right knowledge) means proof, logical reasoning or measuring. (Reasoning is a form of measuring.) For instance, if your arguments are measur–ing up to his expectations then to him you are reasonable and correct. It is scientific. As long as your argument satisfies his measure, you are right—which means that you must talk in his language. For instance, if he is a physicist you must talk to him in the physicist's language. The same argument towards a psychologist is not acceptable. He won't understand, because he has a psychological measure, but if you talk to him in his language he is quite pleased. Then the theologians don't agree. So each of us has some measure which keeps on measuring everything.

Measuring also involves the dualistic principles of 'this is beautiful', 'this is not beautiful'. You say that something is beautiful because it satisfies your measure. There is absolutely no reason—but this is *called* reason!

When we use the word *pramāṇa* (proven theories or

right knowledge) in the context of yoga or vedanta, it is right knowledge according to tradition, to one's own belief; but these are *vṛttis,* fragments, and a fragment is not the whole truth. What is fragmentary is false—not in the sense that it does not exist. For instance you cannot say that the true ocean is a waveless ocean; but when the mind says it is a wave apart from the ocean, that is the mistake.

From where do we derive this right knowledge? Firstly, what has been seen—*pratyakṣā*—is right know-ledge. For instance, that this is a book, is right knowledge. The grounding of our knowledge is arbitrary! For instance, when teaching geometry the schoolmaster puts a mark on the blackboard with a thick piece of chalk, and says, "This is a point." It isn't, it is a big circle. We have to go on these axioms and never question the teacher. If you advance in mathematics you will learn that a point is only a concept in your mind and that there is no such thing as a straight line. So, because our sight is limited, right knowledge is also limited.

Pratyakṣā is what *seems* to be obvious. What seems to be obvious keep changing all the time. For instance, you look at somebody and you think it is obvious that he is a good man; but a few days later you yourself change your opinion and think it is obvious that he is not so good! What is obvious is obvious only because you think it is obvious for the time being. It is a mere play of words which has no sense at all.

Anumānā is inference. Because the body that you cut up in the medical school had a heart on the left side of the chest, each person must also have a heart in that place. That is inference.

Āgamā is the word of an expert. Your grandfather was breathing and suddenly the breathing stopped. You get a death certificate from the doctor, who wrote, "He died of heart failure." You don't question a doctor, because he is an expert.

What has been cognised by the senses, inference and the word of an expert are the three sources of right knowledge.

I. 8 viparyayo mithyā-jñānam atad rūpa pratiṣṭhaṁ

Unsound thinking or wrong knowledge is based on error, on mistaken identity, where the cognition is unreal and faulty and hence the knowledge is faulty, too; and where there is no agreement between the expression and the experience, between the substance and the description.

After this comes *viparyaya* (wrong knowledge). You don't want to accept something, so you create your own ideas. I will give you an interesting and humorous example of wrong knowledge.

A friend of mine, who was a doctor working for the World Health Organization as a malaria expert, went to Boston about forty years ago and was invited to talk to a wonderful group about Indian culture and philosophy. At question time one lady asked, "Is it true that in India, even today, as soon as a female child is born it is choked to death?" The doctor was a very good man and didn't want to offend the people by being rude to them, so he replied very politely, "Yes madam, I guess so. And you see in front of you an Indian born of two fathers!" Her knowledge is a perfect example of wrong knowledge.

So wrong knowledge is when you think that an object is what it is not. Children think that the earth is covered by a blue glass dome—the sky. You know it is wrong.

In our scriptures there are some standard examples where a description does not tally with any existent thing, e.g. in the dark a rope appears to be a snake, or when you walk through a desert a mirage appears to be water. But you know it is wrong knowledge.

Wrong knowledge is based on error, where the knowledge is faulty and there is no agreement between the substance and the description.

I. 9 śabda jñānā 'nupātī vastu-śūnyo vikalpaḥ

Fanciful or hallucinatory expressions and even experiences or imaginations are 'sound without substance', empty words and phrases or descriptions which have no corresponding reality, however realistic or inspiring or satisfying they may appear to be: hence they are the most deceptive and least trustworthy.

Even what you call knowledge, theory or doctrine are born from ignorance, whether they are accepted as right or wrong knowledge; a kind of confusion of all this is what is called imagination (*vikalpa*).

Imagination ruins our lives in a million ways. All of us are subject to this. The stronger the imagination the more real it appears to be, and nothing that we do can enable us to jump out of it. Here is something which we can neither confirm nor deny, which can neither be proved nor disproved, and it keeps tearing at our vitals. Almost eighty to ninety percent of our miseries are born of imagination.

What is imagination? Imagination is an image created in. It is in you, nowhere else. It is merely a thought, and it has no independent reality.

One must acquire the faculty of distinguishing between imagination and the reality. If imagination grips you it is very difficult to get out of it, and it is continuous sorrow. Even if your imagination presents a very pleasant picture it is sorrow, because at the same time the imagination stretches a little more and is worried about the loss of the thing which you wish for.

In imagination one can see that the understander or the ego functions totally irrationally. When it comes to relationship it is even more complicated. No two people see another person exactly alike. If you really contemplate this you might become frightened—or enlightened!

But, imagination as imagination is alright. For instance, if you are sitting in what is called a meditation exercise and you imagine a figure of your *guru,* that is all right, because you know it is imagination. But when you imagine something and go about as if that imaginary object or happening itself is real, then you are trapped. This happens to all of us all the time. You give the imagination more value and more reality than it need have.

Imagination is one of the favourite activities of the mind, and it leads to endless difficulties and problems. Therefore a yogi is cautious not to allow it to interfere in his life.

I. 10 abhāva pratyayā 'laṁbanā vṛttir nidrā

When nothingness or void is the content of the mind, when the idea of nothingness alone prevails, or when the mind thinks that it does not think at all, there is sleep, which is a state of mental or psychic inertia.

Patanjali also includes sleep (*nidrā*) as a *vṛtti,* as another of these fragmented experiences, because we regard sleep as only a temporary feature of our life. You are not asleep now. The rest of the time the sleep experience is contradicted, and therefore sleep is also a form of limitation.

When a man thinks he is asleep and does not know anything at all, and thinks he does not think at all, that single thought is sleep. (I am using the word 'thought' in a very loose and vague sense.) Sleep is not the total annihilation of the mind substance, of the latent impressions formed by the conditioning that has been brought about in the mind, of the *vṛtti* that are there; but the whole thing has been blanketed.

In sleep there is whatever there is—plus an ignorance of whatever there is. The purest of experiencing and of happiness itself were there; but in that state of sleep even that experience was not experienced.

However, sleep is not non-experience, it is experiencing a thing called nothing. Normally you think 'now I am wide awake, when I am tired I dream, and then I sleep' and that these three are distinct and different states, one following the other; that is, when the waking state comes to an end dreaming starts, and when dreaming ends sleep starts. But there is a commentary written on the **Mandukya Upaniṣad** where the author says that these three exist all the time. When you think you are awake you are already dreaming and sleeping at the same time. For instance, when you are absorbed in a lecture or conversation you have temporarily forgotten where you are, that there is a carpet underfoot and that your friend is sitting next to you. Therefore you have been asleep to everything around you. But you have also been dreaming. Every word stirred up an image in you, so that as you are listening the mind is also displaying its own pictures. That is already a dream. When you are dreaming you are also awake. Similarly, when you are fast asleep you are also in another world called the sleep world, where you are experiencing another type of experience comparable to the dream state and to the experience of waking.

So right now there are three worlds: the world of

ignorance, the world of dream and the world of the waking state. The three *together* is the reality. In and through all these there is something which remains undivided and indivisible. That is the reality, that is the truth. Once the truth concerning the awareness that exists even during sleep is clearly understood, then one realises that there is an unbroken awareness in waking, sleeping and dreaming.

When that becomes a realisation you are free. That is what is called enlightenment, *samādhi, satori,* etc. All these words denote one thing, a direct awareness of this simple and fundamental truth that there is no division between what is called waking and dream, and between these two and sleep.

I. 11 anubhūta viṣayā 'saṁpramoṣaḥ smṛtiḥ

Memory is the non–abandonment of the impression created by past experiences, which is revived with much the same impact on the mind–stuff as at the time of the original experience, but with or without the original details and emotional response.

Smṛti is memory. Right knowledge, wrong knowledge and imagination are gathered together, registered, accumulated, preserved and remembered, and therefore there is memory.

Memory is past experience. The impression created by a past experience has not been completely lost. You can recall the memory, the impression or experience left on the mind stuff, and observe it; but it is not the experience. It doesn't have the same emotional impact; and yet it can create great sorrow.

Yoga says let the mind be mind. Past experiences float in, but let them not colour the mind. *We* don't retain the memory, the memory is always there. Even memory doesn't jump up of its own accord. The attention scans, looks at memory, and picks it up.

So when do memories interrupt the flow and when do they not? Memory in itself does not go about inviting or rejecting experiences. It is like plain glass, which is absolutely transparent. It does not discriminate at all, it is just memory. When a memory is coloured, it evokes emotional responses. Memory *itself* doesn't colour. Colouring involves memory, but it also involves a lot more than memory. It cuts a groove which invites the memory to flow there.

Every time there is a strong memory you are almost possessed by it. Depending upon the intensity of the past experience, sometimes it seems to invoke emotional responses and sometimes it is just a matter of revival of thought. The experience is gone, and yet you can revive the impression of that past experience and suffer as if you are undergoing the experience now. Many of us indulge in this pastime. My *guru,* Swami Sivananda, was the only person I have seen who was totally free from this, especially if it was an unpleasant experience.

When there is doubt and confusion you look to authority for its removal. "Someone told me," "I read somewhere," "I heard somewhere," are all stored in the memory bank and you draw upon that in order to drive doubts away. It doesn't help, because in that memory bank are stored not only *these* ideas but contrary ideas. When you want to join with me you pick up that, when you want to argue against me you pick up something else. It doesn't help.

Memory is mixed up with imagination. In course of time the distinction between what is real and what is unreal becomes blurred, because all the time imagination is distorting that memory.

Memory is just past conditioning. It may have its own uses, but when it is allowed to generate action it spoils life. When you have a family and a firm circle of friendship you probably understand how little things add up in memory and become a big thing. If memory is not allowed to interfere in our relationships they will be most wonderful.

I. 12 abhyāsa vairāgyābhyāṁ tan nirodhaḥ

The right understanding and the realisation of the real nature of these five categories of mental states is gained by

(1) right exertion, and

(2) the simultaneous, effortless and wise avoidance of the distracting influences. The latter includes the non–arousal of cravings and attractions that compound one's confusion, and the steady perception in the inner Light that the mistaking of the mental states for the undivided intelligence, is both the cause and the effect of the clouding of the Light. Such perception is sufficiently strong and wise to know that the intelligence is forever uncoloured by ignorant waywardness.

There are several different interpretations of *abhyāsa, vairāgya* and *nirodha.*

Abhyāsa

Traditionally, *abhyāsa* means repeated practice which does not become repetitive and dull. This practice can either augment the inner light or put it out. The same agent can have two opposite effects; just as if you blow a spark too hard it goes out but if the breath is rightly applied it makes the spark glow. So *abhyāsa* can either lead to more and more vigilance and alertness—or dullness and sleep. If the mind is dull there is no zeal in it, and such a mind should not have taken up yoga.

What is practice? "Whatever enables us to be steadily rooted in enquiry, in vigilance." Unless this is borne in mind you may start doing something which might lead you astray, instead of helping you. One must ensure that at every step there is some light, otherwise there is something wrong with your practice. If you are proceeding towards enlightenment, every step you take must result immediately in some form of minor enlightenment; and from there on it must gradually spread to your whole being. Doubt must lessen in intensity, grief must disappear, confusion must clear, and occasionally you must get a glimpse of the truth. Only then are you proceeding in the right direction. If, as you go on practising this yoga you become more and more moody, more and more morose and dull, stupid, confused, grief-stricken, with a long face, then there is something wrong with that practice.

Mahatma Gandhi said that hatha yoga *āsanas, prāṇāyāma*, study and *japa* all come under *abhyāsa*. (That is the traditional meaning.) It doesn't matter what practice we undertake, as long as it has some relevance to our life. Yoga means joining, but it is a tragedy that often our yoga has no relevance to our life at all. It seems to be completely disjointed, disconnected. Why not be a part of the life stream and live such a life as would be in strict accordance with the spirit of yoga? Then you become a yogi, never mind your appearance.

Practice implies a certain repetition. The need for repetition arises because the understanding is still not there. It is not possible to try to develop this understanding.

Why must a thing be repeated? You have a second piece of toast for breakfast because the first piece was not adequate. If the first piece of toast was adequate you wouldn't have to repeat it. In a manner of speaking, *abhyāsa* means both repetition and not repetition. Your hunger is not satisfied with the first piece of toast—only the second piece really satisfies your hunger. You may say, with sufficient reasoning and logic, that it was because the first one lay in the stomach that the second piece was satisfying. But you can see that there can be at least two points of view to this argument. Does *abhyāsa* mean that every time you attempt to meditate you are making some progress, or does it mean that no progress is made until actual progress is made? If you want to jump over a well ten feet in diameter, the ability to jump six feet or eight is of precisely the same value—anything less than ten is useless! (Similarly death can be looked upon as an instantaneous phenomenon or as a gradual phenomenon. As a man gradually gets old you notice that the symptoms of death are ever present in him, gradually increasing in severity and spreading from one part to all the other parts of the body – but until he is dead, he is still alive.) This is one way of looking at it. There are others who say that as you go on with your practice, you are gradually rubbing out impurities little by little—as long as you refrain from adding further impurities to those that existed already. So one can look at this phenomenon called *abhyāsa* or practice from different sides, but it does imply *repeated* practice. It looks like an effort, but it is not; it looks like an attempt, but it is not. It may take time or it may not.

Vairāgya

The word *vairāgya* has about a page full of meanings. It is the opposite of *rāga,* which means anything that promotes your pleasure instinct—for instance, what music is to the ear and colour is to the eye. Anything that pleases the senses is *rāga,* and the result is also *rāga.* When there is infatuation or inordinate, irrational affection, that is also *rāga.* Its opposite is *vairāgya.*

So *vairāgya* has two essential meanings, one being the absence of all attraction, passion or infatuation, and the other being the absence of mental colouring, which inevitably goes with attraction. First the mind considers something as pleasure and that object or experience is thenceforth coloured with that evaluation. If you wear coloured glasses when you look at a man you are not seeing him as he is. The absence of such colouring is *vairāgya.*

Vairāgya is not a commandment to run away from truth, but to discard colouring. If the coloured glasses are thrown away then you see him as he is, irrespective of whether he wants to please you or harm you. Can you see another person without distortion? Can you break the mask that you are wearing of yourself and come face to face with him? To do that is *vairāgya.*

The essential thing is to uncolour the mind. In order to do this you must become aware that the craving that arises in you for a certain object is because of that colouring. The eyes looked at that object, but the mind registered it, and took a picture. Now the mind is coloured by that picture and that keeps on recurring and creating a desire, a craving. That must somehow be undone.

The craving arises even when the object is not present. Is it possible for you to realise at that point, "It is not here, what am I craving for?" For instance, you have a scripture in front of you which you want to read, but this face jumps on to that page. Can you at that moment say, "No, what I have in front of me is this book." It is simple logic at that moment. You want to read the book, and that thing which you crave for is not here. This is step number one. If the mind is reminded of this a few times it stops worrying you in this way. This is of tremendous importance to those who wish to meditate seriously. When you sit for your meditation and the same object of pleasure comes in front of your mind, tell the mind, "This is not the time. The object is not here. We will see when the time comes." Then this tyranny of memory is gone. The colouring is still there but it does not bother you at odd hours. Each time you do this successfully you are stronger.

The need to love and be loved are part of life, but in neither of these is there a mad, agitated craving. For instance you have a piece of chocolate in front of you. Look at it. Is it necessary or not? If it is natural and necessary you will have it. If the intelligence decided that it is not natural, that you are not hungry, then you don't have the chocolate. It is the inner intelligence shining through the mental conditioning that considers this an object of enjoyment and wants it, and in this there is no 'me' at all. The chocolate still tastes good, but there is no longer a craving for it. (This includes pleasures which the sight or the ears enjoy, as well as the taste.) The pleasure is still there, but it is had because it is (in a way) necessary. As the contact is renewed, watch how the impression is formed. The yogi sees directly, "Do I really like this, or is it simply that the impression left on the mind by a past experience demands a repetition?"

When temptation arises, immediately turn it in on itself. Is there an I, an ego, that demands this pleasure, or is it merely the memory of the past experiences that demands this repetition? In the light of that observation it is clearly seen that it is nothing but memory. What is the stuff of memory? The same intelligence. That intelligence is totally free of impressionability. Being eternal, unpollutable, it does not take an impression any more than you can write on water, nor does it hold an impression. There *is* an impression, but it is lost immediately.

It is only when you turn the light of enquiry away that you once again see the shadow on the wall. The yogi's light shines constantly on this shadow, and therefore the shadow is not seen, only the reality behind the shadow is seen – the cosmic intelligence.

One who has developed *vairāgya*—the ability to turn all temptation upon itself—finds that there is no obstacle at all to the practice of yoga, wherever one may be, but unless practice is accompanied by *vairāgya* it is likely to bump into a million obstacles.

Nirodha

Traditionally, *nirodha* is understood as control or suppression. These explanations may be valid, depending upon the point of view from which it is examined.

Here we can look at it from another dimension:

Nirodha means 'when the whole is seen, when the totality sees itself'. If this is so, how is this *nirodha* effected? It is not the 'I' who controls this. Here the control or the restraint is directed at the 'I' itself, and here vigilance is necessary.

Abhyāsa Vairāgya

The traditional meaning of *abhyāsa* is practice, and of *vairāgya,* dispassion Another meaning of *abhyāsa* is 'standing steady, unmoving, and observing the changing moods of the mind'; and of *vairāgya* 'not being distracted from this stand by temptations'. Vigilance (which was considered the best translation of *nirodha*) can be achieved by *abhyāsa* and *vairāgya*.

Yet another meaning is that *vairāgya* is uncolouring and *abhyāsa* is remaining steady in that uncoloured state. It seems to be very simple when it is explained, but if it is realised that it is the total abandoning of all this conditioning and colouring, then it doesn't seem to be very easy. But the constant practice to remain in this uncoloured state of mind is the only way in which the nature of the mind can be understood.

What we call sorrow has no existence apart from cosmic intelligence, and yet in ignorance it comes to be seen as if it were an independent entity. *Abhyāsa- vairāgya* is a twofold process by which this ignorance is enlightened. Ignorance itself is illumined by throwing light on it in order to see the background.

There is another interesting feature. It looks as though *abhyāsa* is one thing and *vairāgya* another. They are not two, but one. When it is seen that the action does not spring from the 'me' when it is seen to be a pure movement in consciousness, that is *abhyāsa. Abhyāsa* is related to expression and *vairāgya* to experience. When it is seen that the action does not spring from the 'me', the *vṛtti* when it is seen to be a pure movement in consciousness, that is *abhyāsa*. The realisation that the experience does not relate to the me is *vairāgya*, the me itself being part of this experiencing—just one little ripple or wave in this ocean of cosmic consciousness.

What is it that gives something a psychological value—that it is pleasant or dangerous? Hearsay has so coloured the mind that it regards something as pleasure. No habit has pleasure built into it.

There is no desire to suppress these actions or to

promote them. To say no is as good or as bad as to say yes.

A very old man in the Himalayas once said, "*Abhyāsa* means to remain established in God. *Vairāgya* means never to let the thought of the world arise in your mind." Marvelous, but almost impossible!

My *guru* Swami Sivananda used to say, "If you want to be firmly established in *vairāgya* before beginning to practise *abhyāsa,* you can postpone it for at least the next three lifetimes!" So, try both of these side by side.

The two things to be borne in mind whatever be the practice you undertake are: one, the spirit of yoga should not be forgotten at any stage; and two, that practice should have immediate relevance to your life, otherwise it is not yoga.

What is needed here is zeal, urgency. Very few of us have the urgency. It cannot be learned from somebody—it must develop from within oneself.

I. 13 tatra sthitau yatno 'bhyāsaḥ

Any steady and continuous or persistent and vigilant endeavour to stand firm in the understanding of the truth of the indivisibility of cosmic intelligence is known as spiritual practice (right exertion).

Ābhyāsa is to stand firm. When one's foothold on this step is firm, a vision devoid of division becomes clear.

The beauty of the yoga philosophy is that it does not restrict you to a certain set of practices, techniques or methods. Whatever is going to lead you on to establishment in this Cosmic Consciousness is *abhyāsa,* no matter what practice is adopted, but in order to get established in Cosmic Consciousness you should continuously persist in that practice for a considerable length of time. The need for repetition arises because the understanding is still not there. It is not possible to try to develop this understanding.

Practice is to enable us to realise the real to be real. Then all actions spring from the totality. If you touch the truth once you are instantly liberated. The effort to stand firm in that understanding belongs to the movement of energy in consciousness. That steady effort to remain established in that consciousness is *abhyāsa.*

Abhyāsa, therefore, means when the entire life is offered to God and given a single direction.

I. 14 sa tu dīrgha kāla nairantarya satkārā 'sevito dṛḍhabhūmiḥ

But, when is one said to be well grounded in practice?

When this spontaneous awareness or cosmic consciousness continues without interruption, for a long time, and one is devoted to it with all one's being, in all sincerity and earnestness.

It becomes firmly established when you continue this repeated practice of reminding yourself that God is omnipresent. Repeated practice becomes necessary when the practice is interrupted by *samskāras* (tendencies), doubts and physical and psychological habits. When they interfere there seems to be a need for practice again and again. You don't have to do this repeatedly if it has been really and truly done once. The trouble is that we are only thinking that we are thinking about God. (Even thinking about God is a very difficult thing. Usually we are only thinking that we are thinking about thinking about God. It is three or four times removed.) So go on repeatedly, till it sinks in. You see the ocean and you see the wave, you see them as different. You blink—no, it is one. Ah! ... but it is gone! Once again you struggle and struggle and try to reach that point where confusion arises in the mind. This goes on for some time.

Once you have clearly seen the ocean as water and the waves as water, theoretically the doubt concerning their identity or identification or names should not arise at all. When there is doubt it means that the vision is not clear. Therefore there is both understanding and misunderstanding. When this happens keep repeating it.

This is where the student of yoga may appear to be leading a double life. Life has not been totally and completely integrated. There are moments of awakening, moments of dullness; moments of alertness, moments of non–vigilance. By persistent practice, *abhyāsa,* these moments of intelligence stretch further and further, and as this happens ignorance is eliminated.

This self–awareness or awareness of the search for the self must be unbroken. If it is broken, in that period it regains its mischief. Patanjali does not say that it can manifest itself only after a long period of time. In the Yoga Sūtras he says that you can enter into this unconditioned state (*samāḍhi*) instantly, but you may not really be established in it until you have been in it for a long time. He merely suggests that you have this delight and remain in it, with your heart and soul completely surrendered to it with all sincerity and earnestness, for a long period of time, without losing it. Then you are firmly established in it, and it is not possible to disturb it.

I. 15 dṛṣṭā 'nuśravika viṣaya vitṛṣṇasya vaśīkāra aṁjñā vairāgyaṁ

How does one avoid distracting influences, without being distracted by such effort?

When the consciousness functions in a masterly way so that the compulsive and overpowering craving for objects seen or heard of, suppression or expression, inhibition or indulgence) turned upon itself—there arises an intense and consuming quest in quest of the what, how and where of the craving itself: that is known as uncolouredness or dispassion.

When there is craving for some experience or object the whole attention seems to be moving out towards it. When you ask yourself, "Where does this feeling arise that this is an object of pleasure (or pain, etc.)?" the attention that was flowing outwards suddenly begins to flow towards yourself. That is called *vaśīkāra*—which means that it comes under your control. That is control of a very different kind. There is neither expression nor suppress–ion, but intense self–awareness.

When in the light of self–awareness the mental colouring is seen and the object is then seen not to have that value, simultaneously the craving disappears. If you are constantly aware of the play of the mind and the ego, then there is no craving—craving does not arise. And if you are constantly watchful every moment that this craving arises, and observe the craving, self–awareness also increases.

So it is only by self–awareness, by looking straight into the mind and becoming aware of its content, that you are going to achieve total uncolouring of the mind. This is not achieved by merely changing the colour. If, for instance, you are watching a movie at a drive–in theatre, you do not see the screen at all. When another car is driven in behind you and the headlights flash on the screen, suddenly you see nothing *but* the white screen. Where have the images gone? In exactly the same way, where is that which you call pleasure, pain, sorrow, jealousy, hatred, love, affection, infatuation etc.? When you suddenly become aware that the brain has become polluted by what you see, hear and feel, in that moment the contamination has been washed away. It is only when the powerful beam of inner light is flashed on it that the whole colouring disappears. When that is gone, the truth is seen.

This continues until the totality is realised as the only reality. Then there is no effort or struggle—no restraint as restraint—at all. All action is naturally restrained. When there is no individuality, no conflict, division or contact between the 'me' and the other, when one alone exists, there is no effort, no craving, no rejection. (Alone means all one. When it is realised that all is one, one is alone.)

Life goes on. The natural enjoyments of life will still continue and they will be pure, fresh and uncontaminated by hopes and fears. We should not go to the other extreme of asceticism, because such an attitude first of all might mean pure suppression (which might lead to some kind of reaction) and, even more than that, at the same time might give a big boost to the ego. That is not yoga, because you get so dreadfully committed to the *vṛtti* called control. Yoga has slipped through your fingers.

The craving wants to possess the object; *vairāgya* (uncolouredness or wisdom) merely means possessing the craving—embracing it so tightly that it does not function independent of wisdom. Possessing the object of enjoyment is the nature of craving; wisdom says, "I will possess this craving so that it does not get out of hand." It behaves as wisdom wants it to behave. That wisdom in you may want to eat a chocolate cake—go ahead. There is no need to suppress it. But then craving does not eat the cake, the wisdom eats it. A big difference!

If you understand the difference you have understood what is called moderation. Wisdom knows moderation; craving is completely mad. This is what we saw in Swami

Sivananda. He could do everything in moderation. Whereas craving leads you completely astray, wisdom allows you to graze, but neatly tethered by restraint—always at the end of a leash, never loose.

When all the desires and cravings re–enter oneself, return to the source, there is true *vairāgya,* true dispassion, the direct opposite of craving.

I. 16 tat paraṁ puruṣakhyāter guṇa vaitṛṣṇyaṁ

Whereas in the earlier stages of yoga–practice, this 'turning craving upon itself' may be (i) blind suppression, or (ii) an act of self–sacrifice with a reward in view, or (iii) at best an active expression of unquestioning faith in accepted authority—the spiritual quest transcends such qualified self–discipline, when THAT which is 'beyond' the conditioned and therefore fragmented inner personality is directly seen to be free of all craving.

When the inner light shines the practice becomes different. This light is not a physical light, but a light which shines within you all the time, that is awake even when you are asleep, that knows for instance, that your right leg is exposed to the chilly wind, and draws it under the blanket. Although the yogi undergoes the same experiences that you and I undergo, in his case, from moment to moment, he sees the screen even though he sees the colouring on top. Because he sees that, essentially that intelligence is free from colouring and therefore free from attraction and repulsion. Experiencing still continues, but attraction and repulsion, likes and dislikes, are greatly weakened. Life and death or night and day are not contradictory, but complementary; the content is one. There is nothing contradictory in this world.

You are looking at the truth of what was previously

seen as the two sides of the coin. What were seen as opposites have become complementary, have blended into a whole. One does not exist without the other, simply because there *is* no other. When that truth is seen it is called *para vairāgya* (supreme dispassion). Supreme *jñāna* (wisdom), supreme renunciation and supreme delight are all the same; they all merge in the absolute. Then there is supreme non–attraction and supreme non–hate; there is love which is not the antithesis of hate, but which is indescribable—a mere 'experience–expression–put–together' of oneness. All experiences blend and there is nothing called pleasure and nothing called pain, there is just pure experiencing. The experiencing consciousness is the same—it is 'I' that feels tickled, it is 'I' that feels pinched. When the body is subjected to what is called a pleasurable experience, the nerves twitch; when the body is subjected to a painful experience, the nerves also twitch, the twitching of the nerves being the common factor. When there is anger, the facial muscles react; when there is love or happiness the facial muscles react. It is all the same movement of energy.

How does one sustain this? Is there a method by which this supreme dispassion can be reached? The next Sūtra suggests a few steps to make this possible.

I. 17 vitarka vicārā 'nandā 'smitā 'nugamāt saṁprajñātaḥ

The realisation of the unconditioned being is at times associated with logical reasoning or examination, deep a–rational enquiry, an experience of bliss or of pure I–am–ness. Yet even at those times there is consciousness of the subject–object relationship, and knowledge of the physiological and psychological states, experiences and deeds.

This Sūtra has been interpreted by some commen–

tators as signifying three or four different types of *samāḍhi.* (I don't know if there *are* different types of *samāḍhi.* The same technique or procedure seems to lead us from one to the other.)

Vitarka means logic. In order to treat this pain as a blessing, you may have to use logic to reach the logical conclusion. (A logical conclusion means neither you nor reason can answer this question. You know that when you have sincerely and honestly applied this reasoning and taken it to its own logical conclusion, not before.) So we begin with logic. For instance, let us say you are disappointed because your wife left you and ran away. That is her business—but why are you disappointed? Can you see logically that it is your 'appointment' or expectation that led to disappointment and despair? You expected something, and when that expectation did not eventuate, you were disappointed. So the disappointment is related to the expectation. If there was no hope there would be no disappointment. Why should a man entertain hope? What kind of logic is there that can answer that question? You shrug your shoulders—that is a logical conclusion. Logic comes to an end there.

Again, it may appear to you that your unhappiness comes from an outside agency, but you realise that you are the one who is suffering. If you accept that you are all right, but everything in life is hostile to you and that is why you are suffering, even then the yogi's logic leads to two wonderful steps:

1. Even if the whole world is hostile, you are part of this world, one with this world, so you are also responsible for that.

2. Never mind who causes the pain, know that it is *you* that is hurt.

A little bit of logic, of reasoning, is used in this way—neither by imagining pain or sorrow, nor by imagining a proper source for it either inside or outside.

Vitarka does not mean analysis. When you are examining fear, jealousy, anxiety, etc. it is better not to enter into an analysis at all. It often leads us nowhere. Finding the psychological cause of fear or jealousy is almost a waste of time, because if you observe very carefully within yourself you see that fear is there and that fear goes looking for a cause; the tendency to be jealous manifests as jealousy, and also goes looking for a cause. You can always find some cause! The serious student of yoga doesn't indulge in analysis, because then the attention is taken away. If you are sitting with this fear or jealousy and you are not able to look at it and see what it is, how can you look at *why* you are jealous? So no such self–deception is allowed.

You must be able ruthlessly to cut down all thoughts with counter thoughts. (We are not discriminating here between good thoughts and bad thoughts.) This cutting of thoughts must be ruthlessly done with the tool of *vitarka*. Then you see the fear and the jealousy directly, without any reasoning or logic.

When you try to meditate, the first thing is that the mind throws up all kinds of arguments, pro and con. As this happens you confront these arguments with counter arguments. So argument and counter argumentation is the first stage in this meditation. This goes on for some time until the mind reaches its own barrier, which is the rational barrier. The intellect does not function beyond ratiocination, the logic barrier, and logic comes to its own conclusion. You have no logic or rationalising intellect now, so you begin to watch and look—not inquiring in the sense of using the mind, because that *vitarka* stage is past. Now you see no argument at all for or against the existence of this indwelling intelligence, you see no reason for or against the truth or the falsity of the ego. The intellect is helpless and so it stops functioning there. When this happens the intelligence which is reflected within you begins to function. You cannot rationally discover this intelligence. Now you can only look—*vicāra*.

Then another movement in consciousness begins. It is not mental activity, but pure attention. It is not a movement in consciousness which proceeds from what is called 'me' towards the other. It is a movement in consciousness which seems to flow towards its own centre. It is neither mental activity, thought nor reasoning, but enquiry, a direct observation within. What is 'within'? What is 'without'? We don't know. For the present it *looks* like within, because a moment ago 'that' looked like without—otherwise there is no within, no without. When the enquiry starts there is a feeling that the attention is moving within towards the centre. That is called *vicāra!*

Vicārā starts when you feel trapped, you experience bondage, unhappiness. *Vicāra* has no proper translation in English, though it has been translated into 'enquiry', which has unfortunately been misunderstood to be intellectual pursuit. It is not enquiry in the sense of asking questions, etc. You may ask once, "What is happening in me, who is repeating the *mantra*?" but once that asking has been done, it is merely looking at it. If that is the meaning of the English word 'enquiry', marvellous! If it is not, the proper meaning has to be discovered. It is merely looking without thought, without thinking.

'Cār' in Sanskrit means movement, and '*vicāra*' means to move efficiently. Without *vicāra* there is no spirit in

yoga practice. In *vicāra* there is neither argument nor rationalisation. There is no anxiety to get rid of unhappiness (then you avert your gaze from the unhappiness and you cannot understand what it is), nor is there a desire to grin and bear it (again you are not looking at it). There is a third alternative—to look within to discover *where* this unhappiness is.

The question of 'what' is the essence of *vicāra*. Here one merely looks at it and enquires, "What is this sorrow?" not "Why is it there?" or "How did it arise?" There is no 'my' sorrow and 'your' sorrow, there is just sorrow. You must be able to extricate this phenomenon of suffering or sorrow (which is independent of the personality and the circumstances) from the circumstances, and see the phenomenon as it is.

Here tremendous concentration is needed, so that you can focus your whole attention upon this phenomenon of suffering and let the energy of the mind flow in that single direction. Then you have forgotten why you are unhappy, you are only aware of sorrow. It is in you.

If you are aware of sorrow, are 'you' and the 'sorrow' two different entities, or are they the same? When you use a *mantra* in meditation and mentally repeat it, you can hear it. Who is saying it and who is hearing it? Suddenly you realise that you are also there, you are watching both these. The sound is emanating from somewhere. Someone is saying this *mantra*, someone is listening to it, and someone is watching both these fellows! Similarly, here you are merely observing this phenomenon of sorrow, and you say, "I am aware of sorrow".

Try this. Stand in front of your electric stove. You can see that the water is boiling in the kettle, but *you* don't have to boil, do you? No. So similarly, you can see sorrow, observe sorrow and become aware of that sorrow. You observe that you are aware of sorrow. As you are becoming more and more intensely aware of sorrow, you suddenly become one with that sorrow. You are not sorry any more, you are not suffering any more, you *are* sorrow. The fire itself doesn't feel hot, it *is* hot. So that if you are sorrow, you don't feel sorrow any more. You are free.

So *vicāra* is a movement in consciousness. It is pure attention. It does not proceed from what is called 'me' towards the other, but is a direct observation within. (You can focus it on sorrow, pain, fear, hate or anything you like.) Unless there is a feeling that the attention is moving within towards the centre, these words have no meaning. There is pure observation and that observation *itself* discovers the true nature of experience. 'Discovers' is meant in its almost literal sense—you had covered that pure experiencing with a big label called 'sorrow' and when this light of observation shone on it, it dis–covered or peeled that label off. That is discovery—'un–covery'. There is an endeavour to merely observe the reality or the content of that experience. (This is like flashing a torch on the shadow on the wall. When the shadow is illumined, its background or substratum is seen.) In that observation there is great stillness, and the object of observation alone exists.

Because of the extreme importance of *vicāra*, let us look at another example—of pain, for instance. Pain, sorrow and suffering are really a blessing, but in ignorance we turn them into a sorrow by blaming someone or something else—the psychologist blames one's childhood and the oriental religious man blames one's previous birth, for instance. Instead of listening to these ideas, if you look at the pain immediately, you may be able to deal with it (A wise man need be hurt only once.)

What is pain, what is it made of? When you begin to inquire seriously, the first thing you notice is that the mind is absolutely calm and quiet. You have pulled away from the pain, and therefore the pain is not terribly painful. You are observing it, inquiring into it, and in the meantime the body takes care of the pain (or whatever it is). There is no pain, only the mind–stuff. In the light of that observation it becomes absolutely clear that there is only the wall (the screen); there is no shadow at all, just the background. There is no wave, there is only the water.

The observation still continues, it does not come to an end, because there is one question which we have not answered. We are using such expressions as 'I observe the mind', 'I am meditating', knowing that all these are mental modifications. Even if these statements are the fruits of direct observation, there are still these questions, "What is I? Who is the experiencer or observer? Is the observer a totally independent entity, independent of the experience? Is 'I' a completely different and independent being standing apart from the mind–stuff?" I do not know.

The whole area of observation has narrowed down completely. The object has gone, the experience has gone, the only thing left now is the observer. If this pure observation asks this question and gets the answer 'I do not know', then 'I' and 'do not know' are the only things left, and these are not two completely different factors, but two sides of the same thing. Here there is no logic and no observation, there is total stillness.

Vicāra is essential in the practice of Raja Yoga and meditation. Meditation helps the *vicāra* and *vicāra* helps the meditation, because *vicāra* needs one–pointedness and introversion of the mind. The mind must be introverted so that both during the practice of meditation and at other times the yogi must be aware of the thoughts and the emotions that arise in him. (That makes it very clear that the yogi is not looking for a blank mind and an emotionless heart!)

The Buddha said, "Live in this world as you would if you were living in a room with a deadly cobra." As soon as you become aware of it you begin to observe—not thinking about it, knowing that your thinking or not thinking does not alter the situation. You are wide awake and full of energy, perfectly concentrated. You may panic for a couple of minutes, but once you realise that you are caught in it the mind is absolutely calm and alert, looking actively but passively. All this is involved in that single instruction of living with the cobra.

If you can dramatise the whole thing within yourself for five minutes, you have learnt all about meditation and *vicāra*. You know what it is to enquire into, to look into, to observe. In the same way, if you are able to observe pain (either physical or psychological) and you have pulled yourself away from it, there is this inner feeling, "I am here, I am not affected by this." (It is not verbal, and you are not trying to bluff yourself.) The pain seems to go away, because you are acting as an observer now, you don't really experience the pain that the body is experiencing. But this does not last long; once this observation comes to an end, you get caught up in the pain again.

If you are serious about this enquiry, if your mind, heart, emotions and life itself all come together and 'functionise' *vicāra*, then you have tremendous energy which is derived from the non–dissipation of the mind. There is nothing that you cannot achieve.

Use whatever pleasure and pain life brings you every day for your enquiry, and if you are sincere and earnest about it, then there is not a single moment in your life when this enquiry need be really absent. For example, when you are singing can you forget about everybody else and listen to your voice? How and where does it originate? How does it feel inside? Even as you are listening, you can look at the process of listening—not the anatomical and physiological aspects, but how listening takes place. If while you are singing you are merely observing the singing, neither thinking about it, analysing it nor examining it, it is a beautiful sensation. So whatever the experience—singing, walking, driving, eating or having a shower—you can utilise it for pure awareness or *vicāra* .

It is definite that whatever path you may take and wherever the observation or enquiry leads you, when that awareness is functioning, when all your mental disturb–ances drop and all the things that are torturing you have gone, there is momentarily a sense of great joy and happiness. Pain ceases to be tormenting and pleasure ceases to be tantalising, and there is an experience of a sort of happiness which is not the absence of unhappiness. Patanjali describes it as *ānanda,* bliss. There is a feeling 'I am experiencing this bliss'. This bliss is completely different from pleasure, and even different from what we normally call happiness.

Here there is only one snag—in spite of this *ānanda* there is also *asmitā* or individuality—'I' am aware of sorrow; 'I' have become one with sorrow; 'I' am fire itself, there is nothing burning 'me'; 'I' am ice itself, there is nothing making 'me' cold. When you get to this stage, there is bliss. But, *you* are experiencing this bliss, the 'I' or the individuality is still there. Up to this you can reach unaided, there is no God necessary here.

From there all division of me and the thought, me and the feeling seems to melt away and 'I' (*asmitā*) alone remains. There is a state of homogeneity within.

You ask yourself, "Who is it that enjoys this bliss?" and you get the answer, "I am". There you have reached your limit. This is a very high state of *samādhi* or consciousness which can help you in real life, but even this is subject to being lost, because as long as the feeling 'I am' or a belief in the existence of the egotism is there, so long the veil of ignorance is also there. You have not completely discovered the inner indwelling omnipresent intelligence, and therefore. there is the ever-present danger of falling from that height.

Beyond that it is difficult for the unaided human being to go, and that is where we need the grace of God. That grace manifests itself when you knock. While knocking at this door called 'I don't know', helplessly you fall down— and the door opens. That is called divine grace (or whatever you wish to call it.) When you collapse, the egotism and the ignorance also collapse. There is enlightenment. Did you achieve it? No. Did you not achieve it? Yes. No questions can be answered rationally from there on. (This approach needs a certain psychological, mental or inner discipline. This may not suit some people, in fact it may sound ridiculous to them)

Vicāra, especially, needs tremendous psychological discipline to keep the mind from straying. If we don't succeed we end up in a beautiful vicious circle—if you cannot control the mind you cannot do *vicāra,* and if you cannot do *vicāra* you cannot control the mind.

There is a different type of inner psychological equipment in different people. In other words if you are emotional, if your heart rules your head, the *vicārā* approach may be difficult. If heart and head are perfectly balanced it is all right; but if—as in the case of most of us—either the head rules or the heart rules, then there arises a slight difficulty. Either the whole technique (if it can be called so) is rejected by the heart as dry, or it is seen as just emotionalism.

Some people don't like any of these. They like hands and feet to be put to work. In their case neither this nor that is of any use. They must be doing something, working. So you have to look within and gauge for yourself whether you should adopt the method of *vicāra,* the method of surrender, or the method we will discuss later—*aṣṭāṅga yoga.*

If *vicāra* is appealing to you that is all that you need to worry about. Raja Yoga is over. You don't have to practise *āsanas* or *prāṇāyāma,* or anything at all. If surrender to God—*Īśvara praṇiḍhāna* (see I. 23) is appealing to you, *that* is enough!

On the other hand, if neither *vicāra* nor *Īśvara praṇiḍhāna* suit you, and there is a lot of physical energy which has to be channelled one way or the other, then there are other practises. Other difficulties and other problems have to be solved with other measures.

How does one know? You are going to say that you must look within and see which one is good. That is precisely the problem! You cannot look within yourself. You don't know what is going on. You may prefer to think that you are like Ramana Maharṣi, or the Buddha, just waiting for enlightenment. You close your eyes, enter into deep sleep and think that *that* is meditation. How do you know what is going on?

This is where the guidance of a teacher or a *guru* may

become useful—at least to enunciate the rules of the game. The *guru* is not going to play the game for you—then it is *his* game, not yours. For instance you might read one little thing in Ramana Maharṣi's book—that in *samādhi* the head is erect and in sleep the head is down. This may or may not be the total answer, the perfect answer, but it gives you some guidance. You know that there is some difference between *samādhi* and sleep. So after two hours of tremendous, fantastic meditation if you find your head is upright, *maybe* it was meditation, if it was down—next time!

I. 18 virāma pratyayā 'bhyāsa pūrvaḥ saṁskāra śeṣo 'nyaḥ

Different from this is the practice which is based on cessation of all effort – even at meditating: this practice leads spontaneously to tranquillity. In that, only the impressions or memories remain: of such impressions is the 'me' constituted.

Effortlessness does not drop from heaven. To begin with you may have to make use of some of the aids described in previous Sūtras which imply the application of some effort. It is the effort that keeps all the mental activity awake, that disturbs enlightenment. At that point the effort seems to be useless and so it drops away. Just the memory of past experiences is still left, because the 'I' is there, the *saṁskāras* are there, and it is that which takes body after body, until that is given up in total enlightenment. The master suggests that as long as this effort is in the right direction, you have not reached the goal, but you are safe.

Saṁskāras can be vaguely translated as latent tendencies, predispositions or psychological conditioning. This is very different from memory. Memory is something you can see, *saṁskāra* is something which sees, which picks up the memory. Memory is a thought, *saṁskāra* is the thing that thinks, that registered the memory in the first place. The difference must be clearly understood.

This seems to suggest that some sort of gross substance within yourself receives all these imprints. It may not be. Please work on it yourself, for only then will you understand it. When someone insults you, what is it that responds with annoyance, with anger? When somebody praises you, what is it that responds with pleasure? One has to find the answers to these questions oneself.

When the mind is absolutely still and there is clear observation of the self without an observer, then the play of the mind and the latent pre–dispositions—the *saṁskāras*—are seen. These have been handed down (if you don't believe in reincarnation), from father to son. (If you believe in reincarnation, from birth to birth.)

Saṁskāra to the yogi is a much greater problem than memory. Every action and every experience we pass through in life leaves an impression. You do something once, or several times and it becomes a memory; which is outside you, so you can look at it and feel it. At one stage (heaven knows when this happens) it is no longer a memory. It has taken hold of you so that you don't even know of its existence. It is no longer something which you can see and handle, it has *become* you. Every time you become passionate, angry, agitated or kind, for instance, the *saṁskāras* of passion, anger, agitation or kindness become stronger, and the grooves become deeper. All these grooves put together is the 'me'. So there is basically no difference between the *saṁskāras* and what is known as the ego, or the 'me'.

In spite of all the yoga and meditation you do, *saṁskāras* are something which remain dormant in sleep, and they are there even in the state usually called *samādhi.*

Unless we come to grips with this *saṁskāra,* we have done nothing at all in yoga—we are only experts in bringing about a change in the bookshelf. You can re–organise your life—which is outside; you can re–organise the thought pattern - also outside, you can re–organise your memory by saying, "I will not remember this, I'll remember only that." If you have very carefully followed the ground that we have covered so far, it looks terribly easy to re–organise that part of it. But how does one bring about a change in the *saṁskāra*—not in the memory bank, thoughts or pattern of thinking, but in the thinker, the one who thinks. *Saṁskāra* is the cell of your cell, the soul of your soul, the very spirit which has been assimilated into you, become you. Therefore it is so strong that it is almost impossible to alter it; and unless it is altered there is no yoga!

It is not the *saṁskāras* or the actions in themselves that matter but the experiencer and the doer of action that mysteriously springs up when the *saṁskāras* are there. Even to recognise their existence is already a big step. The only way to deal with them is through eternal vigilance. If one is alert and vigilant, all experiences—whether they are called pleasure or pain—can be used to trigger self–observation or meditation. When the process of meditation we have been discussing is applied to these *saṁskāras,* there is a serious curiosity. Why do I behave in this manner? Why is it that someone else behaves in a different way? What is it that predisposes me to this conduct, whether that conduct is socially acceptable or unacceptable?

Here you are directly observing not only the *saṁskāras* but the bed, the source, the field in which they grow, as it were. The rays of the mind, which were flowing away from the centre, seem to turn upon their own source. During that process there is a stillness and a dropping of effort. The mind, the attention and awareness are still there and there is this sudden movement which is not movement but a tremendous dynamic stillness. (It is comparable to the candle flame which is steady, although we know that every moment millions of sparks flow along that flame.)

In that dynamic stillness there is very clear awareness of observation itself, without an observer. There is tremendous inner stillness and peace. You may call it bliss, God, or consciousness—whatever you wish. When this happens, the colouring of the mind, and the play of the latent predispositions or *saṁskāras* are seen. In this there is no effort. The effort ceases, because the moment you make an effort, the effort becomes the doer which says, "I practise meditation". In the state where there is no effort, there is not even the feeling that you are practising meditation.

When the process of meditation we have been discussing is applied to these *saṁskāras* there is a serious curiosity. Why do I behave in this manner? Why is it that someone else behaves in a different way? What is it that predisposes me to this conduct, whether that conduct is socially acceptable or unacceptable? That is what we want to know. Here you are directly observing not only the *saṁskāras,* but the bed, the fountain source, the field in which these *saṁskāras* grow (as it were).

So the yogi looks at the thoughts, feelings and emotions with some sort of wonder, and suddenly realises that they are all composed of the one substance. What is the content of any of your thoughts? Thought! Can this observation without an observer (which is meditation) see through all this, right down to the bed of *saṁskāras*, the content of the thoughts and emotions? At that level, the *saṁskāras* cease to be. A thought ceases to be a thought and emotions cease to be emotions, because you have crossed the level of these labels.

I. 19 bhava pratyayo videha prakṛtilayānāṁ

When such impressions remain, one retains the possibility (and the cause) of birth again, even after being freed from the present body and after becoming integrated with one's own or the cosmic nature. For, such impressions or memories nurture and perpetuate the awareness of continued personal existence.

The self is the bed of *saṁskāras*, of all the tendencies and predispositions put together. When the *saṁskāras* form in the mind, what is it that claims, "I experience this, I am good, bad, an Indian, etc."? Why does one say that these impressions belong to 'me', or 'I have these bad habits'? There seems to be a cohesive force (the conditioning or limitation) that keeps all these latent tendencies together, so that this infinite consciousness seems somehow to think, "These belong to me. I am made up of these." The single thought that all these ideas and ideologies, notions and concepts, *saṁskāras* and *vāsanās*, etc. form part of me, belong to me and I to them, is another conditioning.

When the present body drops and the elements of which it is composed are returned to nature, the next embodiment and the next world are determined by whatever be the condition in which the consciousness (which thinks it is limited to this body) finds itself. It creates its own space, its own world, and it becomes what the nature of that consciousness deserved to become at that moment. (Or, what determines that is the nature of this conditioning at the time the embodiment is dropped.) It goes on and on until the conditioning is completely abandoned. How long is anybody's guess.

We have no choice but to go on practising, because as long as this conditioning lasts, every time this body falls (*viḍēha*) and the components are reabsorbed into nature (*prakṛtilayānāṁ)* there is an inner change—a new notion or concept is formed.

Only when the colouring has dropped away and consciousness has become completely cleared of the concepts we have fed into it—including the notions 'I am' and 'This is my mind, my consciousness'—is there liberation.

I. 20 śraddhā vīrya smṛti samādhi prajñā pūrvaka itareṣāṁ

In the case of others, when such spontaneous realisation of the unconditioned does not happen, such realisation is preceded by and proceeds from faith or one–pointed devotion, great energy and use of will power, constant remembrance of teachings and one's own experience, the practice of samādhi (the state of inner harmony) and a knowledge or discernment of such harmony—all of these lead one gradually on to that state of yoga.

Yoga is the whole of life. God is not a sort of king or a ruler, or a great grandfather sitting on a throne some–where, governing the whole universe. God is the indivis–ible cosmic existence, the indwelling omnipresent intelligence. It is omnipresent and therefore indwelling; at that indwelling point, the omnipresence is easily reached. That is yoga!

So it is not difficult to see how all our faculties and all

that is happening in this world have to be seen as an integral part of yoga. We need faith in, and remembrance of, the teachings of yoga. We need to hold on to the feeling of harmony attained in the practice of meditation.

What is most important is that we need to have zeal in our practice. We need to put forward the maximum self–effort we are capable of. Usually we are lukewarm, because we are lazy. There is a limitation to what your brain can do. Go up to that, because until you go up to that, there is no vitality, no zeal.

Have you ever prayed for a loaf of bread, for food? No. Because you have never felt hungry. The prayer of a man who is starving and all he wants is a loaf of bread, is a living prayer. If some kind of implement could be invented to measure the intensity of prayer, you would find that that man's prayer is far more intense than the prayer of all of us put together. Our prayer becomes luke–warm, because the urgency is not there. That sense of urgency, of zeal, must be there in our practice of yoga. Put forth all the effort you are capable of.

I. 21 tīvra saṁvegānām āsannaḥ

However, lest it should be misconstrued that such gradual evolution implies cosmological or psychological distance to be covered, it should be added that the state of yoga or the unconditioned intelligence is close at hand, irrespective of the approach followed by the seeker—if they are full of intense zeal, enthusiasm, energy and sincerity, and are thus able speedily to overcome obstacles.

When one's zeal is intense and total, that total intensity brings this unconditioned state of being here and now.

I. 22 mṛdu madhyā 'dhimātratvāt tato 'pi viśeṣaḥ

Yet again it is possible to see a distinction between mild, middling and intense zeal, energy and effort, although yoga (which is spontaneous realisation of oneness) and effort (which implies duality) are contradiction in terms.

It is possible that some are ardent in their devotion to yoga and may be able to reach this soon; some are not so ardent and so they may take a little more time; some are a little bit dull, but never mind, they will eventually reach this point.

I. 23 Īśvara praṇidhānād vā

Or, the state of yoga is attained by complete, instant, dynamic, energetic and vigilant surrender of the ego principle to the omnipresent ever–existent reality or God. This is instant realisation of God as the only reality when the (ego's) quest of self–knowledge meets its counterpart, ignorance, and stands bewildered in choiceless encounter; and when the ego–ignorance phantom instantly collapses.

How does one overcome the *vṛttis,* including the basic and fundamental *vṛttis* of 'I am'—'I am' as independent? Let us go back to the analogy of the wave and the ocean. The wave *as* ocean is ocean, not wave; the wave as a concept is a concept. The wave as something in itself is non–existent.

The wave is not unreal. Of course it is there, you can see it! But while looking at the wave you are really looking at the ocean, not the wave. The wave as a wave is a concept—a certain formation of the surface of the ocean is called wave. It is a name, a word. In the same way, the *vṛtti* is non–different from the mind.

How do you get rid of the false concept that the *vṛtti* is different from the mind?

The method of *vicāra* was given in I.17. Another

method to help us get rid of this false concept is *Īśvara praṇidhāna*. This deals with the emotional or devotional approach to the same truth, therefore no thinking, rationalisation, condemnation or criticism is allowed. There is just a pure heart–to–heart relationship.

Īśvara is translated as God, and *praṇidhāna* means total, dynamic and passionate surrender to *Īśvara*. This is not a dull and passive action. It must be a dynamic, full–blooded, energetic surrender, so that in that surrender there is no withholding. It cannot be partial surrender, because either it is total or it is not at all! So partial self–surrender is a misnomer.

In the case of self–surrender quite a few questions arise, but those questions do not arise in one whose heart rules the mind. Ramana Maharṣi's teachings of surrender make it look very much like *vicāra*. While talking of self–surrender, he says, "First of all find out who you are and who God is". If you do that you don't want to surrender anything! If you have that psychological discipline which is described in Sūtra I. 17, then there is no need for surrender. Surrender just happens.

Īśvara praṇidhāna is slightly different, it is not the same process as *vicāra*. You are unable to discipline the mind and do *vicāra*, because the energy of the mind seems to be incapable of sustained uni–directional motion (which is *brahmacārya*). This energy seems to be disturbed by emotional states. Then you see that if the truth is approached through the heart, it is possible to arrive at the same point.

Therefore this method is as effective as the previous method of *vicāra*, and can also be used independent of it. Even though you may have no intellectual equipment for the *vicāra*, by this method also you arrive at the same place—instantly. They are not different in essence, because in *vicāra* one is interested in the theory, but to the one who is engaged in dynamic surrender, it is not theory—it is his practice!

Here *Īśvara praṇidhāna* might mean the whole system of Bhakti Yoga.

You might take any form of devotional practice that appeals to the heart and moves the heart to offer itself totally to God. Using the approach of *vicāra* you discover that the division in thought—the anxiety, fear etc.—is unreal, and 'I' alone exists'; whereas in this emotional approach you are seriously concerned about who the 'I' is. But you start on a different footing, saying that God alone exists. Only a little bit of intellectual understanding is needed here.

You say, "This is all God's grace, God's will," because you don't *know* anything. All you do know is that you don't know anything! So the devotee takes that step quickly. He doesn't beat around the bush.

Whatever happens to you, you must be able to say, "It is God's will." Don't be half-hearted—as long as it is comfortable for you it is God's will, but if she does something you don't like, it is not God's will, but *her* fault! One who is able persistently to say that it is *all* God's will, has already pushed the ego sense away. In all these waves and cross currents he is able to see the hand of God.

Here is a lovely story: A king and his minister used to go hunting every weekend. One morning the king was cutting an apple and the royal knife was too sharp and he cut off a bit of his finger. The minister was a philosopher. He said, "Ah, it is good for you, Your Majesty."

The king became furious. He had him arrested and taken away. As he was being pulled away from the royal presence, he said, "This is good for me, it is God's will. And that was *also* God's will." (Not only when things are going right, but even when they are going wrong, you must have the courage to say, "This is also God's will." Then the surrender is correct.)

The king went hunting alone. There were a few bandits in that forest who had taken a vow that if one of their robberies was successful they would offer a human sacrifice to Kali. The robbery was successful and therefore they were looking for a human being to sacrifice. When they saw the king they got hold of him. He was alone and they were many, so meekly he walked to the temple. The robbers brought in their priest. Before the sacrifice he had to be bathed ceremoniously, so he was stripped. As the priest was pouring water on his head he saw the little bandage, and asked, "What is that?"

"Oh, I cut myself this morning."

The priest gave him one resounding slap and said, "Get out. You are unfit to be sacrificed. Something which has already been cut cannot be offered in sacrifice."

The king said, "Thank you very much," jumped on his horse and raced towards his palace. On the way he remembered that his minister had said that the cut was good for him. He thought, "But for that little accident I might have lost my life today!"

He went straight to the cell and released the minister, saying, "What you said proved right. But there is one thing that is puzzling me. I had unjustly had you arrested and put in the cell, and you said that it was good for *you.* Can you justify that also?"

The minister said, "It is obvious. If you had not locked me up here I would have gone with you!"

What happens in our own life may not be so easy to

see, but it is true. If you have that perseverance in seeing the divine in everything that happens, you are liberated.

Īśvara is God, but not the kind of God we associate with temples, churches and mosques. *Īśa* and *Īśvara* are synonymous terms in Sanskrit, and *Īśa* is whatever is—not what you think is, not whatever appears to you to be, but what *is*. What is? Pure experiencing is—not as 'I see you'—that is my thought, and my desire to experience; not 'this face is beautiful and that is not beautiful' or 'this is good and that is not good'. That is opinion! What *is* is pure experiencing, and experiencing is God.

What is meant by 'surrender'? Does it imply that when somebody threatens to break your jaw you say, "No, no, I surrender"? Is that how we surrender to God? In that there is desire, fear and hope. Someone wants to hit you; you are afraid. By doing this surrender you hope to be saved—which means the ego is still very much alive and strong, and it thinks that God is something outside of the me. The outside God is a creation of your own mind.

Surrender also suggests that there is an 'I', and that 'I' has to be taken, nicely gift–wrapped and offered at the feet of God. But surrender is not that. 'I' does not surrender something else. The 'I' *itself* must surrender.

How does 'I' surrender? What exactly does it mean? Only when there is direct understanding of the truth that God alone is, is there surrender. As a matter of fact that is what the simple word 'yoga' means. If you can mentally visualise a blackboard and you draw a line with a piece of chalk, that white line seems to have created a division, above here—below there. You take a piece of cloth and wipe it. As you wipe it you see that that which was above and that which was below are coming together. That is yoga. It was never broken, but on account of a certain colouring it appeared to have been broken. When this understanding arises, what is *is*, and cannot be broken at all. That which appeared to have been broken, appears to come together. Where there was apparent division, that surrender restores oneness. This is the process of surrender.

To help us understand, another example is given: a doll made of salt had the power to think. One day it was standing on the beach and it wondered how big and how deep the ocean is. It jumped into the ocean and it instantly knew the length and the breadth and the depth of the ocean—because when it dissolved it became the ocean. (This was possible because the salt–doll was also made of the ocean—salt.) Similarly, there is nothing called 'me' which is other than the cosmos. The body is the cosmos, made of earth, water, fire, air and energy. Air is moving in the body keeping it alive, and air is also cosmic. There is some intelligence, and that intelligence is also cosmic. What is it that you consider 'me'? An examination of the self in this manner is also called surrender.

At each point one has to be extremely vigilant and careful that it is not the ego that does all this. When the ego practises yoga there is no yoga. Surrender means the surrender of the ego or, even more appropriately, the realisation of the *non–existence* of the ego. That is a completely and totally different thing! Neither a desire for God nor a fear of living is left. It is then that you can really say that surrender *is*.

You cannot say, "God, I surrender myself completely to you so that I may be healthy, I may be strong." You surrender yourself to God, comma, so that you will be happy forever after. That is not surrender, but a bargain; and it shows that you are a very good business man! For just using the formula: "God, I surrender myself to you," you want to be happy forever hereafter. That's good business! No, there is not even a trace of desire that on account of this surrender you must be healthy or prosperous or happy. If those desires arise that means the self is still functioning. Even in your day–to–day activities if the whole thing is handed over, life becomes much better. When the mind starts functioning as if it is terribly important, it is then that tension begins.

When the expression 'God is bliss' is uttered, we often get all kinds of romantic ideas—e.g. 'I must abandon this body, I must surrender myself to the God who is in heaven. Then I am going to bliss!' Bliss is here—in the very touch of the carpet, in the touch of the breeze, in the smile of a child, in the sunrise, in the sunset, in the way the gum trees sway in the wind. Can that *be*. (The sentence is complete.) Can that be—without a desire or a craving arising to experience that as though it were something different from you? Can that be? If it is, that is surrender.

One who has really and truly surrendered does not even know. His life has been sacrificed or made sacred; which means that the whole personality—including the ego sense if there is one—has been made sacred. (This may help you understand what seems to be mysterious behaviour in saints like Swami Sivananda. If they had an ego–sense, even that had been made sacred, had been touched by the divine fire. If they were cross with you, that is exactly what God's will was. Take it as a blessing! There is absolutely nothing that is unsacred in that person's personality.)

When *Īśvara praṇidhāna* happens, all the labels have dropped away; there is nothing that is called good or evil. That is the exalted state of the yogi.

Thus yoga is not something which is confined to morning or evening meditation, but something which *is,* all the time.

I. 24 kleśa karma vipākā 'śayair aparāmṛṣṭaḥ puruṣa viśeṣa īśvaraḥ

Who is God?

That unique indwelling omnipresence that is never tainted nor touched by the ground of actions and their reactions, which afflict ignorant individuals; that which is left–over after the ego–ignorance–collapse; that special inner ruler or intelligence which is unconditioned by time and whose will alone prevails even in the body. In it there is oneness, never divided. It is therefore beyond ignorance and its progeny.

What does God mean to you, what do you like to regard God to be? What is your concept of God? If you are so big that you can conceive even of God, you are covering that God with your own conceptions.

Īśvara, or God, is *puruṣa viśeṣa*—a Special Being who is not touched by the fruition of action, which in the case of ordinary people like us leads to distress and unhappiness. The ordinary being is that which controls your senses, which enables you to express and experience. Endowed with certain mental and physical faculties, as it goes on expressing and experiencing in this world, it cannot help being tainted and polluted by the residuum of these experiences and expressions.

The ordinary indwelling consciousness—the *jīva,* the ego–sense, the experiencer who thinks he is subject to pain and pleasure, success and failure—is the one who is sunk in unhappiness.

One step behind this (behind, in front, under, below, above—no words make sense at all) there is the Special

Being, who, like space, remains completely and totally unaffected. This Special Being is behind this personality, this ordinary being, different from it, and yet within it—because this Special Being is omnipresent, and that which is omnipresent is everywhere—*puruṣa viśeṣa.*

Puruṣa is the inner ruler, the indweller or 'one who dwells in a city'. (Great yogis used to regard the body itself as a city of nine gates and the one who dwells in and rules that nine–gated city is a *puruṣa*). That Being is not involved in your *karma* (your actions and their consequent reactions) and your experiences of pain and pleasure. That which is beyond dualism and which is therefore the undivided intelligence beyond the ordinary personality, is *puruṣa viśeṣa.*

There is another meaning of the word *viśeṣa. Śeṣa* means what remains, the residue. (It also means serpent.) How do you find who it is? By seeing what remains after all that is not the reality has been eliminated.

When you peel off all your own notions concerning this *Īśvara,* when you have eliminated all that is not the *puruṣa* or the inner reality, what remains is the *puruṣa.* If you say that the nature of the inner ruler is seen by peeling these things off by the process of 'not this, not this', it means you have already clothed that inner ruler with your own mind substance. *You* have done it. It is good to remember that God or the reality does not have any clothes on. You are unable or unwilling to see the reality and therefore you put on the clothes. When you want to see the real nature of God you take these things away, one by one.

When you have discarded all the *saṃskāras,* thoughts and emotions (all of which made you behave in a certain way), when you have seen through them and they don't seem to matter anymore, then there emerges the true *puruṣa* the true self, that which is the substratum, the *is*. This is; all else appeared to be, came into being and came to an end. For instance, you think that something is pleasure; it arose from a certain experience and it came to an end, but the experienc*er* is still there. You thought that something else was painful; it arose, it remained for some time and it vanished, but the experienc*er* is still there. That which remains when all these have been seen through, that ground intelligence, is *Īśvara*.

That intelligence—which pervades this body but is not confined or limited to it—connects you and me and therefore enables communication to take place. You can understand it from the example of space. Before this building was put up there was space exactly where we are sitting. Now we are calling it the hall. This space was there before and when this building is pulled down this space will still be there. Nothing happened to that space; it is unchanged whatever you do in it. Even when walls are erected, the space is neither occupied, cancelled out, consumed nor destroyed. Nothing happens to it. In other words, space cannot be cut up. Therefore the use of the expression 'this part of space' is absurd. We discover a new definition—'anything that cannot be parted can never be a part'. The finger is a part of me because I can part from it. Space cannot be cut up into parts, and therefore there are no parts at all in space, and there is nothing called the space in one room as distinct from the space outside. God is described in yoga texts as:

ākāśavat sarvagat nitya—like space, omnipresent, eternal. You can do nothing to it.

In the same way in this ordinary person, you who reads this (but not limited in any way; untainted, un–

touched by this person), there is a Special Person, and that Special Person is called *Īśvara* or God.

Kleśa karma—God is not influenced or affected by what you, as a limited individual, seem to be affected by—which means fear, sorrow, grief, stupidity, ignorance, etc. All these do not exist in God, and that is why you can approach him, surrender yourself to him and be freed from your own limitations.

God is unlimited, unconditioned, and therefore by surrendering yourself totally you also become unconditioned—'I' becomes unconditioned. The wave as a wave is subject to being disturbed by the wind that ruffles the surface of the ocean, but the moment the wave merges in the ocean it is no longer capable of being ruffled. It is free. 'I' is conditioned, limited, and therefore is subjected to fear, anxiety, jealousy and so on; but *Īśvara,* being the totality, is that which remains after all these conditions have been dropped away, or peeled off —*viśeṣa.*

This is merely affirmed by the devotee, he does not intellectualise it. He contemplates God, he knows that God is omnipresent, omnipotent and omniscient. To that God he surrenders himself. When the 'I' is surrendered to that omniscient being, there is instant freedom—as long as the surrender is complete and total!

Since the divine, that is omnipresent and omniscient, is not involved in *kleśa karma,* total surrender to the divine is another way of freeing oneself from the *vṛttis.*

The whole concept of *karma* and of Karma Yoga is woven into this *kleśa karma.* How does one overcome *karma*? It is also mentioned later in the fourth chapter (IV. 7). *"In the case of yogis,"* says Patanjali in this Sūtra, *"karmas or actions are neither black nor white."*

Whatever the yogi does is neither good nor evil,

because he doesn't have the sense of doership. Whatever happens to him happens by God's grace. Whatever he is able to do is also by God's will, God's grace—completely and totally. There is no ego sense at all, so that what he does has no focal point for the *karma* to rebound from. The *karma* rebounds on you only as long as the ego–sense projects it. Otherwise it is lost in infinity. It has no starting point and therefore it has no point to return to. So in God there is no *karma.*

It is only in relation to a finite point that one assumes that there is also a finite goal. But when there is a movement in the cosmos, in the infinite, there is no movement. There is a scientific theory that the solar system is dropping in space—from where to where and what to what—in relation to an assumed central point, which they call the black hole. Even that is an assumption. A motion is motion only in relation to something else. If that something else is not there, there is no motion.

So *karma* is *karma* only in relation to something else. An action returns as a reaction only as long as the starting point is a stationary point. If action springs from the infinite it is non–action. Action that is constantly generated in the infinite, (if it is generated at all) is non action. So in God there is neither *karma* nor *kleśa.*

Kleśa is psychological distress, emotional upheaval or trauma—fear, anxiety, sorrow, grief, unhappiness, misery, life and death. All these things do not affect God. He is not subject to any of these, because of the absence of the ego–sense. Movement of energy in consciousness is interpreted as happiness or unhappiness, pleasure and pain only by that ego–sense. If that is not there, if you are not standing outside when a freezing cold wind is blowing, there is no one to say it is freezing. Space does not say it is freezing, wind does not say it is freezing. *You* call the wind freezing. Therefore there is neither *kleśa* (distress) nor *karma* (action and reaction) in the infinite. All these are merely interpretations by the ego–sense of the movement of energy in consciousness.

1. 25 tatra niratiśayaṁ sarvajña bījaṁ

In that (God or surrender to God) there is the source of the highest and most excellent omniscience, for the self–limitation which is ignorance is dispelled by the removal of the ego–ignorance obstacle. (Or, the omniscience in that is natural and arouses no wonder.)

Tatra means 'in that'—maybe in that surrender itself, or maybe in God. It is a laconic expression that one has to interpret according to one's own light.

When you surrender yourself to God *(Īśvara)* who is omnipresent and omniscient, in that surrender there is omniscience. Omniscience is not knowledge of the particulars by an individual. (You don't have to practise yoga in order to acquire knowledge of particulars; you go to school or university for that!) Knowledge of the all by the all *as* the all is omniscience. Omniscience means knowing not only all things, but the ground of all things at the same time, knowing the reality at the same time—or *becoming* that reality, instantly. This only means that in that person there is no confusion.

When this ego–sense, the basic *vṛtti* of 'I am', is totally surrendered and merges in the infinite, all the confusions and divisions brought about by its assumed independence are immediately set at rest. That is all. It is neither omniscience in relation to something else (another event, for instance) nor an interpretation. It is an instantaneous dissolution of all confusion, doubt and questioning, and of all quest.

So in the state of omniscience there is no doubt concerning the non–existence of the self. That shadow which had been cast and mistaken for a personality with an independent existence, is enlightened. The shadow has not gone, but has been enlightened and therefore surrendered, sacrificed, made sacred. It has become one with the infinite. This is something supremely wonderful; there is no wonder greater than this.

In that omniscience neither a desire nor a craving arises. When the oneness is realised, the things that are bothering us—delusion, ignorance, sorrow, fear, anxiety, vacillation and doubt—will all go. That state of consciousness in which there is no shadow of doubt is surely omniscient.

The **Iśāvasya Upaniṣad** says: "*When the oneness is realised, delusion is gone, sorrow is gone.*" In that state of omniscience one sees that these have no existence apart from the foolish assumption of an individual, 'I am'—'afraid' follows the assertion that 'I am'. When this 'I am' is knocked down, fear has no resting place. Similarly delusion, sorrow, anxiety and doubt cease to be, because they have no place to rest.

* * * * * * * * * * *

Omniscience is not meant in the sense that you can read others' thoughts. It is supposed to be bad manners to read another person's letter, and the person who reads your thoughts reads your letter before it is written! How can that be moral and glorious?

Should the omniscient yogi, or God, know where you lost your purse? The omnipresent consciousness—which is ever present at the same time in you, in the purse, in the money in the purse and in the person who took the purse—perhaps doesn't have the idea that the purse was stolen. When you take your pen from one pocket of your shirt and put it in another pocket of the same shirt you have no feeling that it has been stolen. If the pen had been transferred from your pocket to another person's pocket, then God, being omniscient and omnipotent, doesn't feel that it has been stolen. It has simply changed pockets!

In the third chapter of the **Yoga Sūtras** we are given detailed instructions of how to know certain phenomena. After a lifetime of the practices of *dhāraṇā, dhyāna* and *samādhi* are we only interested in knowing how to find a lost purse, or read another's thoughts?

After describing all these practices at great length, Patanjali says that they are distractions, because in all these your individuality is very firmly sustained. You become more and more egoistic, more and more confirmed in your foolishness and ignorance. He says they are wasteful exercises.

1.26 sa pūrveṣām guruḥ kālenā 'navacchedāt

That omnipresent reality (both in its manifest and unmanifest aspects) is the source of inspiration and intuitive enlightening experience of all the sages from beginningless time; for it is not conditioned (or divided) by time. The inner light is timeless. The enlightening experience is timeless, for time is thought and thought is ignorance.

The light that shines in total sacrifice of the self (or self–surrender) is the enlightening experience; and that itself is the *guru*. The word '*guru*' can be easily translated as follows: '*gu*' is nothing more than the gloom of self–ignorance and '*ru*' is the remover. So that which removes the darkness, or the shadow of ignorance, is *guru*. The *guru* is that enlightening experience. This has been the experience of seekers and students of yoga from time immemorial.

Was there the same *guru*? *Kālenā 'navacchedāt*—the *guru* is not conditioned by time, because this inner light is not a product of thought. Time is a concept of the mind, and so that which is beyond time is also necessarily beyond thought, and that which is beyond thought is timeless. When thought is suspended, time is also suspended. The two are interrelated. This enlightening experience, being beyond thought, is also beyond time, is neither bound nor limited by time.

God, *guru* and what was considered self seem to be the same. Each of these three words—*Īśvara* (God), *guru* and *ātmā* (self)—apparently has a meaning of its own; however, they all denote the one essential indivisible consciousness, indivisible truth; the apparent diversity indicated by the different words is fictitious. When you go to what is called a human *guru*, perhaps he will simply indicate that what you have so far considered to be yourself and what you have so far considered to be God are one and the same; and the *guru* illumines that oneness.

Even the tradition that emphasises the need for a human *guru* is emphatic that it is that light which appears to the human eyes as a human person. To us Swami Sivananda was a radiant personality who was able to enlighten our intellect and lighten our burden, to shine the light of his wisdom on the dark corners of our own ignorance and craving, and in whose presence we enjoyed peace, happiness, joy and inexpressible delight. All these are the inseparable characteristics of the enlightening experience which appears in front of us as the *guru*, but we superimpose humanness on that enlightening experience. That which walked in front of us, which listened, smiled, laughed and cried was this enlightening experience. Being human and endowed with only human faculties, our human vision perceived only the human body, our human ears heard only the human voice. It was our limitation and not his; he was not responsible for that.

Kālenā 'navacchedāt—that which is not bound to time or by time, which is beyond concepts and precepts and beyond description, is the truth, the *guru.* If he appeared to have taken birth and to have passed on, that is an unreal superimposition which, on account of our ignorance, we superimposed upon this eternal light. That light is unborn and undying, unconcerned about time.

I. 27 tasya vācakaḥ praṇavaḥ

That indwelling omnipresent sole reality is verbally alluded to as OM— which is the ever–new and eternal cosmic sound that is heard in all natural phenomena (thunderclap, roaring of the ocean, wind rustling trees in the forest, and the conflagration) and even in the reverberations of the musical instruments, the hum of engines, and the distant din of the carnival crowd.

What is God called, so that I may call Him by his proper name? Patanjali says that God has no name, but His presence is indicated by *OM.* When you listen to any undifferentiated sound—the sound in which your mind does not create a division in terms of vowels and consonants, etc.—is *OM.* When all these blend into one homogeneous sound, that is *OM;* and that is heard everywhere and all the time. It is not absent from anywhere at any time.

You hear the sound when you put your thumbs in your ears; but if you think it is the sound of the capillary bloodstream a differentiation, a confusion, has started.

One must learn to listen to this sound, feeling that this is the name of God.

Praṇava means *OM.* It is very difficult to translate *vācaka,* it is a kind of verbal indicator. So we say *OM* is the verbal indicator of God or *Īśvara.* So *OM* is not the *name* of God. It is important to understand that though we do say that *OM, Śiva* or *Kṛṣṇa* is the name of God, It does not need a name because It is omnipresent and eternal. That which is everywhere does not need to be called anything.

This word *OM* is extremely interesting. In Tamil it just means 'yes'. It is also used in some of the **Upaniṣads** *as* assent or affirmation. That is the very essence of surrend–er! (When you say 'no', your ego is born, and when you say 'never', it is well established!) Shall we then say 'yes' to everything that goes on? Is yes the opposite of no? Being the substratum of all, God is not to be restricted to what we call the pairs of opposites. In It, yes is not the opposite of no, love is not the opposite of hate, like of dislike, peace of restlessness. It is not as though God exists only in love, peace and goodness, me and you. God is the basis, the truth, the reality that underlies all (but not in the sense of the all being several things put together). Truth and falsehood both become truth because the mind or consciousness that conceives of that falsehood is true. So reality is beyond what you consider true and not true, love and hatred, peace and restlessness; and 'yes' is beyond what you mean by yes and no. Therefore this yes does not mean that hereafter you won't say no at all.

In the direct observation of this tremendous inner reality you persistently observe within yourself the rising of distractions. You understand them, look through them, without saying either yes or no; you are constantly aware of what is. That *is,* and therefore that is yes. There is an affirmation, a recognition of what is. However, you are not going to say, "Therefore if I am angry I must say yes to anger." You look into that anger to see that it is nothing more than an outflow of energy against the background of awareness. That 'yes' is different. You are not resisting or rebelling against it, but observing it and discovering the *is* even in that.

Even so, the great commandment 'Resist not evil' does not mean co–operate with evil. We have understood only two meanings: either we resist evil, becoming evil; or we co–operate with evil, becoming evil again. There is a lovely saying in some of the Indian languages that if you throw stones into filth the first person to be splashed is yourself. Therefore you cannot resist evil without being tainted by evil.

We have never tried the third alternative, which is to look through what is called evil or good. In this we have really and truly transcended the evil without being tainted by it. We have become totally good because evil is no longer evil; we have become truly good without becoming egotistic about it. That is what is called *OM*. This is beautifully described in the **Katha Upaniṣad**: "*That which is beyond all the dualities, that in which all dualities blend (day and night into day; love and hatred into divine love, etc.) and which is therefore indescribable, has to be experienced as the Is or the reality that provides the substratum for all these; that is OM.*"

I. 28 taj japas tad artha bhāvanaṁ

How to utilise that OM in the adoration of God?

By repeating it and at the same time enquiring into, contemplating and saturating the whole being with the substance indicated by it – that is, the reality or God, which is the real 'meaning' of OM.

Artha has quite a number of meanings and one is the word 'meaning'. When the word 'book' is uttered, its *artha* is this book you are reading. In that sense, what is the *artha* of *OM*? The dictionary says, *"It is indicative of Brahman, it is God, it is the Supreme Being, it is itself the infinite, it represents creator, preserver and destroyer."* But what is it?—Not what it means according to the dictionary. The following hints are merely indicative, because this has to be your own adventure.

OM is breath, life. It is a beautiful humming sound, a sound you hear when you listen to the truck outside, when the wind blows over the roof, when it rains; when there is a fire, the roar of an animal, the sound of the factories working, the heavy rush of wind. It is a sound which is found everywhere. That is the meaning, the *artha.*

The *OM* sound is produced by the breath coming out of the throat. It is divided into three parts—A U M. It starts from the abdomen with A, continues with U in the throat and ends in the lips with M. So it is called a complete monosyllable. When you learn to repeat *OM,* place your hand at the top of the chest so that you can feel the vibration, close your eyes, take a big breath and make the long sound Ooooooommm, slowly closing your lips as you do so. If you listen carefully you will hear the sound of A at the start, the U sound as the lips start to close, and M as the lips come together. A note in the middle of your register will be correct for you.

If you repeat *OM* looking for the substance that it represents, the mind will become calm, one–pointed and alert. Added to this, if you are sincerely and seriously looking for the substance, there will be the passion of enquiry. Here the whole–souled acceptance and emotional participation in what you are doing is most important.

Japa means to repeat this *OM,* without resisting or accepting, to be constantly aware of it. If the first time you say *OM* you contemplate its meaning, there is no need to say it again. Repetition becomes necessary when the first utterance was ineffectual. You go on repeating this *mantra* mechanically, semi–mechanically, non–mechanically, so that some time or other the penny may drop and you may see what was meant. Were all the previous repetitions useless? Perhaps yes, perhaps no. If those repetitions had not been there, perhaps you would never have reached this point.

Japa can be done mentally. When you thus repeat *OM* mentally it does not make you dull, because you are listening to it keenly, attentively, in order to discover for once (and maybe for all) what that sound is made of. When you were saying, "Ooommm", you knew there was movement of life–breath etc., but when your throat is silent you still hear the sound. Where is the sound produced, by what, and who listens to it? When you say that you are doing *japa* mentally, what is that sound made of? The answer to that question is the *artha*—the meaning or the reality of *OM.* All the rest is word–meaning, one word for another word.

When you say you are 'mentally repeating *OM*', where is it? If you answer that question you have answered all questions. Only when you are able to see this thing happening are you seeing the mind, not when you only think you are seeing. At that point you are not different from the mind, the 'I' is not different from the mind and the 'I' surrenders. It is extremely beautiful, but unfortunately it cannot be put into words. You ask a simple question: "What does 'I am mentally repeating a *mantra*' mean?" First of all, how do you know you are repeating the *mantra* mentally? Because you hear it. But what does it mean? And where does it come from? This question has no verbal answer (or the verbal answer is not the answer) because the verbal answer is also produced by the brain. When it is realised that it is the mind, and at the same time 'I' (which is also the same mind) becomes lost in it, there is surrender.

I. 29 tataḥ pratyak cetanā 'dhigamo 'py antarāyā 'bhāvaś ca

When one repeats OM in this manner, then the consciousness which is ordinarily scattered over the diversity, is gathered, concentrated and turned inward. The spirit of enquiry into the substance of OM dispels all the obstacles or distractions without necessarily wrestling or struggling with them.

When you repeat *OM* in this manner, the attention that was distracted and externalised suddenly reverses and begins to flow into itself, so that the scattered ignorance (called knowledge) has begun to fade away and self–knowledge emerges, becoming clearer and clearer. It also becomes clear that the object, as such, has never known the subject—except as a projection of one's own self. Therefore, in a manner of speaking, prior to this we have been living not only in self–ignorance, but in utter ignorance. Now that there is a reversal of the flow of consciousness, the self seems to be more real, sharper; there is a clarity in regard to oneself. Then, based upon that, there is clarity and a better understanding of what were previously regarded as objects, because the projection of ignorant ideas and notions has ceased. Truth is becoming abundantly clear.

Antarāyā 'bhāvaś means that the obstacles do not exist

at all. It is not as though they are dispelled, but they are made non–being—which means the obstacles are no longer obstacles. A distracting thought or a feeling of pain is an obstacle, but Patanjali says that if you repeat *OM* in this manner and contemplate the reality or the truth concerning it, that obstacle ceases to be an obstacle because the attention that was contemplating *OM* with vigilance and alertness suddenly turns upon the obstacle—which immediately becomes almost a help. It is wrong to say that the obstacle didn't arise; some distraction arose, but somehow ceased to be an obstacle. But does it cease to be an obstacle, or does it cease to *be*? None of these expressions make any sense at all in the face of the inner experience. That is *antarāyā 'bhāvaś.*

It is true to say that from there on the yogi experiences no obstacles whatsoever. What appeared to be obstacles before he took up the practice of yoga and what appear to be obstacles in the mind of others, do still arise in him; but he does not regard them as obstacles. To him they are not obstacles.

From there on whatever happens—whether it is called pleasure or pain, happiness or unhappiness, honour or dishonour—is fuel to this beautiful and brilliant flame of self–knowledge.

Which ever be the path you may choose, or technique you may adopt, you come to the same goal (if you want to call it such) in just a couple of steps. That is why it is called Raja Yoga.

I. 30 vyādhi styāna saṁśaya pramādā 'lasyā 'virati bhrānti darśanā 'labdha bhūmikatvā 'navasthitatvāni citta vikṣepās te 'ntarāyāḥ

What are the obstacles?

(1) Disease, (2) dullness, (3) doubt (4) carelessness, (5) laziness, (6) inability to turn the attention away from the obstacles), (7) perverted or distorted vision, (8) inability to find a firm ground for the spiritual investigation, and (9) even when such a ground is found, unsteadiness of mind and attention in the pursuit of the enquiry—these are the obstacles and distractions, for they bring about and constitute the apparent fragmentation of the mind–stuff.

These are obstacles only in the sense that they distract your attention and, whereas the self is shining all the time, you are then unaware of it. Only to the extent that they cause psychological disturbance are they considered obstacles.

Let us take one example, *vyādhi*—disease or illness. When there is a headache, if you are only thinking of it and of the ways and means to get rid of it, then your attention is not focused on the very source of this experience of pain. The attention flows out, and to that extent it is a distraction. If, on the other hand, you have a headache (or any problem you like) and if it is possible for the undistracted attention to observe the source of this pain (we will still call it pain just for the sake of our discussion) without judging, rationalising, condemning, justifying or calling it this or that, that little pain may be a tremendous aid to self–knowledge. We can use logic and then go beyond logic to direct observation and so on.

It is the mind or thought that becomes aware of pain. Pain *is* a thought. Most of us, being conditioned to the basic feeling, 'I am the body' and having learned that pain is something undesirable, become aware of this pain as something undesirable. Because it is undesired and undesirable it is called pain. If it is something desirable, it will not be called pain—such as the boyfriend pinching the girl's cheek. That is a delight, a desired experience!

If it can be reduced to its own reality—neither the opinion nor the diagnosis, but the truth concerning it (which is pure experience)—without calling it pain or pleasure, desirable or undesirable, then that pain or illness, etc. becomes a powerful aid to self–knowledge. There is no distraction at all.

There is another way of looking at it. Illness is an obstacle only to the extent that it distracts your attention. My *guru,* Swami Sivananda, had diabetes and lumbago in exactly the same way as you have a Cadillac or a lovely big mansion—you are not unhappy about it! To him lumbago, diabetes, etc. were no different from the shirt that he had. When that state is reached what happens to the body is of no consequence to the spirit. It has its own natural changes; but these changes do not produce psychological or mental distraction. Inwardly you are not distracted, no matter what is happening. Nothing affects your inner joy, peace and bliss.

Styāna means dullness and *saṁśaya* means doubt. Doubt produces an inner distraction. It is important to remember that it is harmful as an obstacle only to the extent that it disturbs your inner attention. Faith is another form of doubt. You have faith when you really don't understand what it is all about and you mechani–cally do what you are told to do. This effectively prevents you from turning within and understanding the self, because the attention is still flowing out. Blind faith or blind rejection (which is doubt) are non–different; the common factor in both of these is blindness.

We always bring in doubt or 'but' when there is no urgency. I have rather oversimplified advice; when you are on the horns of a dilemma—'I doubt if', 'but'—do nothing. This applies to getting married or divorced, starting a business, etc. Do it, if you are going to do it, with all your heart, mind, soul and being. If something says 'but', leave it alone till the other pressure builds up to such an extent that you do it in spite of yourself; and then there is no regret, because your whole being did it. In most cases we do not experience this urgency and so we do most of what we do half–heartedly, and experience regret and remorse.

Pramādā 'lasyā means carelessness and laziness, and *bhrānti darśanā* means we are conditioned to seeing the external world as we have been taught to see it. (*Bhrānti* can also mean deluded or perverted vision.)

Labdha bhūmikatvā means contemplating on *OM* and trying to discover the meaning. Occasionally you seem to stumble upon it and then immediately the attention wanders away, distracted—*'navasthitatvāni*. These are obstacles only because they are mental or psychological distractions.

These nine can roughly be accommodated in three categories; one, dullness; two, unsteadiness; and three, ignorance. If you study the entire yoga literature and look at all the methods that have been suggested in the name of yoga (*āsanas, prāṇāyāma,* dancing, jumping up and down and singing, worshipping and so on) you will find that all of them have been evolved by yogis, teachers and masters in response to these nine obstacles.

I. 31 duḥkha daurmanasyā 'ṅgam ejayatva
śvāsa praśvāsā vikṣepa saha bhuvaḥ

By the presence of the following symptoms can be understood the extent to which the mind is disturbed and distracted:

orrowful mood, (2) psychological despair, (3) the motions of the body, and (4) inhalation and exhalation. By being attentive to these factors, it is possible to arrive at an understanding of the degree of seriousness of the obstacles: for they coexist with the distraction of the mind.

Here the yogi has given us a few diagnostic yardsticks in order to recognise when the mind is distracted. If you find these you can be sure that the mind is not steady. *Duḥkha* or sorrowful mood may be the result of your *karma,* or it may be nothing more than unsteadiness of attention – because if there is no psychological distraction and the attention is steady, you must be able to look at the so–called unhappiness and find that there is happiness in it. You are not able to see the obvious truth that there is happiness in unhappiness because the mind is distracted and you're not looking at it at all. So when there is unhappiness the mind is not steady.

Daurmanasyā means 'bad mind', a distracted mind, full of groans and grumbles, ill will and evil thoughts. Without condemning or rationalising, you merely have to realise that when the mind is in a bad mood the attention is distracted. If the attention is not distracted it should be immediately obvious that whether it is called good mood or bad mood, it is still a mood. You call it good or bad only because you are not looking within, but somewhere else. Look straight within yourself and then whether it is called good or bad, the mood must be removed. When this happens what remains is exactly what there has always been – the mind.

Aṅgam ejayatva means when the body is itchy and restless. If there is shaking of the limbs, the yogi prescribes *āsana* (postures). These are meant to enable you to regain steadiness of the body, so that without distraction the attention may be focused upon the phenomenon of experience. *Śvāsa praśvāsā* means inhalation and exhalation. Patanjali says that inhalation/exhalation was not meant only to ventilate your lungs, but to indicate the state of distraction of the mind. The less distracted the mind is, the calmer the breathing is; the more distracted, the more violent the breathing is. Watch the quality of your breathing and you know exactly what the quality of your mind is.

Therefore *duḥkha*—unhappiness, sorrow, misery; *daurmanasyā*—distracted mind; *aṅgam ejayatva*—unnecessary shaking of the body (whether it is pathological or habitual) and *śvāsa praśvāsā*—disturbed inhalation or exhalation, are the surest indicators of the presence of these distractions. You realise that there is a problem and diagnose it by the way your body behaves. You realise that the attention is not steady and there is a dark veil of ignorance which prevents self-knowledge. This gives rise to mental distraction in as much as you can only observe the source of what happens to you outside yourself.

I. 32 tat pratiṣedhārtham ekatattvā 'bhyāsaḥ

In order to overcome mental distractions one should steadily adhere to the practice of one method. Whereas any method will help one overcome distractions, frequent change of the methods adopted in one's practice will aggravate the distractions.

This Sūtra seems to suggest that if you want to attain self-knowledge, pick up one of these methods and be totally absorbed and dedicated to it. One-pointedness is irreplaceable. There is a very beautiful expression: "*My mind agrees to it, but I have no heart to do it.*" Rationally, intellectually, you accept it, but it doesn't appeal to your emotion. It is the emotional assent that provides the energy for whatever we do. Therefore if this wedding of the intellect and the emotion is not there for the yoga you practise, there is no energy and no yoga.

The moment the emotional block is removed there is tremendous enthusiasm and energy.

When a practice has become routine and dull, something new grips your attention. The problem of craving for experience, even for the experience of mental quiescence or peace of mind, is still a craving; and if you yield to this craving you have deliberately created another disturbance within the mind. The master says stay where you are, there is nothing wrong with what you are doing except that you are tempted away from it. It is a distraction which could take you from what you are doing to something else, instead of watching that distraction. Here is a golden opportunity to enquire, "What is it that is being distracted, and why does the new experience tempt me?" Observing it, finding the mischief there and then, is *ekatattvā 'bhyāsaḥ* —total dedication to one thing, one factor.

Why do these obstacles manifest in us? Because of lack of one-pointed devotion. The biblical commandment: "*Thou shalt love the Lord with all thy heart, with all thy soul, with all thy mind and with all thy strength,*" is a beautiful thing. It may apply not only to someone called God, but it is true in everything that we do in our life. If this one-pointed integration exists in our life and we are able to apply it to whatever we do, that is yoga, the whole life is yoga. The entire message of yoga is contained in this one single commandment.

In the next seven *Sūtras* Patanjali has given us a few different methods which enable us to overcome the distractions of the mind.

I. 33 maitrī karuṇā mudito 'pekṣāṇāṁ sukha duḥkha puṇyā 'puṇya viṣayāṇāṁbhāvanātaś citta prasādanaṁ

The following fourfold attitude to life's vicissitudes and in all relationships, being conducive to peace of mind, enables one to overcome the distractions of the mind:

(1) friendliness towards pleasure or those who are pleasantly disposed to oneself (friends),

(2) compassion for the sorrowful, and, when one is in a painful condition, self-forgetful sympathy for those who may be in a similar painful condition,

(3) rejoicing in the exaltation of the noble or the holy ones, and

(4) indifference to unholiness, not being drawn into it nor holding others in contempt for their unholiness.

A yogi who is established in equal vision and whose mind is steady, has these four basic qualities or fourfold attitude to others in the world:

maitrī, karuṇā, mudita, upekṣā.

This is a very important *Sūtra,* because we are living in this world which is full of these four types of people.

Maitrī means friendliness—friendliness towards those who are one's equals. The yogi does not judge them as equals, but the feeling of equality is the spontaneous expression of his inner attitude, of the equanimity in which he is established. He does not strive to be friendly. It is a purely spontaneous outpouring of his inner vision and inner attitude. (One who strives to be friendly is not friendly. You don't try to be what you are.)

Karuṇā means compassion. In regard to people who are unhappy, spontaneous compassion flows from the yogi. In Taoist and Zen terminology they compare this to water. Water spontaneously flows down. It doesn't want or condescend to go down, but descends spontaneously.

Again, the yogi is not *trying* to be compassionate. One who tries to be compassionate is merely pitying you, with a tremendous superiority attitude towards you. So *karuṇā* is compassion where there is no pity or superiority at all.

Mudita means joy. When you see something glorious, joyous or auspicious, or when you come across somebody who is spiritually advanced, again the heart leaps with joy and happiness towards that person. If the heart can feel happy in the happiness, prosperity and spiritual elevation of others, that is another indication of this equal vision and balanced mind.

To those who are equal to us, we are friendly; towards those who are suffering, our compassion flows; towards those who are happy and exalted, our admiration flows. But there is one more group whom we call *apuṇya* —not so virtuous. What is the attitude of the yogi towards this last group—drunkards, murderers, thieves and rogues, whatever be the robe in which the rogue may appear? The yogi is not blind to the fact that certain people's conduct is not good. He does recognise this. He neither condemns them, shuns them nor pities them, nor does he admire them or join them. He does not say, "You are wicked and I am here to uplift you." That is a silly superiority complex, totally unworthy of a yogi.

It is possible to argue that a yogi might even come down to the other man's level, (watch carefully) in order to uplift him. When you come down to another man's level, he has brought you down. Who is to uplift whom? If you yourself are lost, how are you going to uplift another person? So there is none of these, for they are all tricks of the same mind that has been tricking us throughout our life. The yogi sees the violence, the wickedness and the aggression; and perhaps the question arises, "Why does a human being behave like that?" The honest answer is, "I don't know." That is all. There is neither hate, dislike, disgust nor contempt.

When you say, "I don't know" honestly, faithfully and sincerely, you are looking within yourself, at that which says, "I don't know." The attention is diverted into yourself. What happens then is *upekṣā*—psychological non–contact. It is neither indifference nor detachment (though it is often translated as indifference) towards those whom we consider as bad or evil. To a yogi, *ahiṃsā* (non–violence in thought, word and deed) is one of the cardinal principles of life. When the yogi (who doesn't want to hurt anybody and who is full of compassion and love) sees somebody who spills hatred, he is indifferent to that person, he doesn't even think of him. Why? Because the moment you think of a bad person he is *in* you. The more you think of a bad person and his deeds, the worse you will become.

Will you pity that person? There is no sense in it. If you become friendly with him and say, "Ah, you are my friend, my brother," that is hypocrisy. The yogi is totally free of hypocrisy. If there *is* hypocrisy, it is good to realise that it means, "I am something and I want to appear to be something else." In that you have completely lost your yoga practice (*abhyāsa*) because there is no hypocrisy at all in yoga. When we try to cultivate virtues it is good to remember that these are not virtues, because virtues are not qualities that can be superimposed upon the personality. The attempt leads to hypocrisy, tension and depression.

Spiritual growth is something that happens, often imperceptibly. You are growing with the spirit and so it is the spirit that undergoes this transformation, deep within the innermost core of your being, which manifests as friendliness, etc.

When this four–fold attitude is adopted in our daily relationships, all the obstacles that were mentioned earlier are removed and the mind is still; not in a dull, but a dynamically active way. All relationships continue, because it is relationships that expose our own wickedness to ourselves, that bring the distractability of the mind to the fore and so are of tremendous help in this (quest for) self–knowledge.

These are the attitudes of an enlightened person, because his behaviour is not a reaction produced by his prejudice, memory or value judgement. His actions spring from pure consciousness or intelligence that fills his entire being. The intelligence is pure, uncontaminated, un–polluted—and therefore its actions are always pure.

From this little Sūtra a whole school of thought, called Karma Yoga, has sprung. This is the essence of Karma Yoga. If you can constantly watch your own mind to ensure that these are the four attitudes that you have towards all humanity, you are fast progressing towards self–awareness.

I. 34 pracchardana vidhāraṇābhyāṁ vā prāṇasya

Or, the distractions can be overcome by literally and physically exhaling the breath and holding the lungs empty, or by adopting such other methods like fasting or contemplation of death, etc., by which one symbolically 'expires' and holds the prāṇa or life–force outside, as it were.

Pracchardana does not merely mean exhaling, but vomiting. One does not vomit breath, so we say 'exhale'. *Vidhāraṇa* is to hold, and *prāṇasya* is of the *prāṇa*.

Here a very powerful *prāṇāyāma* is suggested: exhale

and hold. This does not mean exhale, inhale and hold, but to exhale all the air out, and hold it out. Don't breathe. If you exhale your breath and hold, you will very soon see what your life–force is! In a few seconds it will stand in front of you and say, "Please open your nostrils". You will come face–to–face with *prāṇa,* the life–force which springs into action and makes you take the next breath. What makes you take the next breath is *prāṇa.* No definition can ever show it to you as clearly as one moment's experience will. At least for a few seconds you will feel a completely suspended state; not only the breath, but everything seems to be suspended! There is no mind, no self.

Please try it some time, and you will suddenly discover that the mind becomes absolutely still. During that period you think of nothing except your breath. It has to be done on an empty stomach because the purity of this practice can be experienced only if you are able to pull the whole abdomen in and push the diaphragm up to ensure complete and total exhalation. When the lungs are completely empty and you hold them empty even for a few seconds, those few seconds are interpreted by your mind to be about 35,000 years! Suddenly you realise that time is not real at all, it depends upon the mental mood. Death threatens you. What you experience then can also lead to the total absence or avoidance of mental distractions. The Hatha Yoga explanation of this is that it is the breath (or the movement of *prāṇa*) that enables your mind to think. So you suspend that. The mind has lost its fuel, and so it is quiet.

If you are afraid to die, don't try this! But if you want to face the reality and the truth of what life and death mean, then carry on. Exhale completely and hold your breath. You don't want to breathe. See what is going to make you breathe again. Then you will see what *prāṇā* is. You will not see it as an object, you will not be verbally aware, but you *will* be aware of it. It is in that one split second, when you are not able to hold your breath any more, that you realise that you could not even die. Something which is beyond the ego which said, "I am going to hold my breath," seemed to sweep the ego aside and make you breathe. Then you are totally fearless!

If there is no ego sense, why should there be life in this body at all? What have I got to do with this body? That is what the yogi wants to find out.

If at the same time you observe what takes place, you will understand what *prāṇāyāma* means—to gather the *prāṇa* and therefore the rays of the mind together and focus the whole thing on this one – ? I don't know what it is!

I. 35 viṣayavatī vā pravṛttir utpannā manasaḥ stithi nibandhanī

Or, intense and vigilant attentiveness to the activities aroused within oneself by sense–experiences can also act as a binding force to prevent mental distractions. Needless to say one should not get lost in such sense experiences. Of such is attentiveness to breathing or to the movement of the life–force, or to the 'silent' sound of a mantra mentally uttered, to the subtle vision of the divine presence, or to the experience of 'the space of consciousness' within the heart.

Although yoga is to be practised so that you come face to face with the self (which necessarily implies the avoidance of being caught in material or physical consciousness, because the whole idea is to extricate the mind from the physical world and physical phenomena) here is a rather enigmatic Sūtra which suggests that even through these you can gain self-knowledge.

Viṣayavatī vā pravṛttir means when the mind comes into contact with external or non-external objects and there is a certain inner experience of pleasure, pain, etc. If you observe that with tremendous attention, once again your mind is stilled.

Pain and pleasure both have validity in relation to meditation. And so two schools arose. One school of thought says that you can drink wine, and as you are drinking you can feel that you are drinking wine, and it's delicious. But the taste is in your tongue. The taste is not in the wine, it is in you, in the 'me'. Who is 'me'?

If, on the other hand while drinking wine you get lost, the mind is completely distracted. Similarly, when you are having sexual enjoyment and the mind is completely lost, there is no harm, it's something which happens naturally. The only problem is that the yoga is gone.

Seeing this, the other school went to the other extreme. They said that this is dangerous because when one drinks, dances, eats meat and enjoys, the mind is distracted. They said, "Asceticism is the answer! Have a bed of nails and sit on it—the mind does not go anywhere!" Pain has this one great advantage—it is possible for you to become used to pleasure, but you never get used to pain! Every time it is new, every time it is hell.

Not only the yogis of the Orient but even Christian mystics used to punish the body, to whip themselves, etc. That is also right, provided that while suffering that pain you can meditate and find the subject or the experiencer. If that is possible it will have the same effect as pleasure; and a state of divisionless experiencing might result.

You don't need to go out of your way to buy pleasure and pain. Life brings all sorts of experiences. Every day you have some pleasant and some unpleasant experiences—ordinary, normal pleasure and pain, nothing extraordinary. Why don't you use them? Instead of reacting to all those experiences, find the self in them. When there is a little pain, don't endure it or suppress it, but become aware of the whole process! Where there is a little pleasure and you are in the seventh heaven, don't go up in smoke, but become aware of that experience.

The yogi does not suppress his emotions, he does not pretend that he does not suffer physical pain or suggest that he can't enjoy some pleasure; but he is aware of them. In his case the experience of pleasure is more intense and the experience of pain is devoid of imaginary suffering. When he is enjoying some pleasure he doesn't get lost in it, he is aware of the whole mechanism. There is no fear, no hope, no craving and therefore there is no restlessness. Whatever pleasure is natural, he enjoys to the utmost. In the same way when it comes to pain there is still no restlessness in the mind; and because there is absolute absence of restlessness there is no confusion. The present pain is the present pain unrelated to the past; and therefore the imaginary suffering, that most people are subject to, is absent.

As you see here the entire process of yoga is nothing but becoming more and more aware of that which is called the self. Whether it is ordinary life or meditative life, it is constantly observing and becoming aware of the arising of something called 'self'.

Possibly *ṭantra* was based upon this teaching. In *ṭāntrika* practices anything and everything was allowed—dancing, singing, sex, etc.—and while indulging in all that the yogi looked within to see the substratum or the content of that experience. By observing these inner experiences one can once again arrive at the same self–knowledge that is the so–called goal of yoga.

1. 36 viśokā vā jyotiṣmatī

Or, one may be keenly attentive to an internal (the psychic blissful inner light) or an external person or phenomenon devoid of sorrow and full of resplendence, and thus overcome distractions of the mind–stuff.

What the master suggests here is that there is an inner light (though not until you discover it) in which there is no sorrow and no mental distraction. If your attention is focused on it and flows towards it, then the mental distractions will cease. Sorrow being an indicator of distracted attention, if that attention is focused upon the inner light which is free from sorrow, you can be free of mental distraction; but in order to do so you should not create this inner light as if it were an object, and then meditate upon it. That is a useless pastime. Meditating upon any kind of object is a waste of time, it takes you nowhere. It is merely a prop, an external aid for internal vision.

Calmly and with an undistracted mind, observe the light within yourself (which is the self) that shines even when your eyes are closed, revealing your own thoughts, feelings, experiences, memory and imagination. That inner light is beyond sorrow, just as in the darkness of deep sleep you do not experience any sorrow. By contemplating the inner light that is beyond sorrow, one overcomes all distractions.

1. 37 vīta rāga viṣayaṁ vā cittaṁ

Or the mental distractions can be eliminated by the adoration of the consciousness of one or which is free from conditioning (or the psychological colouring or attachment or passion). To this category belong even divine images, celestial bodies like the sun, and enlightened living beings—or even babies—though surely one should constantly bear in mind that it is their unconditioned nature which entitles them to be thus adored.

That which is beyond this contamination of conditioning is the pure, untainted, uncontaminated mind; if you do not want to call it mind, you may call it the self, God or anything you like, it doesn't matter.

If there is no thought–wave on the *citta*, it is God. That is why Patanjali allows us to meditate upon the *citta* itself, when there is no thought and no desire in it—*vīta rāga viṣayaṁ vā cittaṁ.* It is abstract meditation and difficult, but it can be done. What is your intelligence if there is no desire in it, if there is no thought in it, if there is no attachment in it? It is God. When one contemplates that, one can overcome psychological distractions.

Therefore Ramana Maharṣi said, "Find out where this thought arises, where this desire arises. If you go along with it and trace its roots, you will find God."

This Sūtra can also mean some person or object which is free from the twin forces of attraction and repulsion. In this category you can include the great masters who are free from love and hate, passion and anger, who are pure crystals; babies, pictures and statues of any image of God, anything that suggests the divine presence; any natural phenomenon—the sun, moon or stars—in fact, anything that shines but is not contaminated by love or hate. Any person, any thing or your own innermost consciousness in which the taint of likes and dislikes, attraction and repulsion, love and hate does not exist—that consciousness which is unconditioned, uncoloured—is also worth contemplating. By contemplating these one's mind becomes steady and undisturbed.

1. 38 svapna nidrā jñānā 'laṁbanaṁ vā

Or the distractions can be removed by holding on to the wisdom gained in dreams, whether they are para–psychological visions or symbolical dreams, as also the wisdom gained by a profound reflection on the `message' of deep sleep, in which there is total absence of mental distraction and in which one experiences no diversity at all. In this state, free from obstacles, one 'experiences' peace and happiness which are 'recollected' on awaking from sleep.

This Sūtra has been variously interpreted. Some yogis even suggest that if you have a vision during your dream, you can meditate upon that dream vision; and if you have a *mantra* given to you in your dream, you can repeat that *mantra.*

You dream, and on waking up you realise you were dreaming. It was a very pleasant dream or a very unpleasant nightmare. When you have a nightmare you are pouring with sweat; and you realise it was unreal. Yet while you were dreaming it was real, otherwise you wouldn't sweat!

What is the wisdom concerning a dream? The dream experience teaches you (if you wish to learn) that time, space and substantiality are not imaginary, but 'dreaminary'—something like what happens in dream. Look at sleep and dream. In sleep you forget the world; even the I–am–the–body consciousness does not exist. The 'I' experience does not exist in sleep; that is, the sleeping person does not say 'I sleep'. So time, space and substantiality are not as real as we take them to be. Sleep and dream teach us not to take things at their face value.

There is another way of looking at it. It is possible that we are all still dreaming, and that it is time to wake up from this long dream. If you begin to meditate upon this wonderful truth—neither accepting it as dogma or inviolable doctrine, nor rejecting it as childish—a tremendous change takes place in you. If, when somebody comes to fight with you, you think, "Maybe I'm just dreaming," (you may even scream—why not? You screamed in your dream) you do not react violently or aggressively and thus promote or perpetuate this conflict. The conflict ends there. At that very moment your attitude towards life and all its events has undergone a change.

These are the only things that one can really say concerning sleep.

1. 39 yathā 'bhimata dhyānad vā

Or, the distractions can be overcome by adopting any contemplative technique, using any object of meditation one likes most, for that which one likes most holds one's attention, and the technique one likes most makes contemplation easy – provided, of course, that neither the object nor the technique itself involves or invites distraction.

Choose any object of experience you like—seeing, listening, imagining, reviving memory, tasting or touching—but be totally centred on that experience. Become totally aware of this phenomenon called experience (though not in order to experience it, because then you are distracted. If you do it with a wish to experience it you are lost.)

Do anything you like, but do something somehow to come to grips with this mental distraction. Use any means whatsoever—whether orthodox means suggested by the various teachers or something that you invent to suit your own particular needs—to try to discover how the mind and the attention are distracted, how a *vṛtti* arises. Become aware of the phenomenon of experience itself, till the only truth you are left with is 'I experience.' (It is never just 'I experience', it is either I see, I know, I taste, I hear, etc.) Go on till only that remains as truth. Then you wonder: where is the experience? In you. What is the distance between you and the experience? What is the relationship between you and the experience? Is there an experience apart from you or is the experience inseparable from you? If the experience is in you, how do you touch it? How do you come into contact with it at all?

Please remember that all that is your own creation. Whatever you have put together with the help of your mental activity is very nice, a beautiful dream. In that there is still a division—the seer and the seen, the meditator and the object of meditation, the subject and the object. As long as there is this division you are sure that ignorance and its consequent ego–sense is also there.

Perfection is there, it has not vacated its omnipresent throne, but you have covered the whole thing with your own mental activity and concepts; you are playing with these creatures of your own mind. All these are related to the ego. That is why in one of Ramana Maharṣi's talks he says that enquiry into the self alone is the right path, because meditation is based on the ego. It is the ego that does the meditation.

Patanjali's meditation is intended merely as an exercise to acquire the power of concentration, of entering into oneself. First you learn to concentrate the mind, to focus it upon something which is chosen; but all the time you remember that this is merely an exercise. One must go through this and come out the other side of ignorance, where there is enlightenment. If that is not remembered, one gets hooked onto a thing called meditation which is nothing but ego–based mental activity and related experiences. You can have all sorts of experiences, but all these are ego–related.

1. 40 paramā 'ṇu parama mahattvānto 'sya vaśīkāraḥ

The mind or the intelligence thus freed from distractions encompasses or comprehends the smallest as also the greatest – for it is free from all limitations, from all conditioning, and from all colouring, and is therefore like the purest crystal.

If the attention is thus undistracted, and if the inner vision is uncoloured, there is a steady concentration of attention.

If at the same time the attention is not attracted (not only not distracted) one way or the other, then that mind is able to comprehend the smallest and the greatest. No problem is too great or too small, no truth is too subtle or too great. That attention, freed from all its limitations, is instantly able to bring into itself whatever there is.

Freed from all conditioning, that attention becomes one with the entire universe and it sees that what was the substratum of 'me' and what was in 'me', is in all and therefore the 'me' is all. There is no limitation, either as an individual or as a cosmic whole; there is no feeling that the self is limited only to me, nor that it is only universal.

What was within me is the self and that self is not only within me, but is within all.

I. 41 kṣīṇa vṛtter abhijātasye 'va maṇer gahitṛ grahaṇa grāhyeṣu tatsthatad añjanatā samāpattiḥ

Lest it should be misunderstood that the intelligence freed from conditioning and colouring is dull, inactive, unresponsive and void, it should be remembered that, like a pure crystal that reflects without distortion or confusion any object that is placed near it, the steady and ever–alert intelligence, too, receives and reflects the colour (nature) of the subject, the predicate, and the object in all situations, instantly, spontaneously and appropriately.

The world outside is not seen in its real form by anybody but the yogi. What you see outside is the projection of your own mind, your own conditioning and fancy. You see the world as you like to see it, as you dislike to see it, or as you are afraid it may be.

When the *vṛttis* are gone, when your thoughts are not governed by your own moods and fancies, then that which is real *alone is*.

The life of that person is like the purest crystal—he reflects everything as it is. In his case there is neither an expression nor a suppression. He neither says that he won't do this, nor that he wants to do that. He neither restrains himself, nor lets himself go. The crystal merely reflects, without ever intending to do so.

In the abstract, it is almost impossible to understand this; only if you have met a yogi like Swami Sivananda is it easy to understand. For instance, he hardly ever used words like 'thank you' or 'please' until someone of West–ern culture walked in, and then automatically he said, "Thank you very much." As soon as someone of Eastern culture appeared, without intending to do so he folded his palms and said, "*Namaste*". When a child went to him, his face was a child–like face—the child was reflected there immediately. If there was an unhappy person that unhappiness was reflected in him immediately, but always without his intending to do so.

Kṣīṇa vṛtter abhijātasya ñ when the *vṛttis* are gone, one becomes a clear crystal. Colouring is taken on, but the crystal is never actually coloured. It seems to reflect the colour, but the colour neither belongs to the crystal, adheres to the crystal nor stays with the crystal.

This crystalline purity of the self is not a thing that can be acquired by directly *aiming* at crystalline purity. Most of us go on pretending that we are absolutely pure crystal and that our whole personality is absolutely divine; but then nothing seems to happen. The mind is not yet absolutely still.

1. 42 tatra śabdā 'rtha jñāna vikalpaiḥ saṁkīrṇā savitarkā samāpattiḥ

In the case of the understanding reached through logic or reasoning, there is confusion on account of the discrepancies that exist between the word (description), meaning (in both connotations as the substance described and as the knowledge of the word–meaning) and imagination or assumption. Hence, it is unclear and uncertain.

As long as logic and reason function and the mind tries to understand, there is the possibility of the taint of misunderstanding, because the mind functions on a dualistic basis. When this happens understanding and its correlative, misunderstanding, must both exist. For instance, when I use the expression 'I love you', many things are implied by it. 'I love you' possibly means that I don't love someone else, that I do not hate you, that I did not love you before, or that I may not love you later.

So understanding or misunderstanding can also be attributed to a confusion that is inherent in thinking and in reasoning. We use a word, and the word unfortunately has a load on it which we call 'meaning'. This is one of the most terrible problems that all teachers have to face. The teacher says something and it is translated by the student into his own idiom. If we *do* seem to understand one another, usually it is purely accidental!

So when the rational mind is used, there seems to be an understanding—*jñāna*—and when this manifests in the mind there seems to be a certain state of inner balance. Even that has the semblance of knowledge, self-knowledge, equanimity or balance, but it is only a semblance. Patanjali's approach to all this is extremely scientific and therefore he does not dismiss even *this* as worthless. He says that it is there and that you can use your own logic and come to its conclusion. Beyond this point logic is useless.

When you have reached this point, again there is an inner peace and tranquillity; but the tranquillity is often shortlived and it is violently disturbed in its reaction. That it can also lead us astray, goes without saying.

1. 43 smṛti pariśuddhau svarūpa śūnye 'vā 'rthamātra nirbhāsā nirvitarkā

But, when the mindstuff is cleansed of memory, the self or personality which was nothing but the fragmentation, the conditioning or the colouring (the impurity) is wiped out as it were; and the substance or truth alone shines without distortion, logic or reasoning which is the function of the limited personality.

Smṛti is the load on the brain which we have regarded as reason, intellect or memory and which was confused with knowledge. This can be cleaned from the mindstuff by realising that this is only memory, pure conditioning, junk. Every time you respond you realise that the response comes from memory, from the junk. When you abandon this, the rational intellect has been silenced and has reached its own conclusion. When this happens the intelligence begins to respond, and therefore there is intelligent responsibility.

When this intelligence moves towards its own centre there is almost no movement. *Svarūpa śūnye 'vā*—as if the observer does not exist. When the ego (the 'I', the observer) is absent, or as if absent, then meditation happens; otherwise there is simply thinking. In meditation it is not 'I' that is observing it; there is pure observation. In this observation the observer is still observed, so that there is still some duality; but the observer seems to be nearly gone, and the observed object seems to fill the entire space. There is a movement in intelligence, but that movement is totally within; that is the observed, the object of observation. It is then that one becomes clearly aware of the object, whether it is a person, an experience or a relationship.

At that point there is no mental activity or rational 'intellection' at all. There is this pure and simple observation. The observer is still alive, but only just; and the observation or the observed object is shining radiantly. If this can happen there is likely to be more understanding and less misunderstanding.

1. 44 etayai 'va savicārā nirvicārā ca sūkṣma viṣayā vyākhyātā

Whatever has been said above also applies to similar distinctions between the other methods already suggested (like the method of enquiry) and spontaneous awareness. Thus, by this they and all the subtleties involved have been explained, leaving only the subtlest experiencer of awareness to be dealt with.

In the same way you can understand what is known as *savicārā*. In *savicārā* there is a definite and positive movement towards the observed object. Take the phenomenon of fear as an example. In the first stage you are merely thinking about it, rationalising it, rejecting it, accepting it and so on. Once that has come to an end you make a positive effort towards this observation. For instance, you are definitely making an effort towards observing this phenomenon called fear within yourself. The mind is trying to understand it; the mind continues to call it fear, and that is how it becomes fear. When that labelling is gone the idea of fear is gone, but there is still some experience of commotion within. In order to observe this commotion the intelligence turns upon itself, and while turning there is still the commotion within; that is, the intelligence is also in motion—*savicārā*—where you are pushing this intelligence towards that experience. Then at the end of that there is *nirvicārā,* where without any movement at all you become aware of the experience—and there is pure and simple awareness. At that time its definition as fear ceases.

When you observe something that is extremely subtle within yourself the fear is no longer an emotion, a gross experience. *Sūkṣma viṣayā*—what is it that is happening in you? You want neither a name, a definition, some intelligence, movement of *prāṇa,* a thought, an emotion or a sensation. When you reject all definitions and descriptions, you realise it is neither tangible nor gross, but something very subtle. It is even more subtle than a thought; and it is more subtle than you thought it was! Then meditation becomes so very beautiful; and it is then that anything that happens to you, at any time in your life, can become meditation.

I. 45 sūkṣma viṣayatvaṁ cā 'liṅga paryavasānaṁ

When thus the subtle experiencer of the inner awareness is observed without interruption one arrives at that which has no identification or distinguishing mark, but which is at the same time not a void.

When you go on observing it keenly, with all your heart and soul, the characteristics with which you identify this disappear. When you are afraid or are shaken by anger, lust or anxiety, and the heart begins to pump very fast, if you observe the fear that produced this (and you go on doing so) the heart seems to respond in a very beautiful co–operative way. It becomes softer and softer, so that all the characteristic marks with which you associated fear (or excitement or anxiety) cease and there is a state which cannot be described or defined. 'I' is still there observing and experiencing this, but all the distinguishing marks have gone.

I. 46 tā eva sabījaḥ samādhiḥ

That indeed is the realisation of the homogeneous cosmic essence, though even in it there exists the seed of potential fragmentation, which is the consciousness of the individuality or the observer.

That is *samādhi,* deep contemplation or total equanimity and equilibrium; but in it there is still the seed of the whole previous commotion. It's like a baby that seems to be totally free of our defects, weaknesses and prejudices—not because it has solved these problems, but because it has not yet become awake to them. That's the difference between the baby and the sage. The sage has overcome these problems, the baby has yet to be awakened to them.

I. 47 nirvicāra vaiśāradye 'dhyātma prasādaḥ

Proficiency in such observation dispenses with even self-enquiry, on account of the uninterrupted self-awareness being natural: then there is spiritual enlightenment, peace and bliss.

When you go on practising *vicāra*, turning the intelligence upon itself without mental activity, you have gone beyond the rational intellect (where logic has reached its logical conclusion) and have trained yourself in this pure observation. Here you are observing intensely whatever happens within yourself. First you strive for this —there is certainly an effort to begin with. When you become expert in this exercise it becomes effortless and natural, and there is pure motionless observation of yourself. You are able to switch on this self-observation without any effort or strain whatsoever.

When the 'I' or the observer has totally surrendered itself to its own substratum (which is the cosmic intelligence), that movement comes to an end. There is the grace of God. That is the only sense in which God's grace, the grace of the infinite self, can be rightly used. God's grace is understandable only in this context where the whole being has been surrendered.

It is important to remember that self-knowledge is not knowledge acquired by 'I' of myself. The 'I' can never know the self. The 'I' being just a *vṛtti,* a wave, it cannot know the ocean. It is the ocean that knows itself and it is the ocean that knows all the waves and currents that are flowing in it or on it.

The next is a very important and beautiful Sūtra:

I. 48 ṛtaṁbharā tatra prajñā

Such enlightenment is saturated with harmony, order and righteousness.

We have been told by every great teacher that the yogi

should be a man of great virtue. You are only filled with virtue when there is total surrender and spontaneous awareness of the content of all experiences and expressions. You do not even strive to be good and to do good, because goodness becomes spontaneous. The inner light banishes all shadow and therefore there is no darkness within. In that state there is neither suffering nor sin. The whole of your consciousness is saturated with *ṛtaṁ.*

The word *ṛtaṁ* is very difficult to translate. It is something that makes goodness good, that is at the root of goodness, that is natural to being, that is naturally good. That goodness is called *ṛtaṁ.* That order is not what you and I would characterise as order, but something which synthesises and transcends all perfection, which sees death and birth as the same event. It does not make any distinction between good and evil, or pleasure and pain. It is order in which all things exist as all things, and yet as a whole, a totality. It is virtue that is inherent in the soul of being, that need not be taught or imposed; it is natural order, something that is natural to the soul. It is not the goodness that we practise towards each other, but the goodness that is non–different from the infinite God. When divine grace has manifested in this life because the whole of life has been totally surrendered to the infinite being, what happens is *ṛtaṁ,* supreme order, supreme good.

Possibly the word rhythm comes from *ṛtaṁ,* the rhythm of the universe, where nothing can be isolated and considered good or bad, where there is neither a thing called relative morality nor absolute morality.

I. 49 śrutā 'numāna prajñā 'bhyām anya viṣayā viśeṣā 'rthatvāt

This enlightenment, this understanding, this realisation is quite different from what one has heard about or deduced from teaching obtained from external sources. Whereas in the case of the latter the object of study, investigation and understanding is outside of the consciousness, the realisation arrived at in the former is of a special category.

This *ṛtaṁ* or natural order has nothing whatsoever to do with what you have heard and what you have inferred to be good. All these are book–virtues that are found in your books and dictionaries. They are no better than the vices that are also found there. Love and hate are both composed of letters of the alphabet; one is not necessarily better that the other, until you reach this natural order. When this happens, the love which manifests in your heart at that point is completely different from what you heard about love, or what you inferred, or what your own mind suggested to you to be love (or a desirable virtue).

Viśeṣā 'rthatvāt can be translated in two different ways. One, this virtue has a special meaning in itself. Two, you have eliminated all the previously learned and loaded definitions of the word virtue, and what remains is pure virtue. You do not regard that as love which someone suggests is love—love of man, love of God and so on. All that is gone. What remains is love which is beyond any description whatsoever. *That* is God.

I. 50 tajjaḥ saṁskāro 'nya saṁskāra pratibandhī

This special realisation of spontaneous self–awareness completely transmutes the entire being and there is total change. All other habits and tendencies are overcome by habitual self–awareness.

That virtue is something that can eliminate all *saṁskāras* from your life. That vision, that experience of natural order being natural, it eliminates all disorder without creating disorder. If there is violence, can you stop that violence without being violent yourself? If he cheats you, can you put him right without cheating him? Can evil be opposed? Opposition itself is evil—isn't it? If he is fighting with another and you try to restrain him, you are as violent as he is. Can you deal with restlessness, the absence of peace, without losing your own peace of mind?

All this is difficult, but when there is this natural order it is able to eliminate all disorder from life without becoming disorderly.

I. 51 tasyā 'pi nirodhe sarva nirodhān nirbījaḥ samādhiḥ

When even that special realisation (with the seed of fragmentation still present) is transcended, everything is transcended, and the seeker has, as it were, come one full circle. The seeker is entirely absorbed in the seeking. The Reality realises itself (it is) without the need for the individual even in his subtlest state. This indeed is the enlightenment in which there is no seed at all for the manifestation of diversity.

When the self has been surrendered, nothing but pure virtue exists. There are neither *vṛttis* nor mental activity. One must be very cautious here; it is not as though the mind must be stilled; floating mental activity may still continue to be, but the one thing that is absent is identification of the self with those mental activities. That also is gone.

Who makes that go? Not 'me'. What is there that can rid the 'me' of a misconception concerning itself? One does not even associate the self with this natural order. Can you pretend that you have understood the basis of this natural order? And can you stand outside it and look at it as if it were an object? The whole thing is absurd. One does not know how this happens. The yogi says that it is God's grace.

Therefore Patanjali does not say, "Stop this identification." You cannot do that. You have reached a completely transparent situation where there is no identification of the 'me', which seems to exist in a transparent way. How does that come to an end? How does the seed of all thought, of all consciousness, of all experience, come to an end? Who crushes that seed? Not 'me'. And the seed cannot crush itself.

We don't know who crushes that seed. Patanjali says *tasyā 'pi nirodha* – somehow the seed also comes to an end. When that happens you are in a state of perfect yoga—not you, but *yoga* is in a state of perfect yoga. God has realised himself, the infinite has once again become the infinite.

Even that is wrong, for if you say the infinite has once again become the infinite it means that in the meantime it was not the infinite, which is absurd. Nothing more than that can be said, because even the seed has come to an end – *nirbījaḥ samādhi*.

If what we have so far discussed in our study of the first chapter is clear, then what follows in the second chapter becomes natural and effortless. (If you are fairly cautious in studying the second chapter, you might discover that more or less the same truths that were expounded in the first chapter are repeated here in different words.)

CHAPTER TWO

II. 1 **tapaḥ svādhyāye 'śvara praṇidhānāni kriyā yogaḥ**

The kindling of the inner psychic fire that at once burns away all the impurities (colouring) and limitations of the mind-stuff, the study both of scriptural texts and one's own reaction to situations from moment to moment, and the meaningful, dynamic and devotional surrender to the in-dwelling omnipresence—these three simultaneously constitute active yoga, or practice of the indivisible unity.

Kriyā means action (*kriyā* and *karma* are synonyms)—so Kriyā Yoga means yoga in action, or doing. It is a universal failing that after listening to the exposition of knowledge that is contained in the first chapter, one says, "I have understood all that, now what must I do?" If you ask that question, that means you have not understood correctly, you have merely heard the words. When the words are no longer words—*vṛtti*—but have become assimilated, these words have become flesh. If this does not happen, either they have not been properly heard or they have merely been stored as undigested words—only then is there an anxiety concerning what has thus been swallowed. For instance, if you have indigestion and the food you have eaten sits there like a stone in your stomach, it creates an anxiety. This does not happen when it is assimilated.

Strangely enough, that very food that has been assimilated demands more food. There is a lovely statement in one of the **Upaniṣads**: *"Food is that which is eaten and that which eats."* Similarly, if this knowledge has been properly listened to and assimilated, it creates its own hunger and receives more knowledge.

Kriyā Yoga is the answer to the anxious enquiry, "What must I do now?" We ask the question, "What must I do?" only when it comes to the understanding of yoga, self-knowledge, God, religion, etc. If, for instance, you are standing right in the middle of a busy street and the traffic-lights turn green and the traffic starts pouring into the middle of this road, you don't ask, "What must I do?" If the understanding has been real, then the understanding *itself* acts. When the truth is assimilated, the word becomes flesh. Your whole being *is* the truth and it knows how to act.

Yoga is not something which is done, but which has to happen, yet the expression 'Kriyā Yoga' is used here. Kriyā Yoga is yoga in itself—yoga expressed in other words. It is composed of three practices. The first is *tapas*—discipline or lifestyle or attitude towards life—which seems to be a fairly vital subject and therefore it is emphasized twice, as part of *niyama* and as the first of the Kriyā Yoga practices. (It is also elaborated in the **Bhagavad Gītā** and other Scriptures.)

We shall look first into the literal meaning. If we know what the word means we may be able, with sufficient insight, to know the spirit as well as its perversion. Language undergoes tremendous change.

You associate a word with a spirit and you express that spirit through a word—and then the word has taken over. So it is necessary for us to understand the literal verbal meaning of a word (not merely the word and meaning). If you pursue this quest, it is then possible for you also to glimpse the spirit and see the perversion.

Tapas

Tapas means austerity, and also to burn. What does burning mean? To ascetics in India austerity sometimes takes the form of sitting under the sun surrounded by four fires. The spirit of the word *tapas* is not merely to light a fire on all sides and sit in the blazing sun, although that has been accepted as one of the articles of *tapas*. There are other sorts of burning—for instance if you get into ice-cold water the whole body seems to burn, but after some time it stops. There was a young man in the Himalayas who had not folded his knees for ten years. He had a thing that looked like crutches almost as high as his chin, with a canvas sling attached. He slept like that—holding his hands on top of the canvas. Whatever he had to do, he did standing. Each leg had become like an elephant's leg. It must have produced intense physiological burning for months.

This sort of *tapas* is also found outside India. For instance, there is a cathedral in Montreal, Canada, which has a flight of steps, in the centre of which there is a narrow segment built of wood. People take a vow that they will walk these wooden steps on their knees in order that their knees may be terribly bruised and burning.

There are other practices which produce burning. For instance, when you fast, there is a burning in the stomach. When you don't sleep, your eyes begin to burn. Every form of burning is *tapas.* As long as it burns you are safe. These are some of the forms of *tapas,* though they may or may not be spiritually valid. There is no objection to any of these things.

What happens to you inwardly when there is severe physiological burning? Can you extend that? '*Ex*tend' is not the correct word. There is another word which probably gives you a clearer meaning—'*in*tend', interiorise—which means it must tend inwards, go deeper and deeper. It is meant to burn or cause psychological burning. Try to understand it in that spirit. Can you intend this burning within yourself in such a way that it also involves your mind? Or does it merely stop with a physiological burning? (The physiological burning will eventually come to a dead-end.)

The body is so tough that it takes people only three weeks to get used to anything, so when you subject your body to the kind of *tapas* which may burn or be a self-torture, that itself becomes enjoyable after some time. It has lost its original intention. The original intention can be satisfied if you are wise and intelligent enough to intend this physical, physiological burning before it disappears, and discover that there is a more real burning—which is psychological burning.

When you are laughed at or ridiculed it hurts—there is a burning within. As long as you pay attention to that, the enquiry is alive. If you are sensitive it must hurt. When you intend this whole *tapas,* you see this inward hurt, insult or disrespect, and you hold that steadily in focus till you know what it is that gets hurt. Then you reach a stage where you are perpetually hurt and yet never hurt. He insults you. As an insult it hurts you just for a few seconds, but as soon as the attention is focussed within, the classification of this thing as an insult has gone.

Again, when you calmly say "No" to a desire or habit as it arises, the mind gets into a commotion and the whole being seems to burn. One is neither enjoying it nor suffering it, one is *in* it. Each time the same desire crops up, one looks at it in that way, going on and on with the enquiry: "Where is it arising? What is it? What makes me want to do this again?" until after sometime this particular problem has dissolved. It has been 'burnt' away!

Tapas and Burning the Ego

Any activity or practice that burns up the false sense of ego is *tapas.* One of the most important ways in which the self-idea manifests is the feeling, "I am this body". The orthodox people suggested that anything that tortures or mortifies the body is good, but these don't work because you are punishing only the body. The idea of the self, that, "I am this body," still persists. After all these wonderful practices you say, "Look what I have done!" which strengthens the ego; whereas if something is practised that directly attacks this idea that you are the body, that might be useful.

What sort of practice should you adopt in order that the false idea that you are the body might be removed?

When you are insulted or get upset, it is the idea that you are this body that is insulted. When you are injured because somebody hit you, it is the body that is injured. Therefore it is possible to work on that area which gets hurt by insult or injury, so that this false identification can be overcome. This is a very beautiful form of self-enquiry or meditation, and it is something that can provide us with the key to solve most of our problems. For instance, somebody calls you a fool. 'Fool' is a word, and that is his opinion, but when you hear this you are hurt—which means you feel almost a physical pain. What has this incident to do with the physical pain that you experience?

We have never asked ourselves this question and therefore we go on suffering this hurt in a million ways in our life. If, on the other hand, we can devote some time to it just once, it will disappear forever. What is this pain and what is it made of? Where does it arise? (Not why does it arise, because then you are tempted to blame others or say that you are a very sensitive person. These things do not help you.) Someone says something and you feel physically hurt. If you contemplate this really seriously and earnestly, you arrive at this simple and beautiful realisation: that person was referring to a nothing and nothing got upset. There is an idea, "I am this body, I am So and so," and that idea is hurt. That is all.

Tapas and the Colouring of the Mind

Tapas, however, also refers to the great energy required to discover the colouring of the mind. The most important factor is the destruction of the colouring of the mindstuff that makes all judgements and evaluations. What is it that is coloured? What does all the evaluating? What we are interested in is to find the colouring agent that gives value to these things that attract or repel us. Without condemning or justifying the mind-colouring, you look at it, discover it, thus de-colouring the coloured understanding. Instead of artifical suppression, you bring it up so you can see it and be able to deal with it. As one comes face to face with the habit (or thought or ego-wish) it dissolves. The cover has been dis-covered! The mindstuff has been decoloured, purified.

Tapas and Enlightenment

Tapas is the inner commotion, the energy of the burning. And *tapas* is the fire that burns constantly—the Light that watches, purifies, illumines—and in the course of time becomes enlightenment.

Svādhyāya

The second practice is *svādhyāya*—study. It is possible for us to discover that sometimes we are on the wrong path and sometimes bluffing ourselves or pretending that we are doing tremendous *sādhanā.* These illusions are kept away by a regular and systematic study of spiritually uplifting texts, whatever they are. It is also possible that if there are fields of non-understanding they may be illumined by the proper study of Scriptures. Very often we may misunderstand a principle, and since that misunderstanding is accepted as knowledge by us, that misunderstanding continues for eternity.

Svādhyāya also means doing *japa* and enquiring into one's reaction to situations from moment to moment, in fact into anything that turns your mind onto itself. When you realise that there has been a misunderstanding, you have understood yourself. Once you discover—by listening to a talk or reading a book—that you have a distorted vision of the truth, from thereon you are careful and alerted to the possibility of misunderstanding. Yoga has happened already.

Īśvara praṇidhāna

The third practice is *Īśvara praṇidhāna*—dynamic surrender to the omnipresent God. It is not a passive surrender, "Oh, God will take care of everything,"but dynamic surrender. This is mentioned three times in the Yoga Sūtras in order to bring home to us the message that self-knowledge is not the end-product of a series of actions (actions being actions of the ego), but it comes into being when the ego has ceased its activities. *Īśvara praṇidhāna* is the total surrender of the ego-sense, not the ego itself. The ego is part of the world-happening. This body will still go on living even if you are the Buddha himself, but you do not have the feeling that you are a sinner, nor the opinion that you are great. Your self-estimation, your regret and remorse have gone. Then one is happy—one is *happiness*!

The 'I' itself is a mere figment of the imagination of the totality, the cosmic consciousness. What is the nature of that consciousness? What is the nature of the personality that is aware of this truth? If there is constant awareness that the 'I' is merely just one ounce of sea-water in the ocean of conciousness, conceptually capable of being isolated from the rest of the ocean, but not in reality, what would your life and behaviour be? That is called *Īśvara praṇidhāna*, surrender to God.

Yoga is not just accepting everything that someone else says. If somebody says, "You know you must surrender yourself to God," question it. In that one little sentence there are four things which you do not understand: you, surrender, yourself and God. What is you? What is yourself? How can you take yourself out and surrender this yourself to God? Where is God? If God is in you already, how do you surrender yourself? So when you hear this simple expression, if you do not blindly accept it and imagine you have understood it, what do you do? If you are an intelligent, sincere, earnest student of yoga, you immediately start studying the whole statement, trying to figure out what it means. What is God? And how do you surrender yourself to God? Even when these questions are asked there is an inner enlightenment or understanding. That is yoga!

So surrender to God cannot be explained, but we may get a glimpse of it. It can happen through different ways. One way is to realise that everything is God—the so-called holy as well as the apparently unholy. One day you begin to wonder, and realise, "I am, but I am not mine; the body exists, it is not mine; the world exists, it is not mine." You realise that this God who is omnipresent—in one and all and pervading all creation—includes you also. It is God who functions even through this body, as it functions through all bodies. There is nothing other than the divine. (Please do not think that God especially manifests in your heart only when you are in an exalted mood. When you are in a sleepy mood also, God is manifest in you. God is always there—but not in those moods, because God is not confined to anything.) You are not exempt from It—but not as 'I', because the 'I' has dissolved. Then every moment you are surrendering, whatever happens you are surrendering—surrendering in the sense that there is no idea of 'mine'.

Surrender to God should not make God look like some kind of armed policeman. That is not what is meant by surrender. *Praṇidhāna* means not passive, but dynamic surrender. In such surrender the 'I' does not say, "Alright, I have surrendered myself to God, let

Him look after me and mine." Let us go back to the analogy of the ocean. That little ounce of seawater is one with the ocean, and the totality of the ocean determines what it shall do. It may be deep in the ocean or on the crest of a wave, it may be dashed against a rock. It seems painful only if you still want to feel 'I am independent of the totality, and the totality must answer my prayers,' which means there is no surrender.

When Patanjali suggested that self-knowledge—the total elimination of self-ignorance—can be had by surrender to God, it wasn't as a technique. Total surrender (the surrender being only of ignorance) doesn't form a technique, but is one of the vital disciplines.

Surrender to God is not something about which you say, "I have surrendered to God. When will I have my next cup of coffee?" It does not mean that after the surrender you will not drink coffee! The body wants the coffee and will have the coffee, but the ego-sense has dissolved.

Surrender also happens when the fire of enquiry burns through all the components of the self and through all its activities. The three questions: "What is beyond the senses, the mind and the self?", "Is the observer different from the observed?" and, "Is 'I' independent of the totality?" burn without an answer, because there is none (no self) to hear the answer! Unable to find the answer, the self collapses in surrender. The observer is the observation—pure awareness. The experiencer is the experience—pure experiencing. There is total freedom, *kaivalya.* One alone is, as all-one.

In these three themselves, there is the spirit of yoga, so it is not the yoga of action in the sense of doing something and forgetting all about it. In *tapas* there is yoga, a total self-knowledge; in *svādhyāya* or self-study, there is self-knowledge; and in *Īśvara praṇidhāna* or surrender to God, there is selfknowledge.

One practises Kriyā Yoga in order to remove psychological obstacles so that one may be predisposed to *samādhi.* However, these actions in themselves may not produce *samādhi. Samādhi* is itself and is not the end-product of some activities.

II. 2 samādhi bhāvanārthaḥ kleśa tanū karaṇārthaś ca

When it is clearly understood that the instant realisation of cosmic oneness which is yoga is not the product of any effort, how can one 'practise' such unity?

Surely active yoga is taught, not because such practice results in the realisation of oneness, but because it can aid in the direction of one's attention towards enlightenment and away from the elements that cause mental turmoil; which, as a result of such turning away, are weakened.'

This Sūtra is extremely important and often its vital message seems to be overlooked. Self-discipline and surrender to God are practised in order that the path to *samādhi* may be smooth, that you may be firmly established in *samādhi,* and the psychological disturbances may cease—or at least be weakened. If this does not happen,. your self-discipline is useless. Whatever be the causes that create confusion in your life, those causes must be weakened, even if they may not completely disappear. If while disciplining yourself you get more and more nervous, excitable, irritable, etc., what are you practising self-discipline for?

Samādhi bhāvanārthaḥ—we are lead from moment to moment to the understanding of the reality. Yoga opens your eyes to the reality. *Samādhi* is a transcendental state. In the absence of self-knowledge this 'transcendental state' becomes another expression which consists of two more words in your dictionary. The transcendental state has to be defined as you define your present state as waking state. But *samādhi* is neither a state, a stage nor the absence or presence of something. It is the reality existing as it is without the least interference by the self. When the self—which describes, identifies, sticks labels on and projects its own ideas upon it—is absent, it is then that the truth concerning it shines. You can't then say, "I understand the truth," because that implies that there is an 'I' which understands, so 'I' and the truth are separate. No! The truth alone shines.

Without *samādhi bhāvanārthaḥ* you are just disciplining yourself, so you become a very good man, and people will admire you. It doesn't work. No motivation other than the direction of your attention towards enlightenment is valid, because all your motivations are going to weave a greater and more deadly web around you, to trap you. So your study of Scriptures, *japa* and surrender to God must lead you to this self-knowledge, *samādhi.*

If, in surrender to God, you are looking within to see what surrender should mean, i.e., "Now that I have surrendered myself to God I must be totally non-resistant," once again the self defines surrender as this, or that. Can the self completely vanish from sight and surrender just *be,* without being so defined by the self?

So surrender to God, in relation to *samādhi,* has a different meaning. It is not a mechanical thing at all, but a constantly self-renewing surrender in which only the defining, destroying self is absent. There is perpetual vigilance, because the whole universe is full of this consciousness, which is aware.

These practices also weaken (not destroy) the *kleśa.* What are the *kleśa*?

II. 3 avidyā 'smitā rāga dveṣā 'bhiniveśāḥ kleśāḥ

The mind is restless because of the many unresolved problems. The elements that disturb the mental equilibrium and thus generate psychic distress are:

(1) ignorance of the truth concerning

(2) one's self or egotism which seems to be the obvious truth in ignorance, and the belief in the separative individuality,

(3 & 4) psychological and unnatural extension of attraction and repulsion which, as neurological phenomena, are natural, and

(5) blind clinging to the present physical 'life', born of the ignorant division of timeless eternity into life and death.

Patanjali says that the whole world is full of sorrow, for a man of understanding, until he realises that suffering is experienced by him because he does not know what his self is. Sorrow and pain do not come from outside, but are experienced within yourself. Nobody in or outside this world, no god, demon or star is responsible for your unhappiness. Unhappiness is within you; it is experienced by you.

It is not an event that makes you happy or unhappy, but your reaction to it. Why do you respond in that manner? Why do you experience pain, suffering and psychological sorrow?

Patanjali suggests a five-fold ground for this unhappiness—*avidyā 'smitā rāga dveṣā 'bhiniveśā.* These are the *kleśā.*

Avidyā

Avidyā is the inevitable ignorance of our spiritual nature, of Self-knowledge. (To help you remember the meaning clearly, *avidyā* sounds like 'I've no idea'.) Ignorance is a non-entity from the philosophical (or the Absolute) point of view, though it is yet capable of very real and frightening results while it lasts. It is similar, in a way, to a nightmare. It is not only like the darkness of the night which veils the reality, but it is like the illusory dream which conjures up false entities which enjoy momentary existence. Anything positively said about it is a cancellation of its own true nature.

The absence of ignorance cannot be easily understood or known. That which thinks, "I am ignorant," is ignorant. That which thinks, "I am not ignorant," is even more ignorant! Someone defined *avidyā* in a very beautiful way. He said, "That person who says 'What I say is right and what all others say is wrong', is suffering from terrible ignorance."

There is absolutely no way in which 'I' could come face to face with *avidyā,* and understand it. One might 'feel' that there is *avidyā,* and 'understand' the description of it, but one can never know what it *is.* Either one is in a state of *avidyā,* or of Self-knowledge. The moment there is Self-knowledge there is no more *avidyā.*

Asmitā

Let us go back to the example of the wave and the ocean. The wave is non-different from the ocean. The entire volume of water—currents, ripples and waves—is the ocean, one indivisible mass. The diversity arises because *we* have created it. There is no motion independent of a static entity. Air moves only in relation to something else—the trees, etc. Similarly, water does not wet itself. If you get into water, *you* get wet. So when we say that there are waves and ripples and currents in the ocean, that is only in relation to you who are not part of that, but to the ocean itself there are no waves, no currents. In the same way, in the physical body, as you sit there calmly and quietly, millions of cells are sparking in your body, there are all sorts of funny rivers flowing, there is tremendous activity going on. And yet, because you *are* the activity, the thing itself, you are not aware of it.

Similarly, when *avidyā* manifests itself, the ignorance is ignorant of the cosmic nature of intelligence and it creates the idea of individuality, the feeling 'I am'—*asmitā*. *Asmitā* literally means 'I-ness', the very idea of 'I', the ego-sense—not egoism in the sense of vanity. As soon as this idea of 'I' arises, it itself creates you, and then the others. By repeatedly affirming this error it has attained the status of truth. The whole thing was born of ignorance (*avidyā*), which somehow manifests in this Cosmic Being—which is Cosmic Consciousness or Intelligence.

The closest you can come to understanding *asmitā* is when you know that you do not understand! If we examine seriously, we will note that problems are all related directly to the ego-sense which labels, classifies, judges and conceptualises. When we make any statement, the 'I' is assumed as a fixed point of reference, from where we relate ourselves to everything. This assumption has to be questioned. As the eyes look at an object, for instance paper, there comes the thought, "I see the paper". Then you stop and start to enquire, "How does the feeling 'I see it' come?" It is when the ego-sense mysteriously springs up that the paper becomes 'paper'. The ego-sense gives a name to itself and another name to the 'other end' of any happening.

What is 'I'? What is the ego-sense? From where does this 'I am' feeling arise? This is the fundamental question which no one has ever been able to answer; but we all assume there is an ego. That assumption *is* the ego. In 'I have no idea' there is hidden this 'I' that refuses to give in, and stands as an unbreakable pillar. So in the ocean of indivisible space a wave arises and the understanding of the ocean-ness of the ocean has gone. Somehow this wave thinks, "I am, I am an entity, I am independent."

Rāga-Dveṣā

When you assume that the fragmentation—the personality—is an independent entity which has to fight for itself, then you begin to develop a relationship with those whom you consider others. 'I' (whatever that 'I' is) seems to experience suffering, because somehow it responds to the environment by neatly dividing it into two halves—one which it likes and one which it doesn't like—*rāga dveṣā*. *Rāga* means attraction, or approval; *dveṣā* means repulsion or disapproval. Why is one terrible and one not so terrible? Because 'I' is the centre of creation and 'I' determines what is right and what is wrong. The activity of the mind begins to distinguish,

"This is beautiful, this is ugly," "This is pleasant, this is unpleasant," "I love this, I hate that." You like something because it gives you pleasure; it gives you pleasure because you like it. It's a vicious circle, constantly torturing you on this rack, stretching and pulling in two directions at the same time—without ever revealing the truth that all this is nothing but the activity of the mind. Minus these two feelings there is no relationship. Swami Sivananda used to say that if you remove these two expressions completely from your mind and your heart, perhaps the world will disappear as the world (as matter, as energy) and you will have a vision of Cosmic Intelligence.

Abhiniveśāḥ

There is only one more category which the keenly observant and wise mind of the author has recognised, and this category seems to have baffled even him. That is *abhiniveśā*—mad clinging to one's own physical life. Patanjali says this is universal.

Because of ignorance, egoism, selfishness, lust and hatred, you cling to what you have and to life itself. Though you know that life is full of miseries you still cling to it, for the simple reason that you imagine that life after death is going to be something dreadful. Even an old man of ninety-five still wants to continue to live in his miserable body, and he will spend a fortune trying to prolong life for another three days. No one knows why it is so.

This love for one's limited life is the trend away from the centre, from this Cosmic Intelligence, and it seems to carry on under its own steam. It's also part of the dichotomy expressed in 'I like this, I don't like that'.

We like to live, we don't like not to live. We dislike death and dying. We invent some nice theories that we are really not dying, but going to heaven, that the soul is immortal and somehow enters into another body. I'm not questioning all these theories, but trying to show how they came into being in the first place because of the fear of death. Why are we afraid of death? Because we dislike it. Why do we dislike it? Because of ignorance.

Day in and day out people die, every day the undertaker is busy. And yet those whose time has not yet come believe that they won't go! What greater wonder is there than this? Even Patanjali says it is a mystery.

It is very good to remember that the sources of psychological distress cannot be *completely* annihilated or destroyed as long as the personality functions as the personality, which means as long as life lasts in this body.

Conclusion

The fundamental truth that *avidyā 'smitā rāga dveṣā* and *abhiniveśā* are *kleśā* (or the roots of sorrow) cannot be taught from a book. You must have arrived at this understanding by a very clear observation of life as it is; where you can quite clearly see that both attachment and aversion (love as opposed to hate) create misery in your life. This you cannot get from a book. If you say, "Patanjali says that attachment is bad, therefore I will not be attached," this is only borrowed knowledge. That there *is* sorrow and misery and suffering in your life has to be seen by *you*, it cannot be infused into you by somebody else.

II. 4 avidyā kṣetram uttareṣāṁ prasupta tanu vicchinno 'dārāṇāṁ

Obviously, ignorance of the truth of one-ness (or indivisibility of cosmic intelligence) is the cause of all the other sources of psychic distress—whether these latter seem to be completely hidden or dormant, veiled or weak, or actively spread out, creating the notion that they are not related to spiritual ignorance, that they are independent of ignorance, and can, therefore, be dealt with by means other than self-knowledge.

This ignorance is the ground on which all these psychic disturbances arise, thrive and exist. They disappear once this ignorance goes. *Avidyā kṣetram*—field of ignorance—is a beautiful and extremely subtle truth expressed in a simple way which one must see for oneself.

You are ignorant of your own true nature. You do not know what this I is that suffers, or why it suffers. While you are in the shadow of that ignorance, if someone says that you are a nice fellow, you are happy. The happiness is within you, but since you do not know the springs of your own inner experience you attribute that happiness to him. You like him because he scratches your back. If someone else says that you are an idiot, you are unhappy, and the unhappiness is in you; but you think it comes from him and that if he (whom you call your enemy) is eliminated, then the unhappiness will also be eliminated! It is not so. The enemy is in you.

Eventually everything—greed, fear, anger, etc.—come out of this ignorance. So until that ignorance is handled, none of these things will disappear. For instance, non-greed cannot be introduced into you the way you can put a slide into a slide-projector.Just as ne goes in and the other one comes out, non greed goes in and greed comes out. But it is not that simple! The greed probably comes from fear, the fear from something else, and that from something else again. So ignorance is the primary cause of all psychic distress, whether dormant or manifest, weak or strong.

We can say that the baby has no ego-sense, no likes and dislikes, no ignorance. Is the baby then enlightened? No, because in ,his case all these are asleep, dormant. Can you say that a sleeping man does not tell a lie, and therefore he is enlightened? No. When he wakes up all these problems will wake up too.

When the truth is not seen, then what appears to be for the moment is given the dignity of a real substance—real in the sense that it will be there forever and ever. This appearance regards itself as a permanent entity in the place of the total truth. That is, a small fragment takes the place of this truth, of the totality—which is absurd. When this totality is realised as the real, as the truth, the illusion is gone—without disturbing anything that exists. If you clearly understand the existence of the ocean as a totality in which waves arise, exist and dissolve without making any difference to the ocean, then there is no ignorance. A tremendous inner transformation has taken place and life takes on a completely different quality.

Self-knowledge can only come after a clear understanding of what life means, of what 'I' is. Only then is it possible for you to even suggest to yourself which way you want to go. First understand yourself, your mind and then you will know which way. The tree knows how to turn itself towards the light and the creeper knows how to twine itself around the tree, because in their case there is no identity problem. The tree, as it were, knows itself. Can you also, in a similar way, know yourself—completely and thoroughly? We are not aiming at self-knowledge as a goal, but suggesting that the basis of our whole life is self-knowledge! If it is so, then what follows is yoga. If it is not so, what follows is unhappiness, misery. It is quite simple. If you want to be unhappy, forget all about it and go on—ignorance is bliss. If you don't want that messy life, here is the simplest thing: "Know yourself," not as a goal, but as a basis for your whole life. So this self-knowledge is not a goal, nor is it the self as the knower of knowledge (which then is the object of the self: e. g. 'I know this'). It is the self *as* knowledge. This is a misunderstanding which language has created.

Knowledge has come to mean 'the object of my comprehension'. When you say, "The object of my comprehension," the 'my' gets swallowed and therefore it looks as though it is an absolutely correct statement of truth. But when you also emphasise the 'my' in it, you find the problem. 'The object of *my* comprehension is knowledge' means that 'I' is here, and there is some kind of relationship or connection between me and that knowledge, so the knowledge becomes an object. And therefore, based on this misunderstanding, one tends even to create an image of self. "I know my self'.

What is meant by that? I have never really understood this expression. The knower *is* the self—not knower in the sense of 'I am the knower and you are the known', not a certain idea or ideal or image comprehended by me, but knowledge which *itself* is the self. Hence self-knowledge is not the goal. Only if it is looked upon that way does it become an existential fact, and not a goal.

II. 5 anityā 'śuci duḥkhā 'nātmasu nitya śuci sukhā 'tma khyātir avidyā

Ignorance gives rise to a 'knowledge' of ego-sense—an assumed fact of the non-existent ego-sense. It is only in a state of spiritual ignorance that one identifies or confuses that which is impermanent with that which is eternal, that which is impure or coloured with that which is pure and unconditioned, pain with joy, and the unmodified consciousness (Self) with thoughts and modifications which are not-Self. Realisation of the spiritual truth or enlightenment, on the other hand, enables the impermanent, etc., to be seen as such, and the permanent etc., to be seen as such.

The ultimate source of psychic distress is ignorance, which is indefinable; but its effects can be detected in the perverse way in which the mind functions: it imagines permanency where there is no permanency; the pure to be impure and vice versa; pleasure and happiness where it does not exist; and it assumes the existence of a self where there is no self. These indicate the state of confusion or ignorance.

Ignorance in itself cannot be seen or understood. You cannot know what ignorance is, but you can know it by its fruits. Its function is exactly like darkness. You have not seen darkness. You only sense when it exists by the fact that in darkness you are unable to see. In order to perceive any object, light is necessary; and if you want to see darkness with the help of a light, you are not seeing darkness at all! Even though you do not know what ignorance means, you can sense its presence and influence by the way you behave and the way that your intelligence is incapacitated or perverted. All the way through it is ignorance. Right from the start it was ignorance, but *in* ignorance you assumed that the cause of this was something else.

What is painful is somehow considered pleasure—smoking is a very simple example that comes to mind. When you started smoking it was painful and yet you thought it was very fashionable. You had to be 'with it' and then somehow the thing that was painful became pleasant. Then you can't give it up, and that's another pain—the pain born of your smoking habit which is difficult to break and which leads you towards illness, suffering and destruction. That which gives rise to pain must also be pain. In the list that Patanjali has given, good and evil are not discussed at all. He does not indulge in good and evil, right and wrong. See the truth for exactly what it is. If you still want to smoke, that's your business.

It is ignorance, perversion, which sees pleasure in what in fact is pain. When this ignorance prevails, the faculty of energy inherent in the universe itself seems to assume what is regarded as the ego-sense. This ego-sense cannot be intellectualised or understood by the mind, because it is something that is born of the mind, is part of the mind, is the mind itself. Once the knowledge arises that the ego-sense is not necessary and therefore non-existent, ignorance also is gone. The ego-sense came into being when it was assumed to exist, and the moment this game is seen for what it is, that very moment it disappears.

(The realisation of the non-existence of the ego-sense is also the role of Kriya Yoga.)

II. 6 dṛg darśana–śaktyor ekātmatevā 'smitā

In cosmic consciousness all activities happen. Thus, for instance, seeing happens: the power of sight sees. However, when the consciousness fragmented by the shadow of ignorance identifies itself as the see-er, there is the ego-sense.

Dṛg is the see-er. The see-er is all the time independent; or, he doesn't exist as an entity, as reality, as truth. *Darśana–śakti* is the power which enables sight or perception to come into being. Though the see-er has nothing whatsoever to do with the experiencing process, he somehow gets involved in it. Experiencing is natural, it is there everywhere. You keep your eyes open, and since you are a living being you cannot help seeing something.

Eyes see, ears hear, nose smells, tongue tastes, skin feels, mind thinks, lungs breathe, stomach digests and life lives—whether you want them to or not. As soon as the eyelids are parted, seeing happens When the sound waves enter the ears, hearing happens. What is it that sees and hears? The sense of sight sees, hearing itself hears. When your eyes are open can you stop seeing? No. That implies that seeing is a natural phenomenon, inherent in light. So there is nothing called the self, the 'I', the ego-sense here; it is merely the sight seeing. Every event comes to an end as spontaneously and instantly as it came into being. There are no problems.

In this pure and simple experience there is no division, just the sense of sight merging in the seen. There is no divided experiencing, no ego-sense at all, and there is the same peace and joy as in sleep.

While all these things go on, when the powers that are inherent in what we call nature manifest themselves, from somewhere in that cosmic intelligence a notion arises, "I see". (One has to experience this in order to understand it.) The moment division has arisen in this pure experiencing, there is a desire to experience. That desire to experience creates the ego-sense, or is *itself* the ego-sense. Instead of allowing the experiencing to continue to be experienced, the 'I' springs up: "I am experiencing, I am seeing, I am hearing." Therefore that experience is treated as an object, and the 'I' rises up as the subject, to experience it: 'I see you'.

In that split second, thought which thought 'I see you' became a space, and in that space a feeling arises 'Ah, you are nice, I like you. ' This means that this energy—which momentarily became aware of you as an object—likes to flow in that direction. When it comes to the practice of yoga, the same feeling arises as 'I must realise God, I must see God, I must have a spiritual experience. ' Wherever you go and whatever you do, the 'I' is there, and because of this becomes more and more deeply embedded.

Theologians all over the world loudly proclaim that God is omnipresent. Omnipresent means everywhere. If God is omnipresent, what stands between me and God? Me. There can be nothing else. If that is so, we come back to square one. What is me? What is 'I'? The 'I', the egoism, is the other side of 'I don't know' and since that is so far away from our daily experience we have treated it as the experiencer. 'I' see, 'I' talk, 'I' hear, 'I' sit. We have taken that 'I' for granted, and from that all of our experiences and expressions flow. , "What shall I do now?" Even in that question 'I' am taken for granted and the 'doing' becomes so terribly important, so that the 'I' is there, accepted as a solid reality. It is not questioned at all.

Therefore when it comes to what you call meditation, a monstrous error is committed. The 'I' being taken for granted, the 'I' meditates—so 'I meditate upon myself'. How can you do that? I have seen fantastic feats performed in circuses that you would not have believed possible, but I have not yet seen someone stand on their own shoulders. If you cannot stand on your own shoulders, how can you meditate upon yourself? What does it mean? And yet it has to be done. Therefore what do you do? You learn to recognise the expressions or extensions of the ego. First you get hold of these expressions and extensions of the ego, and from there you go on slowly feeling your way.

II. 7 sukhā 'nuśayī rāgaḥ *
II. 8 duḥkhā 'nuśayī dveṣaḥ **

**Attraction* (or mental conditioning or colouring) follows, *rests in* (and is just another term for) the erroneous evaluation of an object or experience as *pleasure*. Because of the mental colouring something looks attractive.*

***Similarly, *repulsion* (which is another phase of attraction) follows, *abides in* (and is just another term for) the erroneous classification of an object or experience as *pain-giving*. On the other hand, what the human mind in ignorance regards as attraction and repulsion exist in nature and are inherent, invariable and constant in the manifestation of cosmic intelligence (e.g. the magnetic polarity). In nature, however, there is neither the cloud of ignorance nor its consequent ego-sense, and hence the attraction and repulsion in nature are of an entirely different quality to that found in the human psyche.*

The see-er immediately divides the whole universe of experience into two—something which you like, something which you don't like. Something which you like you call pleasure, something which you dislike you call pain. You seek pleasure; when you don't get it, as often happens, you are frustrated. You dislike pain without realising that it has become pain only because you dislike it; and when it haunts you, you experience pain again. In one case you want to run after it, and in the other case you want to run away from it. Here, running is common. It's good to understand that all these are different only verbally, in fact there is no difference.

No one in the world can honestly and rationally explain why one thing is considered pleasure and another is considered pain Therefore Patanjali says that even this is born of ignorance. In Sanskrit there are two words to signify pleasure and pain—*sukha* and *duḥkha*. You see that both are almost identical, just as happiness and unhappiness are almost identical. Unhappiness is merely an extension of happiness. So any happiness that you endeavour to extend becomes unhappiness. Leave it alone, it is happiness; try to extend it, it becomes unhappiness.

There is a nice theory which suggests that ignorance is bliss. Patanjali says: "Impossible. As long as you are ignorant you are helplessly bound to go round this whirligig. If you experience happiness or pleasure in this life, it is only because you have decided to call it so, for the time being." This is a remarkable exposure. It is not pleasure as such, but you have *decided* to call it so! And therefore, for the time being, it gives you pleasure. What makes it pleasure temporarily? Only your ignorance of its nature and your ignorance of your own identity.

Once the ego—*asmitā*—has come into being it constantly seeks pleasure. (People can suffer for the sake of pleasure, can find pleasure even in such grotesque practices suggested by the psychological expression 'martyr complex'.) Because you call it pleasure you want a repetition of it, and wanting the repetition sets up a craving (which is pain) and when you cannnot have it when you want it, it is painful.

The stream of life takes no notice whatsoever of what you and I wish to have or wish to avoid, like or dislike; but out of likes and dislikes it fashions its own unhappiness. Even what is known as pleasure or happiness in this life is subject to change. Whatever happiness is sought, once gained it leaves you cold. Apart from that, even as you are enjoying that happiness there is a sneaking suspicion that it will change, it won't last.

The constant pleasure-seeking tendency of the ego loves to avoid all unpleasant experiences. But this stream of experiencing flows on, totally unconcerned about our likes and dislikes. (When the sun set did it ask you, "Have you finished your job? May I set now?" When the sun rises tomorrow will it ask you, "Have you finished your mischief, may I rise now?") There is the wonderful doctrine: "God made the world for the pleasure of man." I ask the mosquito: "Are you made for my pleasure, or am I made for yours?"

Patanjali merely suggests that we look at this phenomenon and see why we like one thing and not another. He does not say that therefore you should seek pleasure and avoid pain, but "This is a fact—look at it".

II. 9 svarasavāhī viduṣo 'pi tathā 'rūḍho 'bhiniveśaḥ

Blind clinging to life is an inexplicable yet undeniable fact of life which is self-sustaining (since it is just another phase or face of ignorance) and is therefore found to be a dominant factor even in wise beings as long as the physical body—which is the operative seat of ignorance—exists. It is the operation of the power that preserves the physical sheath for the unfoldment of self-knowledge, combined with the habit of dependence on objective sources for enjoyment and sustenance and fear of losing them, and the inability to see other states of existence.

Abhiniveśa is translated as 'blind clinging to life'. This seems to sustain itself, and that is the surest indication of the presence of ignorance. You do not see ignorance as such, but here is an incontrovertible proof that there is ignorance. This ignorance confuses the spirit or the undying consciousness with the ever-changing, decomposing body.

Why are we clinging to this life, knowing that it is coming to an end? It seems to be totally irrational and foolish. We are clinging to this physical body even though it is bound to perish. Patanjali has concisely, precisely and scientifically expounded the facts of life and even he says concerning this: "This blind clinging to life is there, it seems to be selfsustaining, and it is found even in wise people." Even very wise enlightened people are irrationally unwilling to shed the body.

Though Patanjali has explained the cause of everything else, when it comes to this blind clinging to life he says, "I don't know". That to me is a great tribute to the Yoga Sūtras.

II. 10 te pratiprasava heyāḥ sūkṣmāḥ

These sources of psychic distress are subtle, and not to be confused with their gross expansion as likes and dislikes, habits (good and bad), vanity and such personality traits. However, these subtle sources of psychic distress can be dispelled by resolving each in its own cause (or by confronting each of them with its own true opposite).

These five sources of psychological distress, disturbance or distraction are subtle in their essence and they manifest in numerous different ways. They appear to be subtle only because they are not on view. It is possible to deal with some of them by dealing with their own individual source. Fear, for instance, may appear to be gross, but its own roots are subtle. If you have fear in your heart even little trees look like ghosts at night. Even attraction and repulsion are very subtle. You tend to rationalise these and to say that you are attracted to her because she is beautiful. You think that she is beautiful. Before that thought arises there is another thought which says, "I like her". She is beautiful because you like her and you like her because she is beautiful. Which one comes first? Again, are you afraid of him because he is vicious, or do you consider him vicious because you are afraid?

Love goes looking for an object to love. If you have love in your heart you'll find everybody beautiful. Fear goes looking for an object to be afraid of. If there is fear in your heart it is that fear that projects itself outside and creates objects of which you are afraid. (This is even more evident when there are racial, communal or religious riots. There it is terribly obvious that the rioters are not interested in discovering the truth. They have a certain fear, emotion or commotion within them, and they act blindly, driven by it.)

In the darkness or shadow of ignorance, there is a feeling that *this* disturbance is caused by *that* factor.

Get hold of that, and by rational approach to it see that this is not the cause of your suffering. Then you have removed one layer. The next layer comes to view. If these sources of psychological distress or disturbance are dealt with in this manner with a little patience, it is possible for everyone, starting wherever he is, to reach the ultimate source of psychological disturbance, which is ignorance. Right from the start it was ignorance, but in ignorance you assume that the cause of this is something else.

Ignorance plagues our entire life, perverting our thoughts, feelings, emotions, expressions and experiences. (At one stage they are called thoughts and at another emotions, experiences or expressions, but basically they are the operations of these five sources of psychological distress or distraction.) These five sources of sorrow fall away when their own source is realised, like a snake shedding its skin. Try to get hold of the problem as it is, go step by step, tracing each one to its own source, without assuming anything or rejecting anything; and eventually you will discover that the whole thing was a big hoax.

If you assume that the cause lies hidden deep in the subconscious and therefore you will go under hypnosis, again you will fail, because you have not taken the whole problem step by step. It may be possible that fear of the dark comes from something that happened in childhood, but go step by step from there to find its immediate cause. Deal with that.

The immediate cause of that suffering or distress is gone; but if you are clever you can dive deeper into it and find the root-cause, and eliminate it there. If you shine a torch on a shadow, the shadow is not understood, it is not seen! That *itself* is enlightenment. If without any doubt whatsoever one is able to say, "I know what ignorance means," there is knowledge. The shadow is enlightened, the self is illumined, the truth is realised.

II. 11 dhyāna heyās tad vṛttayaḥ

Both when these elements of psychic distress are mere ripples on the surface of the mind-stuff and when they become gross and operative, they can be dispelled by contemplation.

By meditation you go right down to the fundamental root, *avidyā.* When the light of meditation or self-awareness shines on what appeared to be the source from where these psychological distress symptoms seemed to emanate, you find nothing. That nothing was called ignorance before. Nothing appeared, nothing disappeared, but a clearer understanding has arisen.

II. 12 kleśa mūlaḥ karmā 'śayo dṛṣṭā 'dṛṣṭa janma vedanīyah

All actions bear to the five-fold psychic disturbance or distress a mutual cause-and-effect relationship, thus sustaining a chain reaction. Hence, actions lead to afflictions (notions of ego-sense) which manifest in the obvious physical life as experiences of pleasure, pain, etc., and also in the subtle mental states (likes and dislikes), here in this life-span or in other not so obvious life-states—and such afflictions (the ego-sense and ignorance) generate further actions. However, this need not for ever be so; for from these effects the causes can be known, and the root cause made inoperative.

If basic self-ignorance is the cause of all this psychological distress, how does that take all these different forms? How does it even give rise to a notion of knowledge? You say, "I know he is a good man and therefore I love him." Is this also a fruit of sheer ignorance? Can sheer ignorance appear as knowledge of goodness in the other person? No. Your understanding immediately acts so that from there on it is a confusion, one feeding the other. You think he is a good person, you love him and when you love him you think he is a better person. It goes on and on. When you think he is an undesirable person you hate him, you don't desire his company; and as you draw further and further away from him you think he is more and more undesirable. From a distance he looks even more horrible, because you don't see any good points at all! The first misunderstanding that he is undesirable makes you dread him, fear him, hate him; and on the basis of this, as you pull back you see more and more evil in him. That is how prejudice grows.

As you go on expressing in terms of your prejudice and ignorance, this expression of your thoughts and emotions strengthens this ignorance, making the veil heavier and thicker so that your further actions become coarser and coarser. The actions that spring from that coarse personality become even worse, and naturally it returns making you worse still. (You can understand this very clearly if you look at some relationship in your own life.)

Is there no relief? Only when you contemplate this cyclic unceasing disaster do you realise how merciful and wise and what a brilliant chap God was to introduce this thing called death! That puts an end to this progressive degeneration.

When you observe the course of life, whether this course is obvious or not obvious, you get an inkling into this truth that you are all the time strengthening or weakening the sources of your own suffering, your own sorrow. And as they are strengthened or weakened, your behaviour begins to change.

Patanjali uses the singular—*mūla*—which means one root, ignorance. This ignorance being a non-entity (like darkness) to become aware of it is the only way in which it can be removed. For instance, it is said in the Yoga Vāsiṣṭha:, *"When the sun rises, where does the darkness go?"* In the same way, when there is enlightenment, what is called ignorance, and where does it go?

If you take any experience that you undergo, or any expression of your personality, naturally the first immediate cause appears to be the real cause—but it is not. We in our supreme (worldly) wisdom think that we can somehow overcome this sorrow or unwisdom by merely manipulating the immediate cause. If you think you are unhappy because of someone or something, you try to manipulate that. If you think that to go to heaven is the way to ensure happiness, then again you manipulate by doing some chanting or performing some religious ceremonies. You are merely fiddling around with what your mind suggests as the immediate causes or sources of your unhappiness. That is what we normally do. The yogi suggests something different: take that opportunity of tracing the whole thing down to its root-cause. Without questioning the normal approach to this problem of happiness and unhappiness which involves remedial measures to get rid of immediate problems—such as goodness, charity, an ethical and moral life and religious performance—

the yogi says make use of that opportunity to find out the efficient cause.

In the Yoga Vāsiṣṭha there is a brilliant doctrine given to us: "*You cannot possibly separate the action from the man. The person and the action are inseparable.*"

The behaviour comes from your own being. How can you separate them? These can immediately be dealt with by a clear understanding of their own immediate cause, just as indigestion can be immediately related to last night's heavy food. Once this relationship is understood you eliminate the immediate cause and you have eliminated the immediate effect. The indigestion disappears when you fast the next day, but you have not removed the potentiality of indigestion, which is the stomach or eating! Similarly, though you have eliminated the immediate effect, you have not eliminated the source. It is still there in a subtle form. How do you destroy it at its very root?

II. 13 sati mūle tad vipāko jāty āyur bhogāḥ

As long as the roots of these psychic disturbances exist, generating their consequent actions, their expansion and fruition are inevitable. Their fruition takes place in different life-spans, perhaps in different species, and in diverse experiences. Such fruition is therefore an unmistakable pointer to the persistence of spiritual ignorance and its off-springs—which are the fountain-source of sorrow.

As long as the root is there, it is going to generate action—whether you call that action virtue or vice—and that action is going to modify (not eliminate) the source of psychological distress—not the rock bottom. The source of psychological distress keeps changing. You like something which you disliked, you dislike something which you liked. You can keep on meddling with it, modifying it, without ever getting rid of it.

As long as the five-fold root exists, you are still within this danger zone. They are going to throw up physical, mental and verbal actions which are going to leave their own impressions called *samskāras*. These *samskāras* are going to crave for their own expression once again, and the chain is seemingly endless.

II. 14 te hlāda paritāpa phalāḥ puṇyā 'puṇya hetutvāt

These experiences which are the results of virtue and vice are the sweet and bitter fruits (causing happiness and agony respectively) that are found all along the path of life.

Actions are sometimes called virtue, sometimes vice, and they yield fruits which are sometimes called joy and sometimes called sorrow. As long as the roots are there, they agitate your consciousness, and this agitation generates action—mental and physical activity which inevitably lead to experiences. While performing those actions, already you are enjoying or suffering: whatever it is, something is happening. When you are doing something, it is not as though the fruit of the action is somewhere else—*then and there* you are suffering or enjoying.

Your actions are sometimes virtuous, sometimes vicious, and they give you sometimes joy and sometimes sorrow, not necessarily related to one or the other. Sometimes you think you are doing a good thing and you are labouring under it: it is miserable. Sometimes what tradition or culture says is not good, seems to be very pleasant. But here is an incontrovertible truth: as long as this ignorance, ego-sense, likes, dislikes and clinging to life continues, you are going to live the so-called individual life, imprisoned in a personality. That is what 'I am' means! As long as these five sources of psychological distress continue, they will continue to throw up actions. And actions must result in immediate and long term experiences and long term effects.

Life is a continuous flow. When do you freeze it to work out whether what happened some time ago has turned out to be good or evil? Good follows evil and evil follows good. Good cometh out of evil and evil cometh out of good! Therefore yogis don't discuss the problem of good and evil very seriously, because whether an action is seemingly good or seemingly bad it is still action, and action has got an immediate result—which is the immediate experience which strengthens or weakens the veil of ignorance; and there is a long-term effect which returns to you as further experience, which you may then call pleasure and pain.

II. 15 pariṇāma tāpa saṁskāra duḥkhair guṇavṛtti virodhāc ca duḥkham eva sarvaṁ vivekinaḥ

However, the wise (though their own mind is totally free from sorrow) consider all experiences painful as they are all the fruits of the actions of ignorance. The very pleasures are accompanied by the painful realisation that they are subject to change. Constant and violently painful craving for repetitive experience of pleasure in a vain attempt to cancel the change fills the interval with pain. All of this leaves an enduring impression on the mind, which (impression) creates the painful tendency to crave for the avoidance of pain which alone is therefore continuous. And, there is a constant conflict in oneself as the psychological mood changes, with every change in the thought-form in the mind-stuff; and the conflict is sorrow.

To the person who is awakened to this fact the whole of life and everything in life is unhappiness, sorrow. Wherever there is mental activity and dissipation of energy, wherever there is haphazard movement of thought, there is unhappiness. Even what the common man regards as happiness—pleasure, prosperity, glory, success—becomes painful to the awakened man. The awakened man neither seeks to discover a supposed external source of his unhappiness, nor even to identify what he calls unhappiness within himself, such knowledge being part of ignorance.

Time is passing, everything is changing. If you seem to be happy now even that is tainted by unhappiness, because there is a recognition (whether at the conscious, unconscious or sub-conscious level) that it is passing away. You get bored with the same happiness repeated often, so there is unhappiness there—which means that either the external world changes, or 'I' changes—change being inevitable. Happiness also undergoes this change and therefore must come to an end.

That which is subject to change has only one content, which is pain. That which is called happiness came in. It seemed to give you some pleasure in the beginning, till the suspicion that it might go away arose and made you more anxious to keep it. The craving increased, the effort to hold it increased, but the pleasure didn't increase. The anxiety that it will go away is pain, the struggle to hold it is pain, and the craving to prolong it is pain; so whether you call it pain or pleasure, life is full of pain.

As long as these sources of psychological distress continue to exist, one has to live in sorrow. When you see that such is life, the immediate effect is that there is no pursuit of pleasure. The human body is endowed with the capacity to experience pleasure that is natural. And this natural pleasure flows down the river of nature; without you seeking, it comes to you.

There is a psychological state which you call sorrow, and a psychological state which you call pleasure. Instead of finding words to describe these psychological states (every state being a limitation) the yogi endeavours to look and to 'discover'—in the purest, simplest and most literal sense of the word—'to take the lid off'. When you take the lid off you don't anticipate what you may find. Anything may come out of it.

Instead of examining or analysing, you should observe the experiences that are experienced by the mind, and the mental states produced by our daily life from moment to moment—whether they are called pleasure or pain. Ask yourself three things concerning them: What is the content of each one of these experiences? What is it that responds to this experience and calls it pain or pleasure? Who is the experiencer? These are the three questions to which the yogi seeks answers.

One who pursues this quest immediately discovers another problem. The thought with which this quest was started creates its own mental activity, which is yet a further distraction. Can you put an end to distraction, without being distracted? Can you counter violence without being violent to yourself? How do you do that? There is a distraction in the mind. Can you stop that distraction without the effort of stopping it? Unfortunately that effort is going to add to the distraction rather than abolish it, because now another wonderful little flashlight is going to sit there, discriminating: this is the right direction, this is the wrong direction. So once again the mind is active. Therefore the enquiry itself is manufacturing distraction and psychological distress.

11. 16 heyam duḥkham anāgataṁ

Yet, all is not lost. For sorrow that has not yet 'arrived', not yet reached the field of experience, can be avoided; unhappiness that has not yet befallen may be avoided, by avoiding psychic contact with it.

Here Patanjali gives us a philosophy of yoga which is able to show us the way to deal with our problems, and to eventually arrive at that point where the problems do not arise at all. It is probably the only positive description of the aim of philosophy given in the Yoga Sūtras.

The unhappiness that has not yet reached you can be avoided. This is a fantastic and beautiful teaching given to us. Don't say that because you are unhappy and involved in all this complicated process, you must go on inviting suffering throughout your life.

You know of people who bash their heads against a wall when they have a migraine headache. That aggravates the headache. When they stop, the aggravated form of headache stops and they pretend that the whole thing has stopped. That is not what we are looking for. We are looking for a way in which we can intelligently deal with the sorrow that has already arisen in our lives and how to avoid it; how to stop that which has not yet fallen to our lot. That, the yogi says, is possible.

As long as you are pushing sorrow away you are touching it. Why do you want to touch something which is in any case moving away from you? It came from somewhere towards you, and left to itself it will move away from you. Leave it alone, but utilise that situation of unhappiness you may be in to look within to see how it is that 'I' was caught in this.

It does not mean that you should welcome sorrow, that you should accept or bear it (all these are irrelevant to our discussion). You should try to eliminate sorrow without effort. How do you do that? By keeping quiet and examining the whole dynamics of suffering, of pain. You directly observe pain—which is a completely and totally different thing from analysis. If you analyse pain it becomes multiplied. Without analysis, without intellectualising or conceptualising and creating an image of misery, if you directly observe this phenomenon of sorrow you see it is an experience. An experience presupposes a division into a subject and an object. You are the subject of the experience, the other is the object of the experience (whether the object is material or another person, sentient or insentient, or a psychological phenomenon).

It is the existence or the arising of division that causes experience—whether it is considered pleasant or unpleasant. You have separated yourself from the universe and have lost the reality. Now you can only come into relationship with the universe through mental activity or notions; and this *vṛtti*-activity or *vṛtti*-based life is sorrow.

The only way of stopping the sorrow before it gets to you is not to allow this division to take place in the first place. That is *samādhi,* meditation, *nirvāṇa,* liberation, *mokśa,* or whatever you want to call it.

II. 17 draṣṭṛ dṛśyayoḥ saṁyogo heya hetuḥ

How to avoid contact with the experience of pain? By understanding the structure of this experience. What is the structure of experience? The division or the polarisation of experiencing into the experiencer and the experience, and the subsequent conjunction or contact of the subject and the object of the experiencing—and this can be avoided. Experiencing being the sole reality, the subject and the object are of identical nature, and the thought is the dividing agent. Thought is of pain, pleasure, etc., and thought experiences pain and pleasure, etc. by the psychological action of division and contact. The possibility of the avoidance of pain is because of the unity of the see-er (experiencer) and the seen (experience); without a division.

There are several different ways of dealing with this:

1.) There is a state of what is, the 'being', but mixed up with that there is also a dissatisfaction with that being, and a desire or craving to become something else. The conflict between 'being' and 'becoming' is what is called unhappiness. It is extremely simple if it is clearly understood. It is this conflict between 'being' and becoming that makes us miserable. When the conflict is dropped, they become one—in other words 'being' alone remains. It is an illusory consecutiveness of the being that becomes a becoming.

For instance, I am fifty-four, but the same person two years ago said, "I am fifty-two". That 'I am' is constant. It is not involved in this succession of events, years and dates; and yet there is an illusory misunderstanding, in that, of involvement in this succession called 'time'. When that involvement is realised to be non-existent, there is absolute peace. I am neither fifty-two, fifty-four nor seventy-five. 'I am'. Period. An illusory division that was there has been abolished.

It is vitally important that we remember throughout our study of yoga that there has been no factual division. If there has been it will never come together. Once separated, it can never be put back again. It is the illusory intrusion of this ignorance and craving that produces an illusory division between the being, i.e. what you are, and what you want to be; between what you are and what you want to have. When that illusory division comes in, you are miserable and unhappy. The fundamental basis of yoga philosophy is that nothing has ever happened to you, to the 'being'; and that 'being' is beyond ignorance and therefore beyond the retinue of ignorance—unhappiness, exultation, pleasure, fear or craving.

The yogi realises that the true nature of his being is one continuous being which does not become anything other than being; which remains being.

Unhappiness is longing or craving for happiness. We regard a certain experience as unhappiness because we are looking for something else. That longing for what we consider to be happiness, *is* unhappiness. If the longing for something else is dropped, this *itself* becomes happiness! When unhappiness is seen at a distance (that is, it has not yet reached you) you see a miraculous and beautiful connection—the unhappiness is connected to the craving. If the craving is dropped the unhappiness also drops. The craving can be dropped only when you realise that the division that has apparently taken place within you is illusory and due to ignorance. When that knowledge arises the ignorance is gone, and with that the unhappiness also goes.

2.) It is only an internal psychological division (which is assumed to exist) which creates an experiencer apart from the experiencing itself. If you don't create that psychological division, there is consequently no psychological contact and therefore no experience of pain or sorrow, as such. But, in the process of the eyes seeing, the see-er (the ego-sense) arises and something jumps up and says, "I see". The moment the 'I' (the subject) has arisen in you, that subject is going to create an object. I'm looking at this whole hall, then suddenly, "I see him". It is this assumption of an ego that cuts through the pure sensation of seeing, and suggests, "I see him" The sight sees, but in that you have created an image, a thought form, and from there springs all mischief.

While this experiencing of vision goes on, can this contact be disconnected? Can this reaction come to an end? Can this relationship be seen to be non-existent and absurd? That will happen when you realise that when the eyes are open what happens is merely seeing—the eyes being endowed with the faculty of sight. That faculty of sight being universal, as long as there is light in this universe there will be sight. The action being sight, this sight itself is the see-er. There is no see-er apart from sight. It is not necessary for 'me' to see 'you'. When the 'me' arises, the 'you' also arises, whereas the truth is something in between.

It is easy to illustrate that with a handkerchief. There is a left end of the handkerchief and a right end. That is very clear. Now, there is only one piece of cloth that you call handkerchief and that is between these two ends. But the end is not something *other* than the handkerchief. The whole thing is one indivisible piece called handkerchief. Can we return to that state where what is called 'you' and what is called 'me' are but two supposed ends of a pure, egoless action, something that takes place everywhere?

Does 'I' arise first, then seeing, and then 'you' arise? Or are you there already, and seeing happens, and at the other end of it the 'I' springs up? What exactly is the truth concerning the simple experience of seeing? When this seeing takes place, does 'I', the see-er, the observer, the subject, arise first or does the object arise first? Is the identity of the object independent of the thought arising in the subject? Or is the identity of the object merely a projection of the object?

Both the subject and the object depend upon the predicate. There is only one thing, experiencing. There is only one thing called 'handkerchief" What was merely one has somehow been conceived of or perceived as a trinity. It is an absurd thing. What is it that makes you see this? *Avidyā*.

In the same way, someone calls you a fool. It is just a word, a sound which is heard, an experience. Somehow that experience is notionally (but not in fact) split as 'I am hurt' or 'it hurts me'—'I' being this end, 'it' being that end, and 'hurts' being the middle. If this division is not there it will be just a pure experiencing, a word which has entered through the ears and is heard. In that there is absolutely no pain. Once again, when this division or psychological split between what is called the experience and the experiencer is not imagined (because it *is* imaginary) to have taken place, there is no contact and therefore no pain.

3.) This can also be made possible in regard to physical pain. The condition may still continue to exist, but pain as pain can cease; and if physical pain is allowed to be just physical pain without being called or described so, it will take care of itself. It may even paralyse your limb, but it will take care of itself. It need not necessarily become psychological or personal.

4.) Perhaps most of us would realise that in this effort to avoid sorrow and suffering our whole outlook on life might change for the better. One of the best ways to ensure that all these moral and ethical principles are adopted in one's life, is to point out that in that way lies your happiness. You can be happy if you are friendly with all. If you love all you are happy all the time. A healthy moral life is the best guarantee for the avoidance of suffering and sorrow.

5.) Can you extract the thing called sorrow that is independent of the personality, of the circumstances? Can you pull it completely out and observe it as it is? It is here that tremendous concentration is needed. You focus your whole attention upon this phenomena of suffering and let the energy of the mind flow in that one single direction. (You can focus it on fear, hate or anything you like.) You are only aware of sorrow. It is in you. If you are aware of sorrow, are 'I' and the 'sorrow' two different entities? Or are they the same?

6.) Here we try another technique. We use a *mantra* in meditation, and mentally repeat it. When you mentally repeat a *mantra*, you can hear it. Who is saying it, and who is hearing it? Suddenly you realise that you are also there, you are watching both these. The sound is emanating from somewhere; someone is saying this *mantra*, someone is listening to this *mantra*, and someone is watching both these fellows. Similarly, you observe this phenomenon of sorrow, and you say, "I am aware of sorrow". Well, if you are aware of sorrow, try these:

(a) Stand in front of your electric stove. It is hot, you can feel it. But why should you be hot? If you can see that the water is boiling in the kettle, *you* don't have to boil. Similarly, if you can observe that sorrow, if you can become aware of that sorrow, you are free. This is one way.

(b) The other way is that as you are becoming more and more intensely aware of sorrow you suddenly become one with that sorrow. You are not suffering any more, you *are* sorrow. The fire doesn't feel hot, it *is* hot. So if you are sorrow, you don't feel sorrow anymore. You become one with that sorrow, and the duality has disappeared.

Thus does the yogi utilise the sorrow that has already arrived to find the root of suffering itself.

An interesting feature in the Yoga Sūtras is that there is no condemnation of other points of view, no criticism of anything. For instance, an interpretation of this Sūtra can be very wide and all-inclusive. It does not only mean that in meditation we avoid contact with pain (which means creating an 'experiencer-experience' division within ourselves). That may be one of the recommended methods, but that does not mean that we ignore other methods. Every type of precautionary method that we may take can be included in this. It is not infliction of suffering on oneself that is important in yoga. Suffering comes your way without being invited, deal with it as it comes, but when you see some suffering approaching you, avoid it by any means you can. Whatever be the method you adopt—fasting, diet, *yoga āsanas, prāṇāyāma,* prayer, healing, spiritual healing—they can all be included in this.

Whatever path you may take, wherever the observation or enquiry leads you, the next stage is definite. It is *ānanda*—bliss. This bliss is completely different from pleasure, it is even different from what we normally call happiness. When all our mental disturbances drop, when all the things that are torturing us have gone, what exists is *ānanda.* But here there is only one snag—in spite of this *ānanda,* there is also *asmitā,* or individuality. 'I' am aware of sorrow, 'I' have become one with sorrow, 'I' am fire itself, there is nothing burning me. When you get to this stage, there is bliss. But, *you* are experiencing this bliss, the 'I' or the individuality is still there. This eventually disappears. (See also I. 17.)

Here it is said that one cannot jump on one's own shoulders.

II. 18 prakāśa kriyā stithi śilaṁ bhūte 'ndriyātmakaṁ bhogā 'pavargārthaṁ dṛśyaṁ

What is the object and how does it come into being? The object of the experiencing is threefold in nature (1) the light of intelligence, (2) dynamic activity, and (3) material existence. While the external cosmos is the object of the senses, they themselves are regarded as the object of experiencing by the ignorant, both the external cosmos and the internal experiencer being indivisible from the experiencing. Yet, the 'object' helps the intelligence to realise its true nature by intelligent experiencing, and thus be freed from ignorance.

An object may be what is called an external object—you, it; any physiological experience (pain) or a psychological experience (suffering, anxiety). All these three are objects in one way or the other. A tree is the object of your sight and a pain in the eye is the object of you. An experience of misery is not outside of you, but still you experience it as an object.

The experience of pain is naturally associated with awareness, there is a movement of energy and it *is*. These are the three characteristics of that experience. There is no pain here. That does not mean that whatever is, is not! It is very important to remember that the yogi is not trying to suppress whatever is. That is an absurd thing to do. But, is there an experiencer distinct from that experience who can say that this experience belongs to me; or is the experience the whole truth?

These are all characterised by*prakāśa kriyā stithi śilaṁ*. *Prakāśa*—there is an awareness that characterises these three. When you say, "I see you," there is obviously an illumined object. When there is pain in the eye, there is obviously some kind of awareness connected with the sense organ. even in the case of psychological distress there is an awareness associated with it. *Kriyā*—there is obviously a movement of energy also associated with the awareness concerning that object. In other words, the thing is dynamic. Even when you observe what you consider to be an inert object, there is a movement of consciousness between you and that object, and it is doing something to you. *Stithi*—for the time being it seems to be an existential, undeniable fact that the object exists there and it is there for you to see, the pain is there for you to experience and the fear is there for you to feel.

Bhūte means the gross physical elements that constitute the physical universe—but it is not the physical elements alone which constitute the object.

The sensory part of all physical beings—which is also part of the physical being and yet somehow capable of distinguishing itself—is also needed. Taste seems to be an object, and the sense of taste in the tongue pretends to be a subject, though it is part of the whole physical organism. The whole lot is the object. (What is the object of this object being the object?!)

In this whole concept of object there is enjoyment—*bhogā* and also enlightenment: enjoyment if you are still sleeping under the blanket of ignorance, or enlightenment if your spirit is stirring and trying to see what is underneath all this. The ignorant man comfortably sleeping under the blanket of ignorance is satisfied with it, and treats this contact with the object as enjoyment; whereas the person in whom the spirit has begun to stir—who is not fully enlightened, but awakening—might use the same experience of the object to see his way through to self-knowledge.

II. 19 viśeṣā 'viśeṣa liṅgamātrā 'liṅgāni guṇaparvāṇi

Such objects may even be of different kinds or categories: (1) they can be special—supernatural experiences, (2) they can be commonplace and routine experiences, (3) they may have distinguishing marks or characteristics, or (4) they may be subtle, without any distinguishing marks: and their qualities may be in different stages of development. Simply, the entire cosmos including the external world and the internal sensory system, is the object.

Patanjali says that these experiences which constitute the object may be special experiences or common experiences. They may have distinguishing characteristics or they may not. They may be regarded as something special or non special. 'I see you' is *aviśeṣa*, a non-special experience, because all of us are able to see it. 'I see a blue light around you' is *viśeṣa,* an extraordinary or special experience. Patanjali has nothing but the most objective comments to make on these. He doesn't suggest that one is superior to the other. For instance, seeing of a certain form of god in a vision is a *liṅgamātra* experience, an experience characterised by characteristics and which is at the same time a special experience. It is possible that someone else has an experience of being dissolved totally in this cosmic consciousness, which has no characteristics at all. *This* is one kind of experience, *that* is another kind of experience, and as long as these are objects of a subject, there is division somewhere.

II. 20 draṣṭā dṛśimātraḥ śuddho 'pi pratyayā 'nupaśyaḥ

The truth concerning the see-er (experiencer) is that there is only the ever-pure act of seeing (experiencing). Yet, there arises a polarisation on account of which a concept (which then becomes the subject or the experiencer) seems to experience (the reaction of the senses to the externalised world—all such externalisation being the result of the polarisation and the consequent apparent movement in the subject). An apparently independent entity called experience therefore becomes the object.

Having thus explained the nature of the object, Patanjali goes on to what I feel is probably at the very heart of the Yoga Sūtras—the question, "Who is the *draṣṭā,* the see-er, in this?" The object was very clear and so we took that first. The second thing that seems to be extremely clear and evident is 'I see you'. The next question is, "Who is the 'I' that sees you?"

Draṣṭā dṛśimātraḥ—it is the seeing or experiencing *alone* that is. That experiencing itself, by wishing to become aware of its own experience, creates a polarity.

There are two beautiful expressions in the Yoga Vāsiṣṭha which occur again and again: *"What is cosmic consciousness, what is God and what is anything?"* and, *"Between this and that is consciousness, between that and this is the experiencing or experience."* In that pure experiencing there is neither polarisation nor division. The eyes see one vision, one universe, and that sight is pure, with no division in it.

If sight is realised to be the sole see-er of all sight, in that sight there is no evil, it is absolutely pure—*śuddho 'pi.* All experiences, as pure experiencing, are pure, unpolluted, untainted. The see-er is pure, the action is pure, the sensory action is absolutely pure. So the see-er is pure sight or the act of seeing without a subject-object division, and therefore without any motivation. Therefore in pure experiencing there is neither pain nor pleasure, sin nor virtue.

Draṣṭā dṛśimātraḥ—sight or seeing itself is the only truth.

All experience is pure experiencing in its intensity. Naturally, there is no division between the experiencer as the subject and the experience as the object. One can only think of one universal experience as an example—sleep. One who is in deep sleep does not say, "I am asleep," nor does he even know, think or feel, "I am sleeping". There is a total, homogeneous pure experience. The experiencer is inextricably and essentially non-different from this pure experiencing. (Sleep is brought in merely as an illustration of the existence of such pure experience, not to suggest that sleep is therefore a feature of enlightenment.) In sleep all your good and bad qualities, wonderful qualities and super-wonderful qualities are also lying asleep, and when they wake up there is a lot of trouble!

What you call the see-er is nothing but the action or event of seeing. Seeing happens. Seeing is there, awareness is there. In meditation, pure awareness alone is there. When the eyes are open and see something, only seeing is there. When you eat something, eating is there. When you are speaking, speaking is there. Speaking happens—not I speak to you. Hearing happens—not I hear you. It is even possible for pain to happen. At that moment there is only pain—pain as something without a word, without a concept and without a description. It is not called pain because you are not looking for pleasure.

In this way everything can happen without creating any problem in life. Such a life is a supreme blessing. All the virtues that are described in the Scriptures are naturally formed in that person. But the virtues do not have a goal, a motivation: he is not kind 'because he is going to heaven'.

Such a life is free from motivation and therefore free from despair, fear and hope. When you have no goal, you have no destination. All roads you take are right!

II. 21 tad artha eva dṛśyasyā 'tmā

The existence or the very meaning of the object is but the sum and substance of the subject's fragmentary experience, brought on by the ignorant polarisation. This fragmentary experience is the contact with pain.

This Sūtra suggests that the experience, the object of the experiencer, is also the same stuff.

All sensory experiences happen without any motivation. It is the division of this experience into the subject and the object, into the 'I' and the 'you'—the two ends of a handkerchief—that is obviously absurd; but it somehow happens. When the handkerchief is one, how does it happen that it has two ends? You see the handkerchief, you blink and you see the two ends. When one becomes aware of the two ends (the subject and object) instead of the handkerchief, there is no longer pure seeing, but 'I see you'. 'I-see-you' seems to be incomplete, and so the subject provides itself with a motivation. The ideas that you are attractive, beautiful, ugly, charming, I like you, I don't like you, all follow the initial (shall we call it) wrong perception. It is this division that is the cause of all experience and all contact, and pain is an experience born of contact.

"I think she is beautiful." What is the substance here? 'Think', isn't it? If the thinking was not there, even 'I' wouldn't be there. At the other end of thinking, she is. What do you mean by 'she is'? I *think* she is. So this thing called thinking somehow generates at one end the thing called 'I', and at the other end the thing called 'she is'.

There is no experience without a division; I touch you, the finger doesn't touch itself. Experience means division, experience means contact, contact means division—the three go together. One somehow imagines itself to be divided and, having brought about this imaginary division, comes into contact with itself (which it now regards as its own object) and by that contact experiences pain or pleasure—it doesn't matter which. Now you see that there is no real distinction between pain and pleasure, it is all one. There is only one handkerchief, so how do you see the two ends? Who is going to answer that question? (On the answer to that question depends the entire yoga of self-knowledge!)

So experiencing, as experiencing, creates no problem; thought, as thought, creates no problem; feeling, as feeling, creates no problem. The problem is the granting of an independent status to what is an integral part of the total experiencing, and that appears to create a division. The division itself is illusory and therefore non-existent.

Now, reality or God is not the cause of anyone's suffering. That which *is* causes no suffering or sorrow at all. The truth is pure experiencing. *"Truth cannot be the cause of sorrow; falsehood is,"* can be taken as an axiom. Since that so-called experience has been subjected to falsehood, sorrow is experienced. Thank God it is false and can go! When it is seen to be false the whole game is up.

II. 22 kṛtārthaṁ prati naṣṭaṁ apy anaṣṭaṁ tad anya sādhāraṇatvāt

To him who has attained fulfillment, when the (un)real nature of the polarisation of experiencing is truly understood, the contact with pain ceases: the only way to avoid pain is never to be separated from it (as the experiencer)! Yet, the potentiality of polarisation (separation) and the consequent contact with pain exist in other, ordinary circumstances. Hence, even an enlightened person may still experience pain when not in the total awareness of non-separation.

If we regard sorrow itself as unreal or false, and all pure experiencing as noble, holy, bliss, (even if it be the experience of an amputation of a limb and the crying of a throat) then it is possible that all the religious practices suddenly become meaningless. One who has reached this understanding or realisation is free. He has lost the false idea of sorrow—in his case sorrow has come to an end. It is also possible that when he awakens himself to this truth, he realises that this was the truth all the time. Even when he was weeping and wailing that he was miserable, even then this was the truth, and there is no sorrow in truth.

In his case, the whole game has come to an end. But the world has not suddenly disappeared, for there are other people still creating and projecting this world of pain, suffering and sorrow. They are suffering because of their own misunderstanding, wrong understanding and ignorance. For them sorrow, suffering and ignorance are real. The sage who has been enlightened enters into this apparent diversity and vaguely feels the problems of other people in order that he may be able to solve them.

II. 23 sva svāmi śaktyoḥ svarūpopalabdhi hetuḥ saṁyogaḥ

When the polarisation of the experiencing has taken place, the subject's desire for awareness of its own nature and its own voluntary and involuntary powers of action causes or acts as a link or contact between the subject and the object. (Here the 'subject' is the fragmented concept of self, and the 'object' is both the sense-experience and the external sense-object.)

An example may explain this easily. When you have lost a tooth, the gum starts bleeding. The blood comes from the gum, from the same organism as the tongue, and the same blood flows *in* the tongue. Somehow, now that a division has been made between the blood in the tongue and the blood that comes out of the gum, it tastes salty. That is precisely what happens to us. The blood that flows in the tongue still flows and is perhaps even experienced by the tongue, but since there is total at-one-ment, there is no experience of the taste of the blood, nor the realisation of the inherent faculty of taste in the tongue. But when the blood flows from the gum and falls on the tongue, there is a division, then a contact and an experience of the taste of blood, as also an awakening of the faculty of experience. From there on the mischief starts.

How does this division happen at all? It is still you. Can you quietly withdraw your consciousness from the mouth where all these things are taking place, and sit on the top of your head. You see a little deity presiding over the gums that says, "It's painful," and another deity presiding over the sense of taste that says, "I taste blood". It is one brain, one organism. That is precisely what happens in our relationships. We are all one organism. Because we don't realise this, when one person suffers, someone else feels happy. It is a terrible thing, but true.

If you are in a state of supreme delight, where momentarily you have become completely merged in an experience of pleasure, you then have tremendous energy. Somehow this energy seems to manifest itself only in an extreme situation, when you feel it with your heart and soul. I will give an example from my own experience. Once a lady was driving me to a meeting in her Volkswagen, when one of the wheels sank into the ditch. She cried, "Oh we will be late for the meeting." We got out of the car and lifted the wheel out of that ditch! Normally we would never have attempted to lift such a weight, let alone have done it. From where did that tremendous energy come? From what we might ll

Cosmic Order. But whatever it is, it lasts only for a moment.

Spontaneous action is where the action takes place on its own, not mechanically, not by habit, but when the actor doesn't arise in the action, when the knower doesn't arise in the knowledge, when the experiencer doesn't arise in pure experiencing. When it happens spontaneously it is pure, the 'I' is not involved in it at all. We lifted the whole car, but afterwards if we tried to do it again, our backs would be nearly broken! One can understand more in terms of pleasure than anything else. When we think, "Oh, that was beautiful. I want to repeat it again in order that I may have that pleasure again," it is gone. The self which endeavours to experience its own powers creates the division, and then wanting to contact it, finds it impossible.

It is the pure *śakti* that is doing it. When one surrenders completely to the *śakti*—i.e. when 'I' is not there at all—then what has to happen will happen. When you say, "That was marvellous! I felt the *śakti* rising up. Let me experience it again," then nothing happens. So when the polarisation is forced, instead of being that whole, you are trying to experience your own power, your own intelligence (or even your own ignorance). Then it is gone!

This same thing happens to you when you sit for meditation. You sit down and repeat your *mantra.* You are listening to the mental repetition, and if the sound of the *mantra* is loud enough within you it can drown all other sounds. The wind is howling, it is distracting you, but the teacher says, "Just listen to your *mantra* totally with all your heart and soul, and that howling will not disturb you." You don't hear the wind, but there is a sneaking suspicion, "Has that wind stopped, or am I really in deep concentration?" How do you find out your own powers of concentration? By trying to experience the inaudibility of that sound. Here 'inaudibility' means the audibility of that sound. You are trying to hear, to make sure you are not hearing. That is where you get caught.

Intelligence is there in you, it is that intelligence that manifests itself as all this experience. The 'I', the experiencer, is not necessary for this at all. Where the experienc*er* has not arisen as an independent entity, and where the experience has been dissolved into pure experience, there is bliss and there is no division at all.

When you want to experience it you don't want to surrender yourself to this pure experiencing. It is when you want to sit there and lick it, that the trouble starts.

II. 24 tasya hetur avidyā

Obviously, all this is due to the ignorance of the spiritual truth or oneness. Ignorance alone is the cause of the polarisation, the fictitious separation which is the sole cause for the desire to become aware of 'another' and for the contact of the 'other'

All problems arise from *avidyā*, ignorance. For instance, it is *avidyā* that asks, "How is it that in this single handkerchief I see two ends?" I don't know if there is any verbalised answer to this question; one only sees that non-comprehension of the wholeness creates the two ends, or if you like to put it the other way around, suggestion of the two ends is called non-comprehension of the whole. [Only *Kṛṣna* was bold enough to suggest, in a fantastic statement, that both knowledge and its veiling come from God. (It is very tough, so be careful.) If you want to be knowledge, be knowledge, if you want to get under the blanket, go ahead.] We are only aware that this division and the consequent experience of pain, pleasure (and all the rest of it), have a common ground, and that is non-comprehension, illusion, imagination. In a word, ignorance.

One who is even vaguely aware of the activities of ignorance suddenly discovers that it is not possible, whatever you do, to get rid of it. You cannot live with it, you cannot get rid of it, and as long as it is, it is felt to be present. Whatever is done is done by, and in, its shadow. If you do something good, it is the shadow that does it, or is benefited by it. As long as you keep this body going, the shadow also keeps going. How do you deal with this?

II. 25 tad abhāvāt saṁyogā 'bhāvo hānaṁ tad dṛśeḥ kaivalyaṁ

When that ignorance is dispelled, the polarisation (separation, division or fragmentation) and the consequent conjunction or contact of the experiencer and the experience is rendered meaningless. It is given up. This is liberation for the see-er who is pure experiencing or the undivided homogeneous consciousness which alone existed. Liberation is not isolation nor independence from another, but union in the sense of non-division.

How do you overcome this sequence of psychological distress, or trouble, which has its origin in ignorance, in non-comprehension? When you realise that all these arise from self-ignorance, there could be only one solution—self-knowledge. Nothing else is of any use whatsoever.

Patanjali puts it very cleverly—*tad abhāvāt.* When the shadow is not there, and therefore the illusory division or polarisation does not take place, then there is no contact with pain at all. There is no contact with any object of experience. You immediately see that all your prejudices and so on will vanish, and there is love, harmony, unity and peace. You have stopped sorrow at its very source, before it gets you—the root of sorrow is destroyed.

Because the universe is throbbing with its own energy and that goes on as it wants to go on, pure experiencing and pure expression go on in this world and they do not create any problems or trouble to anybody. It is the conceptualisation of an experience as pain or pleasure, of behaviour as good or not good, that creates problems. When this polarisation comes to an end the contact comes to an end; and when the contact comes to an end there is pure experiencing. Experiencing *alone* exists. Then the experience remains alone—alone in the sense of all one. This pure experiencing is seen as both object and subject, but without the division of object and subject. Then there is freedom. The experiencer is liberated, freed, emancipated from this polarising influence. It is *that* freedom that is indicated in the Raja Yoga philosophy. It is not freedom from another or from pain etc., but total freedom—freedom from the craving for experience, and therefore liberation of the experiencing as such.

This could easily be the finale of the Yoga Sūtras, because the second and third Sūtras in the first chapter define yoga as, "*Yoga is the control of the modifications of the mind,*" and, "*Then the see-er rests by itself as itself*". The see-er, the experiencer, remains in his own true form. In the second chapter the true form is revealed as the pure experiencing itself. When *avidyā*, or the shadow of ignorance comes to an end, then this pure experiencing is freed from conceptualisation, from polarisation. If you can really and truly say right from your innermost being that this sense of ignorance, or 'I don't know' has dropped, and that there is no confusion in your mind, then you are enlightened.

II. 26 viveka khyātir aviplavā hano 'pāyaḥ

Briefly, the constant unbroken awareness of this truth alone is the means to the ending of this ignorance and its retinue.

Viveka means wisdom, awareness, alertness or vigilance. *Aviplavā* means unbroken. The constant unbroken awareness of this truth is *viveka*. *Viveka* is the only way in which the obstacles can be removed. Therefore one should try to get this wisdom, this awareness, and let it be unbroken. When you become dull your vigilance is lost and at that very moment you lose what you have gained. If it is broken or abandoned—whatever be the reason—then immediately you are overcome by self-ignorance or darkness; and the shadow (the ego) comes in again. This interruption *itself* is the shadow, the ego.

Swami Sivananda's vigilance was the constant kindling of the inner light. As long as the light is there, no darkness is possible. However feeble the light, it is capable of keeping darkness away. You cannot eradicate darkness, you must illumine it; you cannot eradicate this notion of 'I' but you can throw a flood of light on it and see what it is. The inner light must burn constantly, uninterruptedly. This is the only way of overcoming ignorance.

So along with the infinite there is also ignorance. The infinite has infinite potentialities hidden in it all the time. There is an enlightening experience which is beyond the dualistic experience; but in that pure experiencing the desire to experience it, to hold it, also arises. The desire arises because it is also inherent in every atom of existence. That which is aware of this is wisdom (*viveka*). When that wisdom is constant and unbroken, the division does not arise; when that division does not arise there is no contact; and when there is no contact there is no dualistic experience, There is pure experiencing which is bliss, there is pure action which is love. There is unity.

If there is no division, there is no pain and no pleasure. Even when there is no division, and therefore no pleasure or pain, there is still awareness. Awareness, experiencing and action are inherent in every atom of existence, in every cell of your body. Pure action is called love; pure experiencing in which there is no division at all, is bliss (whether the bliss comes from cancer or from enthronement) because it is beyond both pleasure and pain.

All the mischief arises from non-comprehension of this oneness. Once again we are back to the riddle. What is non-comprehension? How does it arise if every atom of existence and every cell of one's being is saturated with awareness? I don't think anyone has the answer. One has to look within and see what is aware of this non-comprehension.

When this purity of awareness or wisdom is unbroken, your life is free from sorrow; you live as if in deep sleep—which means that everything that happens to you happens in totality, without an experiencer arising. When talking happens, there is no talker, only talking. When you are working, working happens, you and working have become one, so that there is no you there.

Only when *viveka* is uninterrupted can it be said that the obstacles have been removed. We often behave like a shaving razor. We shave something and imagine the whole problem is solved. It's not solved! Early next morning you wake up and see it is back again. This is the constant problem in our life and our yoga practice. We think the problem is gone but it is not. Our usual old friend and enemy, 'I thought'—'I thought it had gone', 'I thought I was enlightened'—can come and interfere in our lives in a million ways (and the next phrase is important) 'without our being aware of it'. Because our being unaware of it is called ignorance, here the common excuse, "I didn't know" is no excuse.

11. 27 tasya saptadhā prānta bhūmiḥ prajñā

This awareness is keen, intense and operative even in the field of the first seven of the eight states or limbs of yoga practice whose description follows: this practice should therefore not be a mechanical, unintelligent, dull routine.

These seven are not merely a set of yoga practices which you resort to for one hour a day, but something which covers your entire life. The eighth limb is *samādhi* (which is not considered a step or a limb, but enlightenment itself.)

I am often suspicious of defining these seven following traditional concept moulds, because once the mind creates a conceptual mould the awareness is gone.

We have conceptualised and crystallised these seven limbs (or outflows of this yoga philosophy), so that when the words are uttered the mind already thinks it knows.

Patanjali takes immense care to warn us that awareness must be the hallmark of all the seven limbs of yoga, otherwise you are only doing gymnastics. All these practices are wonderful, but they are not yoga unless they are saturated with the serious spirit of enquiry. It is clear that mechanical practise of any type of yoga has no spiritual value. Yoga is what your own inner consciousness considers it to be. If you think it is physical the benefit you derive from it will also be physical. The Scripture is merely a signpost, it is not the business of the signpost to tell you which way you should go.

Yoga is not something which can be practised as a part of life, the other part being left to fend for itself. It has to cover, penetrate and illumine the entire life. The light is there and it must radiate in all these seven directions, so that nothing is left in the dark, no aspect of our being, of our life, is left untouched by that light—neither thought, word or deed; thinking, feeling or will. In that light, which is this unbroken awareness, there is no darkness.

When vigilance or constant alertness infiltrates all these seven, then enlightenment results. The same light becomes enlightenment. It's like walking through a dark tunnel—what appears to be a distant glimmer, with the help of which you walk through the tunnel, becomes a light when you are there. It is not as though that speck of light leads you to something called a greater light. You see the speck of light, it guides you on, you walk guided by that light and you suddenly realise that that *is* the light (of course in a much grander form).

When this little candle (called constant alertness, awareness, or vigilance) infiltrates (that's the right word for it, whether you like it or not) all aspects of your life and personality, that itself becomes enlightenment. Then these aspects of our being get instantly integrated, moulded into one. Their oneness is revealed. That is holiness.

II. 28 yogā 'ṅgān anuṣṭhānād aśuddhi kṣaye jñāna dīptirā viveka khyāteḥ

This awareness shines resplendent with the light of intelligence, when the inner psychic impurities that becloud the vision of truth have been eliminated by the intelligent practice of the 'limbs' of yoga.

Virtue itself comes into being or is revealed within oneself when the spirit of yoga manifests: all the rest is *trying* to be virtuous. So, trying to develop virtues, trying to be good and do good is not only hypocrisy but bluff, because if that intelligence in you really and seriously sees something as not so desirable, or foolish, it drops it.

One should sustain this inner light of wisdom undimmed. When that shines on all aspects of our life, it is then that all these aspects of yoga become spontaneously manifest, without effort. The beauty in yoga is that there is no effort. Effort implies inner struggling, the inner struggling implies disharmony within.

Practise all this. Don't think that thus you create the light, the truth. Truth is always there. The very definition of truth or reality is that which is eternal.

Nobody need create this reality. If reality were in need of such creation, it would not be reality in the first place! So yoga is not an attempt to create self-knowledge. It merely cleans your own mind and heart.

II. 29 yama niyamā 'sana prāṇāyāma pratyāhāra dhāraṇā dhyāna samādhayo 'ṣṭāv aṅgāni

Discipline, observances, posture, exercise of the life-force, introversion of attention, concentration, meditation and illumination (at-one-ment) are the eight limbs of yoga or the direct realisation of oneness. Hence, these limbs should all be practised together, intelligently, so that the impurities of all the physical, vital and psychological limbs may be eliminated.

What has come to be known as the official Raja Yoga is mentioned at this point. After having described nearly the whole of the yoga philosophy, Patanjali gives some practical hints. The sequence is very clear, very beautiful and very important. We all know how to do things, but what we do not seem to recognise is the fact that every action has a philosophy and a motivation, whether you like it or not. When that is forgotten, there is confusion.

Aṣṭaṅga means eight limbs (*aṅga* is limb). It is not unusual even for great masters and teachers of yoga to use another terminology—the eight steps. However, when you look upon these as the eight steps it can give rise to a slight misunderstanding which is later condensed into a doctrine.

When you climb a flight of steps you climb them one by one, so the teaching (from that point of view) is that here also there are these eight steps up which you go one by one.

Instead of regarding these eight as steps, Patanjali characterises them as *aṅgas*—limbs of one entity. The whole yoga is one, these eight are just limbs. This entity called yoga with these eight limbs must be given birth to together every day, so that you have no business to say, "I am now practising purity, and after I have practised purity I will come on to contentment, then the yoga postures, etc." By then you are dead!

However, if you look upon this method as composed of eight limbs you see that one limb alone is inadequate, imperfect, and eight imperfections put together cannot lead to one perfection. A baby is not an assembly of eight limbs—it's a person, a total being. It is possible that some limbs might grow faster than others, but all these must be there at the beginning. Approached from that angle it suggests that on the very first day you practise anything concerning yoga, you ensure that these eight limbs are all intact together and that they are characterised by the light of wisdom, which is indivisible, and this must touch every one of them. If you bear that in mind, then the whole thing becomes beautiful and nothing is mechanical.

Dhāraṇā, dhyāna and *samādhi* together are called *saṃyama.* These three are not independent actions but one continuous movement. *Saṃyama* is this continuous movement. The prefix '*saṃ*' often implies perfection or properly done. So *saṃyama* is when *yama* becomes well grounded, full, total. (See III. 4)

Yama is the first limb of yoga. It has been variously described as restraint, self-control, regulation, holiness and discipline. As discipline it means studying your nature, the springboards of our action. Some explanations tell us that if you do not become firmly established in *yama* you cannot take up the practice of yoga. But then if you accept the above view of *saṃyama,* when you are perfectly established in *yama* you are enlightened. On the other hand, *yama* is only possible if all the other limbs of yoga are also practised together.

Niyama means not restraint, but discipline. Let us call it virtue. *Yama* and *niyama* are not so much things to be done, as truths to be understood. They are simple if one truly endeavours to understand that they are in themselves the faithful manifestations of a vigorous search for reality. They are neither disciplines imposed upon us by others, self-imposed disciplines nor measures of self-control in the sense 'I suppress my inclination and even natural urges'. Non-violence, truthfulness, purity, etc., demand that the self (whose activities are known as violence or the spirit of domination) should be vigilantly watched.

Discipline is not something you have to do with great effort, but it is an understanding of the truth. When the truth is understood, the truth *itself* acts. Kṛṣna revealed a great truth in the **Bhagavad Gītā**: *"You are your own friend and your own enemy. If you lead a life of self-control you are your own friend. If you lack self-control, you are your own enemy."* There is no compulsion here, but an indication of a truth.

So self-discipline in yoga has to be discovered by the student himself, not by struggling to cultivate the virtues listed under *yama-niyama.* The very fact that there is need to cultivate them indicates that they are not there already, and that perhaps their opposite qualities exist! Any effort at such cultivation depletes one's energy. Hence the master suggests that while you practise the *āsana,* observe the behaviour of the body. Regardless of what yoga posture you are doing, the whole body participates; the inner intelligence restores balance and comfort. Similarly, in meditation you will discover the intelligence beyond the limitations of the body and mind (thoughts and emotions) and the limitations of the individuality. That which is beyond these is pure intelligence or consciousness, which is indivisible. The intelligence that functions in the body is undivided; even so, the intelligence in the universe is undivided.

When this truth is realised directly, *yama-niyama* and all the rest of self-discipline follow effortlessly. It is like this: when you want the baby's face to smile, you tickle the foot, not pull its cheeks apart. When you realise your oneness with all life, virtue or self-discipline is natural.

When you realise that self-ignorance can only be dispelled or enlightened by self-knowledge (the enlightenment of self-ignorance itself being self-knowledge), what are you trying to do when you do yoga *āsanas* or when you hold your nose in *prāṇāyāma*? In the fourth chapter of the Yoga Sūtras there is a very beautiful answer: *"All your efforts to cultivate virtues and to discipline yourselves by doing āsana, prāṇāyāma etc., are like the actions of a good farmer or gardener."* A gardener removes the obstacles. The inner light shines unabated and undimmed all the time, but there seems to be an obstruction to its functioning. (When the yogi cultivates virtues, eradicates vices and disciplines himself by practising *āsana* and *prāṇāyāma* etc., he merely removes the obstacles.)

There has been perennial argument among teachers and students of yoga concerning the qualification of yoga-practitioners. Which comes first, *yama-niyama* (ethical discipline) or *dhyāna* (meditation)? Is it possible to practise or even to learn meditation if one is not fully established in *yama-niyama*? On the other hand, is it possible to get one's foothold in *yama-niyama* if one does not learn to meditate, to look within, to observe oneself and to recognise the tricks of the wayward mind? So, which comes first? Gurudev Swami Sivananda said, "Both."

II. 30 ahiṁsā satyā 'steya brahmacaryā 'parigrahā yamāḥ

When the light of intelligence or the awareness of the truth illumines the mind-stuff, psychological order comes to prevail which is manifest as the following articles of natural self-restraint or discipline: non-violence; perception of what is or truth; non-hoarding; an effortless movement of the total being in cosmic homogeneous essence; and non-covetousness. (The fourth article also specifically refers to continence or chastity.)

Yama is the first of the limbs of *aṣṭaṅga yoga*. It is a group of five virtues:

ahiṁsā, satya, asteya, brahmacarya, aparigraha

[non-violence, truthfulness, non-stealing (not taking anything that belongs to another person), continence and non-greed (not coveting someone else's possessions).]

Yama also means restraint or death (*Yama* is the god of death.) If you are really and truly aiming at a life of enlightened living, you must be prepared to abandon non-enlightened, ignorant living. When death comes naturally, there is nothing dramatic. It is so simple: one just stops breathing! Death takes life from this body quietly, without any trouble. *Yama*, in its meaning of self-control or virtue, must also be effortless. There must be an inner ripening. When the whole being is ripe, then virtue happens.

What have these wonderful, positive, noble qualities to do with the god of death? With their practice you are bringing death into your everyday life, every moment. The inner intelligence or light naturally becomes aware of the least obstruction that arises (or seems to arise) in it, and is able to deal with it. Then it is gone before it can gather strength and momentum. That is *yama*. That itself is self discipline, self-restraint.

Yama is self-restraint in a very subtle and beautiful way, not in the manner of suppression or self-denial. Turning attention upon itself is the key. If, for instance, there is a craving for wine, the attention flows towards a glass of wine on the table, and there is tension. Instead of either deciding to drink a glass of wine or not, is it possible merely to watch and see what is happening in you, what this thing called craving is? Then the attention immediately begins to flow towards itself. There is what Patanjali calls *nirodha*. Thirst, which is natural to a living organism, will not go away, but the craving will disappear, the tension is gone. Then picking up a glass of wine or a glass of water just happens, without effort.

When you want to know what craving is all about, how it arises, how it functions and what it is made of, the attention flows upon itself and at that very moment the craving loses its life force. Here you develop will-power, but of a different kind. You neither give in to a craving nor suppress it, but observe it. If you give in to a craving you are finished; if you suppress that craving, the craving is apparently finished for the time being. In both instances you have not understood what the craving is, so that the next time it is going to come back in a different form and take you unawares.

The only way in which you can guarantee that you will not be taken unawares, is to become aware of the origin, existence and function of this thing called craving. When that is done the craving has gone and what is natural happens without your will. Such a person's life is absolutely natural and therefore devoid of tension and confusion. There, another intelligence functions. You may call that intelligence God, divine power or whatever you wish. That is self-restraint of a different quality, and that is the kind of self-restraint that is meant when Patanjali describes *yama* in the Yoga Sūtras.

Restraint of this quality cannot possibly be defined or codified into sets of 'thou shalt' and 'thou shalt not'. These have never really worked. Instead, if we can be aware all the time, this philosophy can be alive in each one of us. That awareness brings about an action which is indefinable, which has to be discovered from moment to moment without being categorised and petrified.

When all hopes, aspirations, fears, anxieties and motivations drop dead, what survives is this tremendous intelligence (you may call it what you like—soul, *jīva, ātma* or God within) which is imperishable, which shines in its own light, untarnished, uninterrupted and undistracted. When it is constantly illumining the hidden springs of our own actions what happens is virtue, *yama*. The shadow called evil does not arise. So virtue is when this intelligence shines uninterruptedly, making it impossible for motivations to arise at all. If on account of past habit, certain motivations, hopes, fears or anxieties come up, this *yama* beheads them. What happens in the light of that intelligence is virtue.

If you entertain a hope that this virtue is going to lead you to heaven or give you a better next life, then you are not dying and it is not virtue. Virtue which has a motivation, either relating to this world or to a future life, is not virtue at all. When death is brought into our daily life the first thing that is completely knocked out of our life is hope. Hope creates a thing called tomorrow, the future, even though it may not exist.

There is a parallel here with Sūtra III. 4 which describes *dhāraṇā, dhyāna* and *samādhi* (concentration, meditation and the superconscious state) as *saṃyama. Saṃyama* is perfection, while *yama* is the preparatory state—one is preparation, the other is perfection. If the substance is the same it means that *yama* also involves inner awareness and vigilance, insight. If the insight is not there, you merely surround yourself with these do's and don'ts, and the self continues to flourish, to get stronger and stronger. What is needed is insight which becomes aware (vaguely in the beginning and later perfectly) that what is called the self—'I', 'me'— is perhaps non-existent.

So in the *saṃyama* state there is direct awareness that the self doesn't exist. In the *yama* state the same reality is not seen so clearly, and therefore how far *ahiṁsā,* for instance, is practised in your life, depends upon how clear the truth of the non-existence of the self is. If the insight is developed, the insight *itself* determines what your life should be.

Ahiṁsā

Ahiṁsā is not something which can be demonstrated or positively defined; that is why it it is negatively worded *ahiṁsā'*. *Ahiṁsā* means the total absence of *hiṁsā*. *Hiṁsā* means not only physical violence or harassment, but harmfulness. Even the intention to do harm to others is *hiṁsā*. To hate, to be jealous, to be rude or crude (either in words or looks) is *hiṁsā*.

Ahiṁsā is usually translated as non-violence and non-aggression in thought, word and deed. You shouldn't harm or insult anybody. This seems to be quite simple and easily understood, but if you watch your mind then, about ninety-five percent of it is busy cooking up how to *seem* to practise *ahiṁsā* without really doing it! That is what we do most of the time when we interest ourselves in the wonderful virtues described here. They are not virtues that can be acquired, so if you want to be non-aggressive, for example, you cannot introduce non-aggression as an element of your character. You do something else and that blossoms as non-aggression—it may be *japa*, meditation or something totally unconnected with what your life-style may be.

Ahiṁsā is not capable of being reduced to do's and don't's—these have no value at all. For instance, whenever this topic of *ahiṁsā* is raised (usually during question time) someone asks, "Swami, you spoke about *ahiṁsā*, that you shouldn't injure anyone in thought, word or deed. What about those mosquitoes which come during my meditation—shall I kill them or not?" The reply is, "You have still not stopped eating meat and yet you are terribly concerned about this little mosquito!" The ideal, of course, is to ensure that we do not even by heedlessness (much less wantonly) destroy even the least of God's creatures—but the wise course is to start closer at home, instead of running away to the extreme.

How often do we see people who love animals and are full of sympathy towards vermin, but hate their fellowmen and treat them with less sympathy. How often do we find people who starve their kinsmen in order to do spectacular (publicity seeking) charity to an orphanage. It is with reference to them that the Tao-Te-King says: *"Do away with benevolence and eject righteousness, and the people will return to filial duty and parental love."*

Exalting love or charity very often leads to hypocrisy; failing to promote love and charity leads to selfishness and hardheartedness.

There are some situations where to be soft, sweet and gentle may be *hiṁsā*. For instance, if your son is doing something which you disapprove of, how do you react? If you do not restrain a child who is behaving badly, you are promoting evil. Apart from anything else you are supressing your own emotions. So with supreme love you may have to be egotistic and chastise the child.

What *ahiṁsā* involves is constant, unbroken awareness in which there is alert attention which avoids *hiṁsā*.

Non-violence, as far as the social structure is concerned, is restricted purely to not hurting other people; not fighting, not killing. But non-violence in the spiritual sense is a subtle inner adventure leading to self-knowledge. Is it possible to lead one's life never hurting another, yet also never being hurt oneself? The definition: *"You must not hurt anyone in thought, word or deed,"* does not say that you must not hurt anyone else or other people, it says you must not hurt *anyone* in thought, word or deed.

What about yourself? It is possible for us to suppress our anger when we are insulted or injured and congratulate ourselves that we have thereby 'practised' *ahiṁsā,* but we are doing violence to ourselves then! We can either think we have learnt to love our 'enemy'—which is surely hypocritical, or to feel 'God will punish him for this,'—which is another form of violence! If my life itself disturbs you, should I jump into the lake? If for your sake I jump into the lake, in order to promote the happiness of one body I am punishing another body!

Is there any virtue in that? It is possible that even in that case there is violence or aversion in me, in the mind, in the heart, in the self. That aversion, instead of flowing towards *that* body, flows towards *this* body—which is mine—and instead of weakening or destroying the self, it makes the self very strong. By suppressing anger I have hurt myself. Is that the definition of *ahiṁsā*? (I am not suggesting that you must retaliate, that is worse.) Instead of punishing him I am punishing this thing called 'me' and in that cosmic intelligence which is everywhere (and therefore in both him and in me), there has been a disturbance. Cosmic intelligence becomes aware that there has been a disturbance, so that is not *ahiṁsā.*

If someone calls you a fool, you may feel hurt; and once you are hurt, you will bear that hurt for all time to come. However much you may mask it, in ten or fifteen years it may still come up as gossip or some other type of subtle character assassination. You have not forgotten. And that is violence. So that heart which is hurt is violent.

Is it possible to live in such a way that you feel no hurt and never hurt at all? If you do not feel hurt at all, then you don't even know how to hurt others. That perhaps is what is meant by *ahiṁsā*. Here non-violence takes a very delicate and beautiful form. If it is realised that the 'I' or the ego-sense is a mere shadow cast on this intelligence, that 'I' cannot be hurt—it is impossible to hurt a shadow. You will not be hurt at all when you realise that what is hurt is only the ego, your own self-image, a shadow which is the product of your own ignorance. *You* are the fool that is hurt. Yet if you are a real seeker, endeavouring to dispel this shadow of the ego, you should mentally thank that person who pointed out the fool. Your goal is to discover the ego, and he has made that ego react! Now you can see that reacting ego and deal with it. If you feel hurt and call yourself a spiritual seeker, you are insincere, you are not honest with yourself.

Is there a way out of all this? How do you know you are non-violent or non-aggressive in your thoughts? Please remember that this discipline is not the discipline of a recluse, an ascetic or a single man only, but is meant to apply to everyone in all circumstances. If this discipline applies to all everywhere, at all times, what is it that is hurt? If the inner light has been shining brightly all the time, it doesn't get hurt at all, because the moment a thought 'I am hurt' arises, it chops off its head. That is the state of perfection. (But what about you and me? If you are hurt mentally or psychologically the light is not unveiled completely, it is still able to direct the attention to that hurt which is within you.)

So, non-violence is essentially the virtue of not being hurt. And the virtue of not being hurt is the virtue of having no self-image. When the self-image is completely rooted out of the heart, then you are love, you are non-violence. Whatever actions proceed from that heart, mind and body, will be good.

It is difficult for these *yama* to be cosmetically cultivated. For instance, if you want to you can make a show of non-violence, you can repress the aggression you feel, bite your tongue, use nice words etc.—and so do violence to yourself! The yogi's approach is different. When provoked by insult or injury he studies (that is what 'discipline' means) the internal annoyance and that which reacts to the provocation. The inner light begins to question, "What is this anger?" He is so busy studying the psychological phenomenon of anger that he has no time to be angry. (Similarly with lust, greed, fear, jealousy, etc.) The yogi works on himself and an inner revolution takes place as a result. Until one realises that the self is non-existent and that there is only one life (which are two sides of the same coin), *ahiṁsā* is not possible. Both must happen simultaneously.

True *ahiṁsā* or non-injury in thought, word and deed and in truth, is possible only simultaneously with this enlightenment. In order for the desire to harm to completely disappear from your heart, you must learn how to observe the arising of the emotions and to remove them from there. If you are able to do that, then you are meditating. When you are spiritually ripe and filled with love, then virtue happens without any inner struggle. This is both meditation (*dhyāna*) and discipline (*yama-niyama*), which Swami Sivananda emphasised. It is natural and effortless, profound and permanent.

So *ahiṁsā* becomes possible when there is meditation; and, it promotes meditation. It purifies the heart and the mind and it enables *yama* to become *saṃyama*.

Satya

Satya is truth. What you say must be truthful, pleasant and beneficial. Truth is not merely saying what you want to say. For instance, if someone says, "What do you think of me?" and you reply, "I think you are ugly, you are an idiot," you may think you are being very truthful, but you are insulting and rude. That is not truth.

Satya may mean being truthful in one's speech. That is a tall order, since there are times when we may have to tell lies. You must have the ability and the daring to tell a lie, and yet be honest and truthful! Because you don't see the sanity of being dishonest, dishonesty must have dropped without your knowledge. That is virtue. You have seen the truth, however momentary a glimpse, and this glimpse has eliminated the vices from your personality. That is what is meant. But generally, instead of the virtue being a fortress to help you on this march, it becomes a prison house. You are imprisoned in it, you cannot but 'be' something. Therefore the 'I' is again important. Do you see the danger here? It is not that yoga gives us a license to be vicious—but when virtue becomes important it means that the ego is still important: "I must be regarded as a holy man." What for? Hence, as you can see, even virtue depends upon a glimpse of the truth. It is not a first step but it is part of the whole. It is one limb of the whole structure of yoga.

Scriptures describe how on certain occasions untruth becomes truth, and truth becomes untruth. If we get hung up on speaking the truth as a discipline itself in a restricted śense, then we not only lose sight of the totality of truth, but we fail even in that restricted 'speaking-truth', because the vision is narrowed and there is no insight.

How can you recognise the truth? Is what you recognise the truth, or is it also picked by your own opinion? You have a number of standards already stored within you, and you go looking for confirmation of those standards. You are good or bad. Who is the judge? Your standard. Who put the standard there? Yourself, or your grandfather. That again is a tradition, an opinion which is totally unrelated to truth. Therefore the concept of truth may have to undergo drastic revolutionary change within us, before we can even attempt to decide what truth is.

For instance, if someone tells you that So-and-so is a holy man, and that you should go and have his *darśan*, the truth is that in *his* opinion that person is holy and you should have his *darśan*. You do not come to any conclusion about it. To come to a conclusion is a dangerous thing—the mind is closed and the quest for truth is lost.

Is it possible for you not to jump to any conclusion about anything? This means to be able to distinguish between what is an opinion and what is the truth. If that is lived (not applied or merely practised as an exercise in our daily life) it leads you to the next stage: "If this is just an opinion, where is it formed and what is the truth concerning it?" An opinion springs from your own prejudice. If you are constantly looking for truth and if you are able at the same time to know, "This is only an opinion, it is not truth," that *itself* is the truth. It is then that you are able to graduate from mere verbal discipline to higher spiritual disciplines. The very fact that you realise, "This is *my* opinion", stops you from expressing it where it need not be expressed, where it will hurt. When what you are about to say is not factual, pleasant and beneficial, say something else.

Satya demands a constant search for the truth, recognising the distinction between fact and fiction, truth and opinion—not only in your speech, but in your thoughts, your actions and your whole life. Then the mind becomes more and more transparent.

One who pursues this quest comes face to face with some shocking truths concerning the mind. There is a realisation that all that the mind conceives of and expresses is untrue, false opinion. Peeling layer after layer of the mind and its prejudices, you will realise how opinion is formed because of *saṃskāra.*

So *satya* is not merely to speak the truth, but to be devoted to the real, not to be led away by the *vṛttis.* The reality is pure intelligence. To draw closer to that intelligence is *satya,* and to be led away into the by-lanes of *vṛttis* is to pursue the unreal. *That* is the truth. One who lives this truth is a true seeker.

It is the truth in you that enables you to recognise truth. And the rediscovery of the truth in you is meditation. Without meditation you cannot know what truth is, without meditation you cannot know what non-violence means. So *ahimsā* and *satya* are closely related, universal disciplines.

Asteya

The third of the *yama* is *asteya*—a synthesis of contentment, simplicity and charity. The literal translation of *asteya* is non-stealing. There seems to be an anti-climax. We were discussing *ahiṁsā*—not to hurt and not to be hurt, and *satya*—living in truth, speaking the truth and expressing truth in thought, word and deed. These are all highly developed, needing much intelligence, love, integrity, courage and grit; and then comes—almost an anti-climax—don't steal!

Kṛṣṇa says in the **Bhagavad Gītā** that if one does not share with others in need the things that one tends to accumulate—food, buildings, clothes, etc. —he is a thief. Can you put on more clothes than you can wear? The body itself teaches us a lesson of tremendous importance: no-one in the world can eat more than a stomach-full of food. One verse in the **Bhagavatam** says that what you can eat now, you are entitled to have. If you have something more you will be sick. The body also teaches you that the maximum space you need is the space in which you can lie down, and the maximum clothes you need are what can cover the body. The rest is all stolen property, accumulated by this pair of forces—hope and fear—that seem to govern our lives from day to day. The yogi merely says, "Look at this phenomenon."

There is another way of looking at it: whatever you have acquired comes from the earth. The body, food, buildings, motor cars, clothes, all metal and wood, etc. come from the earth; so it is possible to recognise that you did not bring anything at all when you were born, and all that you call 'mine' now, belongs to the earth.

Asteya also means non-holding and non-hoarding goods which are in short supply. To take more than you need of the world's goods is greed! Accumulation, even of that which seems to be vital to life, is destructive. Why is there greed, why do we accumulate? There are two motivations or premises: firstly, we think we are going to live for a long, long time. Secondly, we think that that power (call it God) which exists now providing us with nourishment today, is somehow going to die before we do, so we may need a bank balance. These two together form the motivation for greed. It is hope and fear of the future that turns every one of us into a thief.

How do we know what greed means? We think that we only want our necessities. But what does 'my necessities' mean? If the intelligence is constantly awake there is constant questioning. (If that is not there, the intelligence is asleep.) There is constant churning, because the intelligence is awake; but yet the old *samskāras* or life-habit-patterns continue. For every step you take you slip back a little. There is no use saying, "I am improving," or, "I am not improving." This limb is there. It is developing in its own time.

However, neither throwing everything away nor holding has any meaning whatsoever, unless the inner light perceives these two premises to be false. When the inner vision sees both of these to be error, then the desire to accumulate drops away. You do not push it, because when you push it away, the pusher is another greed, "I am going to give up everything in order that I may have . . .". That is what you are supposed to drop! When there is this inner light, these things will not arise at all—and there is *asteya*.

Kṛṣṇa, in an enigmatic and simple statement in the **Bhagavad Gītā**, says: "*Eat in moderation, sleep in moderation, do everything in moderation.*" What is it to be moderate? What is *my* moderation may be *your* starvation! That intelligence which is undimmed, uninterrupted by hope, fear, anxiety and so on, *alone* is the deciding factor. That intelligence is capable of deciding without the interference of thought or feeling, hope or fear. One who understands this manifests in himself the virtue of nonstealing.

Brahmacarya

Brahmacarya literally means 'when the whole inner consciousness flows constantly towards truth, towards what is, towards God, Brahman. That is difficult! And so some holy ones restricted the meaning. They asked, "What is it that distracts a person's attention most?" The opposite sex. So they interpreted *brahmacarya* to mean continence, chastity. This is no doubt one of the constituents of *brahmacarya,* but *brahmacarya* means much more than that. *Brahmacarya* is also part of the search for truth. It means that the mind is constantly moving in the infinite (Brahman), towards the infinite, constantly looking for Brahman. That itself again is meditation.

When the question, "What is truth, what is this?" is burning in one's heart, it is then that both truthfulness and *brahmacarya* are possible. It is said that the yogi who is devoted to truth becomes completely silent; everytime he wants to say something, there is the thought, "How do I know it is true?" This happens also with *brahmacarya* in the sense of chastity. When your mind, heart and whole being are constantly absorbed in this search for truth, towards enlightenment, then craving does not arise and continence happens. On the other hand, suppressing all these emotions is dangerous because it is violence, it is untruth, and there is no *brahmacarya* there.

Aparigrahā

The fifth of the *yama* is *aparigrahā,* which means non-covetousness, non acceptance of gifts given in the wrong spirit and removal of greed.

Aparigrahā, in popular translation, is non-receiving—not to accept or desire what belongs to others. As a matter of fact, the word greed is more appropriate in connection with this than *asteya; asteya* is more non-holding. *Aparigrahā*—non-receiving, non-acceptance of even gifts—is a beautiful thing. It is not complicated at all. Whereas in *asteya* you are allowed to have what you really need, you are allowed to make a living and you can keep in the refrigerator what you need for tomorrow morning, in *aparigrahā* what is indicated is that you don't receive anything at all. The person who practises *asteya,* for instance, may not steal, but if something is given to him he will take it.

In the **Bhagavad Gītā** it is said: "*The yogi is quite happy with what comes unsought*"; but here Patanjali goes one step further and says, "*Stop receiving even that.*"! This is total absence of greed. First we said *work* for a living and here we say work for a *living.* These two are tremendously important. Don't feel that you don't need to work, because somebody will give you what you need. Instead, earn your living. (Here also, in modern society we have so nicely readjusted the economic system that we know how to get what belongs to another in a very legal way: we call it business!)

If you apply the moral principles here these are also very high aspects of *yama*. If you take the attitude which is to first acquire the insight and then in that insight let it be seen that the self does not exist, then even *asteya* and *aparigrahā* appear to be great virtues. The comfort of *this* body is as important as the comfort of *that* body; feeding *this* body is as important as feeding *that* body. The masochistic method of feeding others and going without yourself is also un-yogic. There again the self wants to assert itself, to feel superior and saintly, proud of what he is doing. When the self is seen to be non-existent, all these virtues naturally manifest themselves.

To say that you must be established in all these before you can even start practising an *āsana,* is to put the cart before the horse and run far ahead of it. One who is not mindful, not practising meditation and contemplation—who has not learnt to observe himself in action and in silence, in seclusion and in company—cannot decide what non-aggression, truth, non-holding, *brahmacarya* and non-acquisition mean!

These five disciplines cannot be practised by either forcing them upon oneself or imposing them on others. Imposed virtue is force, not virtue. When the wisdom that there is only one indivisible intelligence prevails in your heart, then these *yama* become natural to you.

As long as this inner intelligence remains undivided and undistracted, no distraction can ever arise. What happens in the life of a yogi whose life is such, is described in *yama*. In his life those qualities will be found. So, to be good comes first and doing good is a mere extension of that being.

II. 31 jāti deśa kāla samayā 'navacchinnāḥ sārva bhaumā mahā vrataṁ

These articles of supreme (because effortless) self-restraint or order are universally invariable in everyone seeking enlightenment. They are compromised only when there is disharmony and contradiction between, for example, one's head—which seeks the order, and one's heart—which seeks the concomitant of disorder, viz., pleasure. They are not affected or modified by distinctions of birth (class, tribal, etc.), nationality or geography, epoch (ancient, modern, etc.) or of circumstances (profession, life-style, contingencies, etc.)

II. 32 śauca santoṣa tapaḥ svādhyāye 'svara praṇidhānāni niyamāḥ

In the light of intelligence illumining the life-style, arise the following observances: purity of body, mind and environment, contentment, psychic fire that simplifies life and purifies the heart, self-study or constant vigilance, and surrender to or worship of the indwelling omnipresence.

Niyama in common parlance suggests a regulated life, not only inwards but also embracing your external life (if one can divide life into something external and something internal).

The five *niyamas* are:

śauca, santoṣa, tapas, svādhyāya, Isvara praṇidhāna — purity, contentment, austerity or simplicity, study and total surrender to God).

You do not try to cultivate these *niyama,* but watch to see if these qualities are there in you. If they are there, then you are heading in the right direction; if they are not there, something is wrong somewhere else. So, something must be done to rectify the cause. You must find where the opposites of these qualities arise, not merely manipulate and cover them up. Covering up our faults doesn't work. (For instance, a friend of mine wanted to stop smoking but didn't, and every time she came to see me she used some kind of inhaler which smelt like cloves—so that when she came and spoke I smelt the tobacco and I smelt the cloves.) Instead we should look for the cause, and when *that* is rectified, the faults go away.

Śauca

Śauca in simplest language, is cleanliness of body, mind and environment. It is purity which can embrace both your inner self and your environment. When your inner being is pure and clean, I don't know if it would even tolerate outer uncleanliness. To say that your heart is pure and soaring in transcendental bliss and your body, dress and room are filthy, doesn't sound very reasonable to me. People have often said, "Some of your great yogi were filthy, or at least the Scriptures say so." Yes, but somewhere hidden in those descriptions are also suggestions that this yogi who appeared to be uncouth in appearance with filthy matted hair and so on, had a celestial fragrance emanating from him. The imitation yogi isn't capable of emanating this celestial fragrance!

If you experiment you will understand this. One day sit for meditation with dirty feet, the next day clean just your feet, and the next day take a bath and see the effects yourself You will understand the difference. It is an Indian custom to wash the mouth, hands, legs and face after meals. If you try it you will discover the benefit. You will find that this practice promotes digestion and assimilation. And seems to have a wonderful effect on the nerves. This is because water contains *prāṇa* and you imbibe the *prāṇa* from the water. You will notice that you feel refreshed after contact with water.

So much for external purity. Let us turn to internal purity. Firstly, the body must be pure. The practice of asanas helps to remove both impurities from the gross body, and blockages to the free flow of *prāṇa.* Then the mind must be pure. No evil thoughts should arise in the mind. Your motives and your feeling must be pure.

So cleanliness is not only washing hands, dishes, etc. and keeping your surroundings clean, but it embraces and encompasses the whole personality. Body, mind, heart and soul should be clean.

Santoṣa

The quality of contentment is so universally acclaimed as the key to peace of mind that it is unnecessary to labour the point. Absence of contentment is an indication of the presence of a thick veil of ignorance. Contentment is not a counsel of despair, or the fruit of laziness or the action of the idle and lazy rich. That sort of contentment is useless. No mechanical contentment is of any use—no mechanical anything is of any use! So contentment is not simple. It is lack of desire, which is the root of all our sufferings, and the cause of our discontent. In order to practise contentment one has to be aware of the arising of discontent all the time. Who but a selfish man will be tormented by discontent? Discontent is the seed for the trees of covetousness, theft, harmfulness and falsehood—all of which were dealt with in *yama.* Hence contentment is a corollary to the practice of the five *yama* already dealt with.

Contentment can arise in your heart only if you have faith in God. Contentment with one's lot has been denounced by materialists and grossly misunderstood by spiritual aspirants, too. The materialist's error lies in the supposition that it is ambition that brings success and prosperity. Far from it. It is work that brings success and prosperity. Ambition often acts as a distracting influence. Minus ambition, work performed as one's duty might bring greater success. Whereas ambition pulls you out and dissipates your energies, contentment turns you within and preserves your energies. Thus contentment is the secret of real achievement too. The spiritual aspirant's error is that he extends this contentment to the performance of his duties, whereas it applies only to his possessions. To be contented with what one has is yoga. To be contented with what one does is laziness!

In the Yoga Vāsiṣṭha it is said that contentment is one of the four gatekeepers to enlightenment. Contentment, therefore, is not a negative attitude of shirking one's duty, but the positive one of aspiring for liberation from the shackles of ignorance. It leads to peace of mind and the greatest achievement possible.

The Tao-Te-King says:

There is no greater crime than seeking what men desire,
There is no greater misery than having no content,
There is no greater calamity than indulging in greed.
Therefore the contentment of knowing content will ever be contented.

Tapas

Tapas means a very simple life, austerity, asceticism, self-purification, penance and penitence. It also means burning—an internal psychic or psychological burning. Any practice or life-style that results in the burning of the psychological impurities (*saṁskāras*) is *tapas*. It may also mean cultivating greater and greater self-awareness; for instance, if you are insulted you enquire into the nature of this inner hurt and your reaction to it, instead of retaliating. Swami Sivananda said, "Bear insult, bear injury, this is the highest *sādhana*," which means that while you are being insulted you are observing yourself.

One has to see the relevance of this teaching in one's own life. That is, if you are angry, for instance, you are boiling inside and a tremendous heat is generated within. Where is this anger, and what is it? You should neither suppress it nor express it, but observe it. Is it merely to earn a word of praise from others, that you suffer all this self-torture, or are you hoping that by doing this battle within yourself you are going to heaven? Neither of these, but the truth concerning this anger must be directly seen. What does that imply? For a few minutes or half an hour you are sitting and watching this tremendous tornado within yourself; you are meditating, using the anger itself. The whole attention is focussed on this inner boiling. You observe this tremendous disturbance within you and the thought arises, 'This is anger'.

Even then the battle is not over. You are still standing aside looking down on yourself as if it is not you. This anger is within you; the you is within the anger. What is the relationship between you and this anger? How is it that you are able to observe it though it is within you and you are within it? Anger is merely a word you picked up from somebody. Suddenly the self that was observing this, disappears. With that the anger is gone, because there is no one to call it anger. There is no self in relation to which it can be described as anger. Then you are doing real *tapas*. It doesn't matter what emotion (whether it is called anger, fear, anxiety, passion or any other name), it will still yield its fragrance—which is self-knowledge. If you can deal with it once, you have dealt with it for a lifetime.

So if one is intelligent, one can use pleasure, pain, honour, dishonour, praise or censure as the road to *samādhi*.

Svādhyāya

While practising some kind of enquiry or mental *tapas*, the masters say it is essential that there should be an intelligent understanding of the truth. Therefore they recommend *svādhyāya*—study of Scriptures and self-study. We need some guidance, otherwise it is possible that we undergo life's experiences and think we are learning from life, but we are getting the wrong message. It is here that we realise the great importance of both the Scriptures and the teacher, which together form what I would call the railroad. They will not take us to the goal, and what is even more important, they will not push us on it; but if we have the energy and the application they provide a sense of direction. The Scriptures keep us on the track and prevent us from reading false lessons from our life's experiences.

There are three different aspects of *svādhyāya*:

1. The orthodox meaning or definition of *svādhyāya* is to study a chapter from a Scripture every day. It can be done in a routine way, till the spirit of enquiry is awakened. Every day there must be some inspiring scriptural ideas, otherwise the mind thinks of something else and it becomes that. For instance, if you allow the mind to think of wars or riots, the whole of you has become conflict. You will be the start of the next conflict. When you read such things you are depressed and worried. Then you pick up the **Yoga Vāsiṣṭha** or the **Bhagavad Gītā** and read: *"Everybody has to die someday."* That thought changes your attitude and outlook on life. So some kind of scriptural study seems to be vital to our daily life.

If you are more deeply interested in all this, it is better to follow it up with a brief period of contemplation, because that piece that is studied has some relevance to your life. Can you recapture that relevance in contemplation?

2. Another orthodox interpretation is the repetition of a *mantra,* or *japa,* which must also be part of your daily activity. While you go on repeating the *mantra,* inevitably your consciousness takes on a certain subtle form. If you go on repeating this *mantra,* hoping that thereby you are creating within yourself a certain form, how is this self-study? If you enquire into the nature, the composition, the why and the what of the image, the sound picture, that is being put up within you, then it becomes *svādhyāya,* otherwise it is mechanical repetition. Swami Sivananda used to say, "If you repeat a *mantra* or do yoga postures, *prāṇāyāma* or what you call meditation mechanically and without understanding the spirit, then it has a negative value."

3. *Svādhyāya* may also mean meditation, which must also form part of your daily activity. When you meditate within yourself—using either a *mantra*, an image or a thought, an abstract form or formlessness—this is *svādhyāya.*

If these three are there they soften (if not completely demolish) the troubles that we are subjected to in this world. If it is used in the right spirit, perhaps it may redeem us from such troubles.

Īśvara praṇidhāna

What is *Īśvara*? *Īśvara* is also abbreviated into *Īśa*—Is. What is, *is* God. Whatever is, is God—not what appears to be, or is liable to change, because what is changing cannot be considered 'is'. If you can arrive at that, that is God. Let us take space, for instance. You cannot destroy space, you cannot cut it, burn it or cancel it. There is nothing as unchanging and as permanent as space, so space can be regarded as God. Therefore that which *is* has to be unlimited, infinite, permanent. What is, and what is everywhere, at all times, is God. That is *Īśvara.*

If this God *is* at all times everywhere, what is to be surrendered, and by whom? A glass of water is an object, so you can pick it up and give it to me. But what will you give to God? It is ignorance that is surrendered to God. What is this ignorance made of, and what sustains it? 'I' is the one that is ignorant of God's omnipresence, who by constantly doing this and doing that, denies the omnipresence of God. So what is the thing to be surrendered? That ignorance, nothing else. And who is the one that surrenders? The one that is born of that ignorance, who perpetrates that ignorance, who clings to and sustains that ignorance by constantly thinking that 'I am' and 'you are', etc.

It is possible for one in a million to understand the omnipresence of God and that the ignorant ego is itself the sole obstacle. If you are not in that category, then surrender to your picture or statue of God, to your father, mother or wife—anything, as long as that surrender is total and the mind does not even ask questions. If your surrender is real then that statue (or to whomever you surrender) is as good as anything in the world, because the omnipresence of God fills that, whatever it is. It is also possible to surrender to a living guru and do exactly the same thing. But here there may be the worry, "What if he is a fake, and misleads me?" 'Fake' is alright, 'misleads' is also alright, but misleads 'me' is the problem. If you want to preserve that 'me', then there is no surrender. If there is surrender, there is no meaning at all to the rest of that sentence.

When there is surrender (to whomever it may be directed), you are free. That intelligence is able from then on to take complete and total care of whatever happens, and to ensure that this 'me' doesn't come in again.

Surrender to God should not make God look like some kind of armed policeman. That is not what is meant by surrender. *Praṇidhāna* means not passive, but dynamic surrender; in such surrender the 'I' does not say, "Alright, I have surrendered myself to God, let Him look after me and mine." Let us go back to the analogy of the ocean. That little ounce of seawater is one with the ocean, and the totality of the ocean determines what it shall do. It may be deep in the ocean or on the crest of a wave, it may be dashed against a rock. It seems painful only if you still want to feel, 'I am independent of the totality, and the totality must answer my prayers'—which means there is no surrender.

When Patanjali suggested that self-knowledge—the total elimination of self-ignorance—can be had by surrender to God, it wasn't as a technique. Total surrender—the surrender being only of ignorance—doesn't form a technique, but is one of the vital disciplines. You cannot attain self-knowledge if there is not this constant and dynamic self-surrender to the divine—the divine being knowledge. The ignorantly assumed existence of a self must constantly be offered in sacrifice (as it were) to the omnipresence.

Knowledge which is the self is veiled by an assumption of the 'me' as an independent entity, and when the light of knowledge shines, that is seen to be non-existent. The self as energy flows down, the self as knowledge flows up to meet the descending grace in the heart and completely and totally surrenders—in the sense of inwardly merges—so that there is no longer a will called 'my' will; and (mark this very carefully) there is no longer a will called 'God's will' or 'your will'. The expressions 'Thy will be done' and 'God's will be done' are used only because there is still someone to say those words, to think those formulas; but in reality even that is not there. If there is no 'my will' there is no 'your will' also.

Only if that is understood in its right spirit can we appreciate it. That is why in some very great saints there occasionally appeared to be a show of vanity, but in their case at that point there was nothing called 'my will' or 'God's will'. There was no division. So if that person used the word 'I' it is God speaking through that mouth. (That is just from our point of view—it doesn't exist in his point of view.)

It is not possible to describe that state. That is *Īśvara praṇidhāna*—where the ego does not say, "I will" or, "I will not" When these two are dropped you realise that action flows without thought or ego inteference. There is dynamic surrender, which merely implies that this inner intelligence is alive to ensure that there is no current private motivation. Let the action flow as the blood flows in your veins, without any motivation whatsoever.

If there is *Īśvara praṇidhāna* one is in constant *samādhi. Samādhi* can be interpreted from one point of view to mean an even keel, a completely balanced state of mind, which is also possible if one is able to apply this to one's daily life. That is, in any tricky situation, you can immediately reaffirm this surrender. The very fact that you have to reaffirm the surrender means that the ego has come up again! Then you realise that the trickiness of the tricky situation is also brought about because of the ego. So to bring about balance necessarily implies the recognition that the balance was disturbed, because the 'me' suddenly raised its head.

Surrender to God cannot be explained, but if you are careful you may glimpse it. When your consciousness expands, and in the light of this consciousness you realise 'this is God, that is God; what is regarded as good is God, what is regarded as not so good is God; what is truth is God, what is regarded as untruth is God; what is holy is God, what is regarded as unholy is God', then something is dissolving within you. That is the ego—which was built up by your own ideas, education, culture and tradition. All these things which have been gathered together to form your ego-prejudices, self-estimation and all your ideas about good and evil—are gradually dissolving.

II. 33 vitarka bādhane pratipakṣa bhāvanaṁ

When distracted by wayward or perverted ratonalisation, suitable counter-measures should be adopted to keep away or remove such obstacles, especially by the contemplation of the other point of view.

Pratipakṣa means opposite, *bhāvana* is contemplation. Contemplation of the opposite has been given to us as a method which will help us in our practice of control of the mind. In the beginning this is possible only when you sit down for meditation practice. When you sit down a thought occurs in your mind; a thought which is the revival of the memory of some pleasure. When you want to deal with this you set up its own opposite. For instance, you think of some cake and you wish you had some now. Then you set up in front of it a counter-thought which says if you eat cake you will have stomach trouble, or your teeth will go bad—contemplation of the opposite. Instead of focussing your attention on your desire for this cake, you focus it on the evils of eating cake. If you want to smoke, set up as a counter-thought the evils of smoking. Thereafter instead of holding the need for a cigarette in your mind, you hold the thought of lung cancer in your mind. These two thoughts jump around in your mind—carefully watch and see how one overcomes the other. If you are keenly contemplating the counter-thought, then you will know how the counter-thought is able to swallow the desire.

In this manner you can develop what one normally calls 'will power'. But enlightenment does not come from will power. If you are not cautious and vigilant, you can get into will power, thought reading, telepathy and all these things, and lose the ultimate goal of enlightenment. But if you are watching the clash of the desire and the counter-thought, you can gain an insight into how to deal with these thoughts, cravings and passions. Once you have the master key to deal with this, then eventually you can overcome all thought and reach enlightenment.

Pratipakṣa bhāvana can also be used in ordinary day-to-day situations to prevent the mind from being agitated and moving from its centre. For instance, if distracting, destructive, distressing thoughts arise in your mind, confront them with their opposite. If you think ill of some person because he has cheated you, let you down or harmed you in any way, think of his good qualities. If the mind suggests all the evil that he has done, confront that thought with all the good things that he has done. I saw this in Swami Sivananda. Once a man who was our postmaster, cashier and treasurer ran away, taking the last cent that was in the ashram. After that we were drowned in debt. It led to police investigation, because some government money had been taken. For a few days postal and police inspectors came into the ashram asking questions. When one of these officers came to see Swami Sivananda he always said, "Oh, he was a good man. He did a lot of good work. He produced these few books." Swami Sivananda would keep these books ready at hand for those few days.

A similar statement is attributed to Rāma. His step-mother was responsible for banishing him to the forest. One of Rāma's brothers also went with him. During their first night in the forest, where they had to endure hard living conditions, the brother said, "But for this woman you would be lying in the palace." Rama turned to him and said, "Don't you have something else to talk about?"

So you have the ability, whenever there is a destructive or distresssing thought in your mind, to confront it with its opposite. If someone is rude to you (and you are seeing him for the first time so that you don't know of any good things he may have done) you can think, "*He* is rude, but that other person is very good to me." You have done no harm to the first man, and yet he is rude to you. You have done no good to the other man, and yet he is kind to you. (I am sure all of us have had such experiences.) Some one bullies you or insults you, and you walk a hundred paces more and someone is kind or complimentary to you. So as soon as the idea that So-and-so is nasty to you arises, immediately confront it with the thought that someone else is very pleasant.

* * * * * * * * * * * * * *

Sūtras are aphoristic and therefore enigmatic. They are not logically and grammatically completed sentences, but they must ignite a depth of understanding within us. *Vitarka bādhane*—'in the case of disturbance caused by destructive doubt'. *Pratipakṣa bhāvana*—'contemplation of the opposite'. What does it mean? Who disturbs? Who creates these doubts? (That is not mentioned.) Maybe yourself, maybe someone else. It may not be quite fair to say that the yogi, sincerely and seriously observing life and becoming aware of this virtue arising, might himself be subjected to destructive doubt. But it is possible in the initial stages—when you are not well-established in either of these—that there is doubt arising within you. It can arise internally, within yourself; or externally, where someone might create a doubt in you either in person or through writings, talks and so on. (It is very important to remember this.)

If you, a sincere and serious student of yoga, are so vulnerable that you can be wafted away from the state of alertness or vigilance that you have so wisely aroused in yourself, then the first condition has not been fulfilled; your yoga is not intelligent, your virtue is not built on intelligence. (See II. 28). If it was, it should have been able to sustain itself. As long as that light is burning there can be no darkness in this room.

Instead of fighting with this external doubt, see that either something has gone wrong, or you imagined that the inner intelligence had been awakened, but in fact it had not. (It was merely a presumption, an assumption, a thought, a notion within your own mind.) In a moment of lack of vigilance it is possible for a doubt to arise. I am labouring this because if you are subject to this kind of destructive doubt, how do you expect to contemplate the opposite? If you have been non-aggressive and loving for years and years, and suddenly something happens and you are filled with aggression, I don't know if it is possible for you to bring up a counter-suggestion within yourself and stop this aggression. So, once what appeared to be deep-seated faith is shaken by a devastating doubt, what is there in which you can prop up a counter suggestion?

I feel that it is not in the seeker's own heart that the doubt arises. If someone who doesn't understand you comes and uses twisted, vicious argument, you become assailed by it. In such a situation, what is your chief anchor? How do you contemplate the opposite so that his attacks become futile?

Faced with this kind of challenge the sincere and earnest student of yoga contemplates

duḥkhā 'jñānā 'nanta phalā

II. 34 vitarkā hiṁsādayaḥ kṛta kāritā 'numoditā lobha krodha moha pūrvakā mṛdu madhyā 'dhimātrā duḥkhā 'jñānā 'nanta phalā iti pratipakṣa bhāvanaṁ

Wayward or pervert reasoning is often indulged in to rationalise violence etc., whether these are direct personal actions, or indirectly caused, or merely witnessed or acquiesced in. These can be mild, moderate, or grave transgressions. However, they have greed, hate and stupidity as their antecedents, and they yield the bitter fruits of endless sorrow, and ever-deepening darkness of ignorance—such contemplation is the effective counter-measure. (Or, hence the need for suitable counter-measure.)

The path of violence, aggression, untruth and falsehood will inevitably lead to endless unhappiness and endless ignorance—*duḥkhā 'jñānā 'nanta.* That ignorance itself becomes the manifestation of your own inner intelligence. Only if that inner intelligence has been awakened properly and sustained in you, is it possible for you when challenged in this manner to produce the *pratipakṣa bhāvanaṁ* at once—naturally, and almost effortlessly. That seems to be the wonderful secret in those two Sūtras. *"Whenever there is an obstacle or obstruction this inner intelligence at once springs into activity and dispels it."*

When the inner intelligence has made the decision it sees very clearly, but either the revival of past *saṁskāras,* memories, tendencies or past habit patterns (or the suggestion of someone else) questions the decision of this inner light, and suggests that there may be a reason for doubt, then the light shining upon that doubt itself instantly dispels it.

II. 35 ahiṁsā pratiṣṭhāyāṁ tat saṁnidhau vaira tyāgaḥ

When there is natural firmness in non-violence all hostility comes to an end in its very presence. Conflict ceases in such a mind.

The fruit of *ahiṁsā* is that beings give up their enmity in the very presence of the man who is established in *ahiṁsā.* Primarily, since he offers no violent resistance to any being, all opposition fails when directed towards him. (As the Indian proverb goes: *"You cannot clap with one hand.")* He serves as a temperamental and emotional 'airconditioner' and anyone who comes within the circle of his influence immediately 'cools down'. By his example, he inspires people to give up enmity, and when they see that enmity is a degrading quality and that love ennobles, they too grow in love.

Wild animals who are natural enemies also become peaceful in his presence. As is said in the Bible: *"The lion will lay down with the lamb."*

II. 36 satya pratiṣṭhāyāṁ kriyā phalā 'śrayatvaṁ

When there is firm grounding in the perception of what is, or of truth, it is seen that action and reaction, seed and its fruits, or cause and result, are related to each other; and the clear vision of intelligence becomes directly aware of this relationship. (Or, one's words are fruitful.)

The fruit of *satya* (being established in truth) is said to be 'bestowal of fruits of actions', or 'the effectiveness of his words and actions is immediately to be seen'. In other words, there is tremendous power in his thoughts, words and deeds, so that they do not need time to bring them to fruition in a later life.

A commonplace example of this we see in our daily life. If a shopkeeper is truthful, honest and not greedy, if he enjoys a reputation for being neither an exploiter nor a blackmarketeer, people will flock to him and his business will prosper. Hence `honesty is the best policy', though truth leads us much further than a business proposition.

Peace follows truth, because peace and truth are synonyms. One who is established in truth is at peace. He has a clear conscience. This is what few people in the world realise. To err is human, but the man who does not go against the voice of truth or his conscience at least has peace within him, to maintain him through all his trials and tribulations. This conscience is our only true friend (and when flouted, our only real enemy). Hence 'unto thine own self be true'. If you make a mistake, the Lord speaking through your purified conscience, will lead you out of that error.

II. 37 asteya pratiṣṭhāyāṁ sarva ratno 'pasthānaṁ

When the intelligence firmly rejects the desire to hoard, and when thus there is natural firmness in non-hoarding, even precious gems stand in front of the yogi, unable to deflect him.

n established in non-holding all the 'precious gems stand in front'. This has been interpreted in various ways. For instance, some have taken it to mean that if you are perfectly pure, you don't steal or cheat, all the wealth of the world will flow towards you. Some have even taken it to mean that in order to test your total absence of greed, the gods will place precious stones wherever you walk!

This interpretation sounds fantastic, but it may be far-fetched. One beautiful saying of Walt Whitman seems to apply: *"A man is as rich as the things he does not possess."*

You do not say 'I want' in connection with that which you have already. So, one who does not use these two words obviously has everything. Since the yogi whose inner intelligence is awake does not use these two words at all, it is assumed that the entire wealth of the world is his. That's a very beautiful poetic way of describing *asteya*. In short, it is a synthesis of contentment, simplicity and charity.

II. 38 brahmacarya pratiṣṭhāyāṁ vīrya lābhaḥ

No effort is involved in living or acting in itself-effort implies disorderly movement of energy in several directions as lust, anger, greed, etc. Hence, when the whole being moves effortlessly in the cosmic homogeneous essence, and thus there is movement of energy in a single direction, which is really non-movement, there is great conservation of energy. It is not dissipated in diverse sensual and psychic activities. The worst dissipation of energy is sexuality. Hence the yogi is wedded to chastity in thought, word and deed, which he carefully preserves through the practice of yoga postures, pranayama, right diet, contemplation, holy company and prayer. Effortless chastity promotes energy.

If you are a celibate *brahmacāri*, you will have abundant energy. *Brahmacarya* does not only mean sexual continence; it means the mind dwells constantly on a different plane altogether. It is then that we stop the leakage of energy not only through sexual fulfilment, but through other things; for instance both talking and eating cause a tremendous loss of energy. When one's whole being moves in truth, in the spiritual centre, then the energy that normally is dissipated in these channels becomes available for this enquiry.

When the attention is wholly and totally directed towards enlightenment, continence happens.

II. 39 aparigrahasthairye janma kathaṁtā saṁbhodhaḥ

When the inner light of intelligence illumines the state of mind that has firmly rejected all greed and there is contentment with what life brings unsolicited, there arises knowledge of the mysteries of life and its why and how.

When you are firmly established in this non-greed (or, as we have interpreted it, when you work for a living) there is intimate understanding of the how and the why of life itself.

How did this life come into being? How did life arise in the first place? You didn't ask to be born here, but you have been given birth to. That which gave birth to you knows how long you should live this life, what life is going to be like, what you are supposed to get and what you are supposed not to get. All that is already known.

If you want to you can bring in your *karma* and reincarnation theory here: *"As you sow, so shall you reap."* I have changed the formula to, *"As you sow, so shall it grow"*. I don't know if you have ever considered this. You sow one seed, just in fun, and out of that one seed the tree grows and yields abundant fruits, with very little effort on your part. If that is not going to teach us how to live then nothing else will! So to the simple yogi who has some fruit trees around his *ashram*, the message is quite clear. In his heart there is a prayer 'May I also be like you, oh tree! Taking little and giving a lot,' knowing that that power which is able to produce this miracle right in front of his eyes is there for all time. That which generates this tree, multiplying the seed a million fold, is capable of sustaining it as long as it has to be sustained. The vision that sees that does not crave, has no greed in it and does not accept or look forward to receiving gifts.

II. 40 śaucāt svā 'ṅga jugupsā parair asaṁsargaḥ

The habit of cleanliness, if it is not mechanical and ritualistic but intelligent with an understanding of the nature of decaying physical organisms, reveals the impure nature of the physical body; and there arises disgust for the body and a disinclination for contact with those of others.

From this practice of cleanliness, disgust for one's own body and that of others' arises. Whereas all the other *yamas* and *niyamas* that we have discussed so far have only one Sūtra following, *śauca* has two, suggesting its importance.

You go on washing this body and it continues to be dirty. Dirt is gathered not only from outside, but it pours from inside. Incidentally, it may mean that the yogi keeps this body clean not in order to make it appear beautiful, but (since it seems to exude all this filth) only to keep it clean. So emphasis is on keeping it clean, not cosmetic cleanliness. When it is kept clean the body teaches you how to avoid polluting it. You are disgusted with keeping it clean, so why will you put into it that which will make it filthier? The yogi is also not attracted to others. He is not worshipping the body, as it were, of others, because that body is also made of the same substance—however beautiful, holy, handsome and charming it may look. This outlook arises from the intelligent practice of cleanliness.

II. 41 **sattva śuddhi saumanasyai 'kāgrye 'ndriya jayā 'tma darśana yogyatvāni ca**

And, such a habit of cleanliness also leads to the purification of the whole substance, peace and basic goodness of mind, one-pointedness, mastery over the senses, as also the ability (and the qualification) to attain self-knowledge.

Here *sattva* does not mean the quality called *sattva* but that the entire substance of which you are made (the body, mind and senses, etc.) becomes pure. Therefore *śauca* obviously does not mean wearing a clean dress or cleaning the skin only, but cleaning the body within as also the mind and the senses and so on. In Hatha Yoga practice there are quite a number of cleaning exercises called *śat kriya* which involve cleaning all parts of your physical organism. In Raja Yoga, when one keeps on practising cleanliness, it extends to your emotions, thoughts—everything.

Saumanasyai—the mind becomes goodness, goodness becomes the mind; *ekāgrye*—it becomes one-pointed. A clean heart is undistracted by distractions. When the yogi is not attracted by objects of pleasure, there will be no distraction of his attention.

Indriya jaya—when the body and the mind are cleansed of all impurities, the senses function in a controlled, disciplined manner, not in a disorderly way. If the senses are freed of toxins and impurities, they function efficiently and in a healthy manner. If the mind and heart have also been purified and all attraction and repulsion in the world have been abandoned, then the senses function in an orderly way.

Ātma darśana—just this simple thing called cleanliness leads to the ability to behold the Self. That again suggests that this cleanliness is not merely cleanliness of the external body or environment (though all these are essential), but it goes right through to your very self, your very soul.

II. 42 saṁtoṣād anuttamaḥ sukha lābhaḥ

From contentment there flows the most excellent happiness and delight.

We do not know why people run after material objects and accumulate them. Even a multi-millionaire who has a huge mansion sleeps only in one bed. He does not eat gold and drink silver, he also has to eat food and drink water. The more possessions you have the more trouble you have in keeping them secure and in good order. If you keep this idea in mind, "The less I have the less worried I will be," you will be happy. This contentment comes only if you have faith in God.

Contentment leads to peace of mind and also the greatest achievement possible. Every nation, race, religion and language has a proverb which is in essence: '*A contented mind is a continuous feast*'. Out of contentment supreme happiness arises; when you are contented there is supreme happiness.

II. 43 kāye 'ndriya siddhir aśuddhi kṣayāt tapasaḥ

The inner psychic fire destroys all impurities of the heart and mind, and brings about the health, sanity, wholeness or perfection of the physical and vital being (the inner senses).

To deaden yourself completely is easy, to let the senses run riot is easy, but to perfect the senses, mind and body, and yet keep them pure, means tremendous intelligence. This is *tapas*.

Kāye is usually translated as the body, but it may also extend (or intend) to cover subtler bodies also. *Indriya* means the senses. Since *tapas* is purifying, the senses, physical body, psychological body and causal body are purified and they become perfect—*kāye indriya siddhir*. (This is the total opposite of what we often come across in this world—most people who do *tapas* are always morose and dull, shutting themselves off from the world as ascetics and living in their own world, as it were.)

Fasting cleans and purifies your body, but then the pure food that you take is already polluted in some way or other, and somehow pollution enters the body. The physical body cannot be kept completely pure, it has its own course and it will inevitably follow, no matter who you are; and therefore *tapas* essentially refers to the inner body—the senses and the mind, which are polluted in various ways. When it shines brightly, the inner intelligence clears this pollution from moment to moment.

When something is purified there is transparency, and when there is transparency there is clear vision. The light passes through that transparency without any obstruction or distortion, and there is self-realisation, self-knowledge.

Patanjali promises that we shall develop occult powers by practising *tapas.* Fire burns and purifies. People who melt gold know that when gold is melted in fire, it becomes pure. In the same way, if you burn the senses and the mind in the fire of *tapas* they will become purer, and therefore they will have wonderful powers. In a lighter vein, and in order to enable you to understand, let me explain. With the nose you can smell. If the nose is clean, you smell well. If you have a cold and your nose is full of mucous you cannot smell even what is near you. In the same way, if you purify the senses by *tapas,* you will develop occult powers.

II. 44 svādhyāyād iṣṭa devatā saṁprayogaḥ

By study, (not necessarily nor exclusively) of Scriptures, and of oneself, the consciousness is united with the desired or loved divinity. This divinity may well be a 'luminous' internal transmutation-experience or its externalised psychic manifestation, or an 'enlightened being.

By the practise of *svādhyāya* or self-study you may have a vision (maybe inward or outward, internal or external) of your own beloved divinity or *iṣṭa devatā,* the form or the luminous thing that you love most. It does not mean God-realisation, but you will see God in the form in which you are worshipping Him. For instance, if you are regular in your **Bible** study and you regularly take the name of Lord Jesus, you will get a vision of Him. If you sincerely study the **Bhagavad Gītā**, you will have a vision of Lord *Kṛṣṇa.* God-realisation or Self-realisation is far away, but even having such a vision is not a small achievement!

Your *iṣṭa devatā* may have a physical shape and it may appear to you in various guises. You realise your unity, your awareness with that luminous being. It is not as though this beloved divinity is up there in heaven and it comes down here and you become one with it. How do two entities become one? It is absurd! One has first to realise one's *non*-entity.

II. 45 samādhi siddhir īśvara praṇidhānāt

Perfection in self-awareness instantly follows total, dynamic and intelligent surrender of the individual ego-sense (in the sense of the realisation of its unreal nature) or the merging of it in the indwelling omnipresence (in the sense of the direct realisation of the falsity of the me', the ego-sense, and therefore the sole reality of the indwelling omnipresence).

This Sūtra is a beautiful safeguard of the spirit. If that surrender does not happen, then the words 'God's grace, God's will, surrender to God' are all absolutely meaningless. Then the 'I', the ego, that is supposed to be surrendered to God, in fact uses these as a whip on the back of God: "*God, thy will be done. Take care of us and do exactly what I tell you to do. By your grace everything is possible. I won't do anything, but everything is supposed to be done. Things must happen the way I want them to happen. I determine what is right and what is not right, what should happen and what should not happen.*"

When there is *Íśvara praṇidhāna*, surrender to God, you are in constant, uninterrupted *samādhi*—total oneness, total self-realisation. Here again is the famous example given in Indian philosophical systems: this surrender is like the attempt of a doll made of salt jumping into the sea in order to fathom the ocean. The doll becomes one with the ocean, and what the ocean decides, happens to that salt doll. It has become one with the ocean—*samādhi.* 'The total intelligence shines as the sole substance or reality.' (See Chapter III. 3). The 'I' doesn't exist at all, only the ocean exists. Naturally, what the ocean determines is what happens!

II. 46 sthira sukham āsanaṁ

The posture of the body during the practice of contemplation and at other times, as also the posture of the mind (or attitude to life) should be firm and pleasant.

The word meaning of *āsana* is posture. This Sūtra defines posture as *sthira*—it must be firm, and *sukham*—it must be comfortable. So whether it is physical, psychological or emotional, there must be physical, psychological and emotional firmness, and the posture must be pleasant and steady. It must not involve confusion, conflict or struggle. When the posture is steady, physically and psychologically, and when you are not struggling, meditation becomes easy.

Why is *sthira sukham āsanaṁ* prescribed? Because Patanjali had mentioned in another Sūtra, *"Unsteadiness of the body or its limbs is an indication of the unsteadiness of the mind."* So if you bring about steadiness of the body there are greater chances of your being able to be aware of the movement of energy in the mind.

Patanjali gives us three hints:

1. There should be mild, steady practice. You should not give up or overdo the practice. This is important in the case of not only *āsana* and *prāṇāyāma,* but also of meditation—in fact of everything.

Sometimes in our Scriptures we are told that we should have burning aspiration or desire for God. The word 'burning' was used by a *ṛṣi* who was living in the forest. He had only seen the burning of a fire which burns steadily, without noise, always going up. Steady, calm and always going up is 'burning aspiration for God'. But take the case of the modern Primus stove. It burns with great sound and fury, but in a moment it goes out and is finished. Modern burning is like that—all sound and fury, and then the fire goes out. Some modern yogis do all sorts of things for a while and then give up. That shows that the motive itself was wrong.

If you are sincere, your yoga practices will be steady and mild. If you are able to sit for a few minutes now, gradually increase it. If you suddenly increase the time, something may happen to your knees and then you will have to leave the practice for some time.

2. The next aid is meditation, which itself will give steadiness of posture. One helps the other. If you are able to sit steadily you will get meditation. If your mind is concentrated, you will be able to sit steadily.

3. In India they have a belief that if you meditate on a tortoise, a mountain, or some other firm object and pray, "Please God let me sit like that," this will help you to have a firm posture. Yoga postures are not just physical postures. The mind must be connected, because it is the mind that gives strength. Power is always there and it is the mind that makes the power available.

Once you have mastered this meditation posture, the mind or the attention is flowing in one direction, there is tremendous energy and your attention is not easily distracted and diverted. So you need a firm posture in order that you may be able to look within, to directly observe the arising of the ego-sense, to understand who the see-er or the experiencer is. You are caught in the illusion of the existence of an experiencer. You must come face to face with this thing which you have regarded as an experiencer, so that in the light of that observation the experiencer must disappear.

It is usual to say that the Raja Yoga *āsana* is different from the Hatha Yoga *āsana.* The divided mind always thinks of differences, but it is possible to see that they may not be different. According to standard commentators, *āsana* is restricted to a few postures which are considered to be meditative postures, where the body is in a state of immobility without discomfort. In other words it does not refer to the other postures like the *sarvaṅgāsana* (shoulderstand) and the *sirṣāsana* (headstand), etc. But I have a feeling that this Sūtra covers even *those* postures. Therefore it is essential while you practice those other yoga postures to hold them steady for some time, not do them as gymnastics or exercises. First it becomes uncomfortable, because the muscles that were lying idle for so long have suddenly been put to work.

Every *āsana* is an unusual posture and when you put the body in an unusual posture there is obviously some discomfort to begin with and the balance is disturbed. But if you observe what goes on, at that point there is tremendous internal activity, the balance is restored and the discomfort that you felt in the beginning is also gone. So in a few moments it becomes more and more pleasant and steady. Here you are really discovering that there is an intelligence beyond the ego, because the ego itself cannot bring about this restoration of balance. If you do a difficult balancing posture you will see that your whole body is alert and very alive. (But of course if you do it mechanically or with violence, then you don't notice all this.)

Soon you are able to maintain that posture for a long time. While doing so, you will discover another fantastic truth. First, you can never hurt yourself. It takes an extraordinary idiot to hurt himself. And second, the powers of this inner intelligence are indescribably beautiful. As you assume any posture, the balance is lost and some discomfort is produced, but then this inner intelligence springs into activity, restoring the balance and restoring comfort. From second to second this intelligence works—it calculates faster than all your computers put together—readjusting and realigning. The intelligence functions as one whole unit, an indivisible unit. The yogi sees this in his *āsana* practice.

The inner purpose of the *āsana* is manifold. One purpose may be to discover the intelligence beyond the me, but it also promotes tranquility and peace of mind, and what is called physical and mental health. When the body is in a healthy condition the mind is also healthy, and you can serve humanity much better. At least you are not a nuisance to anyone. Some yogis in India say that anyone who does *āsanas* in order to gain health is selfish; but it is good to remember that to be healthy is already a great service to humanity. The sick man needs the attention of a half a dozen people, thus you are doing a great service by sparing people that trouble.

Of course the yogi values health only to the extent of the body not disturbing the mind in its search for truth;

so that at one stage it is possible that the mind is steady, regardless of the state of the body. At that point the yogi may not be at all interested in keeping good health. In order to understand that you must have seen someone like Swami Sivananda. His body was almost the house of several illnesses, but still he was radiant. It is not possible for us to undertand how a man can be radiant, peaceful and tranquil in spite of the fact that his body is sick, because in our case the body and mind are closely tied to each other.

Another great yogi said that if you are able to sit steadily for an hour or so the mind will become steady; you may not even have to work on the mind.

Unnecessary moving of the limbs is also an indication of the restlessness of the mind. When you are sitting steadily in a certain posture, you begin to feel restlessness entering the limbs, and it feels uncomfortable. The Zen masters say: "*Become aware of this restlessness; it is this restlessness that affects the body, mind and the spirit. Don't express it or suppress it.*" You *cannot* suppress it; it is there, crying out! Keep it there and observe it. (Of course, if that becomes a distraction, it is useless.) So yoga is not simple do's and don't's; you have to use your common sense and intelligence all the time.

Āsana can also mean seat or mat, so when people talk of *padmāsana* (*padma* means lotus), it may mean sitting in a lotus posture or sitting on a lotus! Let us look at it from a different angle of vision. Take, for instance, *āsana* as posture. *Padmāsana* is the posture of a lotus, not just the lotus posture. A lotus can stay in water without being spoiled by it. This is a fairly common expression in yoga literature: "*A yogi lives in the world just as a lotus lives in water, totally untouched, untainted, unaffected by it."*

So lotus posture may mean what has traditionally come to be regarded as the lotus posture, or the posture of the lotus standing in water. As you go on contemplating this, you get greater and greater insight. The lotus springs out of mud, and yet it is the most glorious of flowers; which may mean don't go to a psychoanalyst, don't worry about where you started and what happened in your childhood or previous incarnation. All that may be mud—but you are a lotus. Don't go on regretting what happened some time ago and blaming others for what happened. Realise what you are now—a lotus. That can also be lotus posture.

So *āsana* can mean mental posture, psychological posture and emotional posture. One must bear all these in mind and not merely get hung up on some definition or description, and feel that that is all there is to it. It is also possible to see in it a vital lesson in your life—that unless your mind, emotions and your attitude to life are steady, well rooted and also comfortable, your life is not going to be smooth. In the same way, if psychologically and emotionally your posture in this life is both firm and pleasant, then life goes on smoothly.

If we accept that yoga is to be practised throughout our daily lives, then this posture may even refer to the posture we take in regard to life. Your attitude to your life must be steady and comfortable. An uncomfortable discipline is not likely to last, because it creates an internal tension or rebellion. And yet a certain discipline is needed. That discipline must be flavoured with common sense. Then it is likely to last.

So posture may mean the yoga posture in which you sit for meditation, and also the postures you assume in your life, in your relationships with people. If there is no disruption or violent conflict in our relationship it can last for a long time, but once some relationship is broken, it is very difficult to mend it. Even if it is fixed, it is still patch work. The least bit of little heat somewhere else is going to melt it!

You must find firm ground. If firm ground is not there, every little wind is going to blow you one way or the other. Once you have struck root and there is firmness, then you can grow as tall as you like, as wide as you like, because you won't be uprooted. All this must be accompanied by comfort and an inner joy, otherwise the mind is going to rebel against everything you do. This is true of both the yoga postures and the posture called life. If you ever have had the misfortune to twist a muscle during a yoga posture, for a long time the body will refuse to attempt it again, because it is frightened. In life too, if you get into a messy situation in personal relationships or in whatever you do, and you invite discomfort, pain and suffering, the mind wants to avoid it. It doesn't want to get involved in that.

Only the person who is at peace within himself and who tastes and enjoys that peace, to whom peace is beautiful and blissful, would not want to be drawn into any conflict whatsoever. Such a person *is* peace, he radiates peace and joy. It is not by struggling that one can establish peace or happiness, but by relaxing and letting the whole thing go. Being rooted in peace and being firmly established in inner happiness, that person can radiate or promote such things in life.

This little Sūtra, therefore, can have all these applications in our daily life.

II. 47 prayatna śaithilyā 'nanta samāpattibhyāṁ

Such a posture can be attained (1) by the abandonment of effort and the non-use of will, and (2) by the continuous awareness of the infinite eternal existence.

To make sure that we get the message, that there is no struggle, Patanjali adds one more Sūtra. Two things are to be combined—*prayatna śaithilya*—that is, almost effortless, without strain. This means go up to that point where you begin to feel strain, and stop there. If you stop before, you are lazy. But that is only half the Sūtra, the other half—*ananta samāpattibhyāṁ*—means contemplation of the endless, which is a very romantic way of saying, "Go on". There is infinite potentiality within you, contemplate the infinite. So the author says, "*Stop when strain is experienced, but go on gently.*"

This is true of the yoga posture and also the posture called life. When there is some strain or trouble in your life, remember this. Don't struggle to get out of it, because that will make it worse. Also remember that you were there before the trouble came into your life and you will continue to be there after. You are the infinite, the trouble is only a little incident in your life.

There should be minimal struggle, knowing that the intelligence in the body which created this body and sustains it, is capable of handling any situation that arises in life. There is no need to get worried about it now.

So, in the practice of *āsanas* and in the posture you take in regard to life itself, the less the effort the greater the purity and beauty. The picture arises in your mind and immediately the intelligence in all your limbs springs into action. It is effortless. By contemplating the indivisibility of the intelligence, the body assumes the posture, and the person assumes a certain posture in regard to life and in all relationships.

II. 48 tato dvandvā 'nabhighātaḥ

Then follows immunity from the onslaughts of the pairs of inseparable opposites—like pain and pleasure, heat and cold, success and failure, honour and dishonour.

Once you are steadily seated, when you have mastered this meditation posture and the mind or the attention is flowing in one direction, there is tremendous energy and your attention is not easily distracted and diverted.

Here is a wonderful exercise. Sit in the lotus posture and tell yourself, "I am not going to get up for another three hours." The knees begin to hurt, you don't endure that pain (if you endure that pain you become a martyr, we will put up a statue for you!), but utilise it and try to discover what it is that calls it pain. There is certainly a sensation in the legs. Where is this sensation (a mere neurological affair) converted into the psychological category of pain? Why shouldn't this neurological phenomenon be left as a neurological phenomenon? Why must this encroach into your psyche? A nerve is paining, let it pain. A nerve is twitching, let it twitch. Why must the brain interpret this neurological phenomenon as pain? Why not as pleasure? Or, why pleasure? Why not leave it as a neurological phenomenon?

If one observes what goes on within oneself during this *āsana* practice, then it becomes yoga. The idea is that as each posture is executed one must see what is happening to the body. What does the body say? What is the sensation? How does the brain or the mind interpret this sensation?

If one understands the spirit of *āsana* in this manner, this Sūtra explains what happens (not necessarily as a result of all this). The student of yoga transcends or is immune to the onslaught of what are known as pairs of opposites. There is a slightly modified expression: 'pairs of inseparable opposites' such as day and night, or heat and cold. You cannot separate one from the other. Even if you go somewhere where it is always hot, you will find that your body begins to perspire profusely. Where there is heat there must be some kind of cooling agency. So everything is accompanied by its own opposite. If you have a friend, in him you have an enemy. You want him to continue to be your friend, so you hope you don't offend him. Already you are making him an enemy, because fear of losing the friendship is already the hidden enemy in this relationship. On the other hand, it is possible that someone hates you and the initial feeling is that he is your enemy. You are scared to death, but because of that you are nice to him, thereby creating a friendship there. These things do not come alone.

So, if the definition that we studied so far concerning the posture—that it must be firm and comfortable, there should be least effort in it and there should be contemplation of the infinite—had been understood, then you are not bogged down by these pairs of inseparable opposites. You realise that he is your friend, you have to be afraid of him now; he is your enemy, you have to make friendship with him now. It is hot, well never mind, you will sweat; it is cold, you will put on a jersey and make yourself warm.

This Sūtra has also been interpreted by orthodox commentators to mean that if you are able to have this firm posture and enter into meditation, you are unaffected by heat and cold. This to me is very childish, a very small fringe benefit; whereas if one understands the whole spirit of this text, it opens up a tremendous vista of beauty. Your whole life is transformed!

If the posture in life (as also the physical posture) is steady, and there is constant contemplation of the infinite without any struggle, then whatever happens in life—honour, dishonour, pain, pleasure, happiness or unhappiness—you become a sort of optimist, able to enjoy the fact that there is always some happiness hidden in unhappiness. (Please don't think that I mean the martyr complex or masochism.) You cannot write the word 'unhappiness' without the word 'happiness' in it. Unhappiness is merely an extension of happiness. It is when we try to extend happiness that we run into unhappiness. Be content with what little happiness that comes, enjoy it, let it go. Don't look forward to that anymore, or try to extend it. Since you are not rejecting what is coming next, it doesn't become real unhappiness.

So when one is firmly and effortlessly established in this posture and when one contemplates the infinite all the time—not only when you are sitting in your lotus posture for meditation, but in any posture that you may assume, physicaly and mentally—that is the sense in which the word *āsana* is used.

II. 49 tasmin sati śvāsa praśvāsayor gati vicchedaḥ prāṇāyāmaḥ

Simultaneously, the interruption and reversal (and therefore the balancing) of the flow of inhalation and exhalation, of the positive (life-promoting) energy and the negative (decay-promoting) energy, constitutes the regulation of the life-force which is then experienced as the totality of all its functional aspects previously and ignorantly viewed as the building up and the breaking down opposed to each other.

If the mind and the nerves are excited and the body restless, the breathing is agitated. If they are calm, the breathing is calm too. So the movement of the breath is an indicator of the state of the mind. Therefore breathing is not only for the ventilation of the lungs or the blood, but an indicator of the state of the mind. *Prāṇāyāma* (control of *prāṇā)* is recommended for that. Perhaps the yogi who invented this system meant even this to be a psychological trick, not a physical exercise.

Watch your own breathing as it goes in and out, and you will know what the state of your mind is; because the mind and the breath being very closely interrelated. When your mind is steady the gaze is steady and the breathing is smooth. (Deep or not deep doesn't seem to matter at all, because if you seriously practise concentration and meditation you might be surprised to see that your breathing becomes shallow).

What is Prāṇa?

It is not easy to understand intellectually what *prāṇa* is. If you ask me what electricity is, I would say that electricity is electricity. In the same way, *prāṇa* is *prāṇa*! If you paraphrase it in any other way it creates more confusion, not clarity. The yogi is not interested in description, but truth—which means direct experience.

Prāṇa or the life force is not something which is identical with the air that we breathe, however pure or holy it may be, but that which makes the body and the mind function. Neither the body nor the mind can understand it. You may say it is life-force, but you do not know what life-force is! The air contains *prāṇa.* The air itself is not *prāṇa,* but something in the air is *prāṇa. Prāṇa* is not the breath itself, but the power that makes you breathe. *Prāṇa* is in water and in food, too. It is not food itself, but the power that digests that food; not drink itself, but the power that produces thirst. So it is not the food or water or air, but something in all of them. The *prāṇa* in you is able to extract the *prāṇa* from the air you breathe, and use it. It is wrong to think that it is the oxygen that makes you live. Your *prāṇa* uses the oxygen.

It is *prāṇa* that connects the body with the mind, and therefore what happens in the body is reflected in the mind. When the body and mind are pure and the *prāṇa* flows unobstructedly, there is a great sense of well-being. When the *prāṇa* is obstructed it will send out signals—either pain or dullness. If you say, "This is a bit painful, so I will just lie down," then there is total obstruction. The body and mind are dull. It is easy to avoid pain and discomfort, but then we make the mistake of doing nothing. The body is not meant to be lazy. Obstruction is brought about by wrong eating habits and ways of living, and dullness is brought about by laziness. If these two are avoided, then one communicates with this *prāṇa* and one senses peace and well-being.

When the yogi speaks of *prāṇa* he has a concept of his own—something which is cosmic, which functions in the body, with the help of which you are able to see, hear and speak, and ultimately with the help of which you are able to think. When the *prāṇa* works in the physical body it generates energy and movement; when it works in the brain, it thinks. The yogi says that it is the *prāṇa* that works through the mind. When you are calm your breath is also calm, and when you are excited your breath is excited. Which is the cause and which the effect? We do not know. Either may be the cause, because it works both ways. If you control your *prāṇā*, your mind is controlled; if you control your mind, the *prāṇa* is controlled. Ultimately, you reach the conclusion that both are somehow one.

Prāṇāyāma

Probably what is known as *prāṇāyāma* is meant not so much to cleanse your lungs and help you purify your blood, etc, but to steady what yogis call *nādīs*. *Nādīs* are extremely difficult to define or demonstrate. *Nādī* has been translated into nerve, artery and vein, but it actually means something like a river, which flows or like a light ray which flows onwards. Nerves don't flow. *Nādīs* can be compared to the sound waves which enter into this room now. If you had a transistor radio and switched it on, the radio would pick up the sound waves (or radio waves). Something like that happens within your astral body. That is a *nādī*.

Prāṇāyāma exercises are supposed to purify those *nādīs*, not just your nerves. Incidentally, these are all side benefits. When you are doing your postures you are being spiritually awakened, but your body also benefits. I would call it a fringe benefit, not the real benefit. In the same way, when you do the *prāṇāyāma* exercises, the mind becomes steady and the *nādīs* become purified. That the nerves and mind are also calmed is a fringe benefit.

The *prāṇāyāma* exercises have a tremendous meaning. Therefore one who does *prāṇāyāma* or breathing exercises as part of yoga has to approach it in a different way—not merely use these as breathing exercises, but as a part of a spiritual adventure. By the practice of *prāṇāyāma* you come face-to-face with the power we call *prāṇa.* You know that *prāṇa.* It is not possible for anyone to show you, but within you you will realise what it is.

When you concentrate your mind on the various plexuses during the *prāṇāyāma* exercises, *prāṇa* flows into them, following the mind. Patanjali says we should have a steady posture before attempting *prāṇāyāma,* because when you begin to practise, the *prāṇa* vibrates more powerfully. With a little practice you will actually feel power being concentrated there.

If you find it difficult to look within and discover this *prāṇa,* use the following method: as you breathe in and out normally, see if you can become aware of the exact moment when inhalation becomes exhalation, and exhalation becomes inhalation. At that point you will find *prāṇa.* The brain has no function here at all.

There is another method. When you inhale until you cannot go on any more, what makes you stop? That is *prāṇā.* Hold the breath, making the whole body like a full pot. How long must you hold? The holding must be as long as possible, which means *you* should not exhale, *prāṇa* should force the exhalation. At that point, if the observation is keen, there is direct understanding 'this is *prāṇa*'. (Don't worry. You won't die before your time is up, and when the time is up nothing will save you!)

Patanjali suggests an exercise in which there is interruption of the inhalation and exhalation. Slowly start to inhale, and stop. Continue to inhale, stop. This can be repeated until the inhalation is complete. Repeat the practice as many times as is comfortable for you. Then similarly interrupt the flow of the exhalation.)It is important that you do not exceed your limits. Watch to see that the breath remains even and smooth. If it becomes jerky, you have exceeded your limits. Stop immediately and do not practise this till the next day.)

The **Hatha Yoga Pradipika**, the ancient Scripture of Hatha Yoga, describes *prāṇāyāma* as three-fold: inhale, retain, exhale through alternate nostrils. (This *prāṇāyāma* is usually associated with Raja Yoga, though Patanjali does not mention this.) While exhaling and inhaling in the alternate nostril breathing, watch and observe this inner intelligence and its functioning. How beautiful this breathing is! Even this perennial action of breathing is beyond the ego. If you have realised this intelligence, then *prāṇāyāma* will lead you to *samādhi*. If there is foolishness in your mind, the foolishness is removed by practice of this *prāṇāyāma*. It reveals to you that you are not living because you want to, but because something has willed all this into being—call it God, *Brahman, Átman* or anything you like. Become conscious of that.

So *prāṇāyāma* is not merely filling of the lungs, the oxygenation of the blood, and holding your nostrils, but is something which covers the whole of life—and death. (It was considered so important that it was woven into the daily life and worship of the Indian.) *Prāṇāyāma* must lead to the clarification of the mind, so that the next time you ask yourself, "Where does a thought arise?", "How does a neurological phenomenon become a psychological factor?" the questions are more meaningful.

We are living mechanically, not knowing what life is, but somehow with the deluded idea or notion that this life is ours. Then we become aware of this breathing. In order to become aware of this, you have to upset that somehow. The yogi would like to introduce awareness into it and deliberately upset that process, stop it, prolong it, make it short; you can do anything you like and that is *prāṇāyāma.*

If you continue to breathe mechanically you will also continue to think mechanically, automatically and therefore you will continue to be a slave to thoughts whose presence you don't know, whose origin you don't know, whose operation you don't know.

It is possible to arouse the awareness by getting hold of this breath and twisting it. There is a constant will to live and there is fear of death. Can that also be interfered with so that you have neither will to live, nor fear of death? Can that also be reversed? You are not afraid to die and you do not long to live. Once you tinker with this, challenge it, you realise that the ego is impotent and it can do nothing, faced with the life force; then you surrender. When you do that, once again you come face to face with this *prāṇa.* That can be achieved by challenging the life force in any manner you like so that instead of mechanically and automatically living, you become conscious of life—this is the life force that is functioning. At that point one realises 'It is not *my* life'.

Once you challenge and get to know this divinity that is in you—making you breathe, making you eat, making you do all sorts of things—you become aware that it is not your slave, your creation. Then you consciously surrender the whole thing to that life force. But this time you are fearless. To begin with the fear was hidden, but now you are truly fearless, knowing that the life force is capable of handling all situations. (I am not suggesting that the yogi is a foolhardy adventurer.)

So *prāṇāyāma* is not merely control of breath, but direct perception of the life principle—the life principle again being part of this cosmic stream which has been crystallised by the ego. By catching hold of that breath, that life-force, once again you are trying to break through this tangle of ego-sense.

All these practices are very healthy and can be of tremendous help provided we use them as fortresses or aids, and do not let them possess us, do not let them strengthen the ego sense. Every one of these practices must thin out this ego sense. But if we foolishly allow these very instruments of thinning out the ego to make it firmer and stronger, we have missed the central essence and core of yoga.

II. 50 bāhyā 'bhyantara staṁbhavṛttir deśa kāla saṁkhyābhiḥ paridṛṣṭo dīrgha sūkṣmaḥ

Different techniques involve holding the breath <u>within</u> (after inhalation), or <u>without</u> (after exhalation), or the <u>suspension</u> of the breath, with conscious effort. There are different types, too, some <u>prolonged</u>, some <u>subtle</u> (short)—different also in regard to the <u>place</u> where the breath is held, the <u>duration</u> of the retention, and the <u>number</u> of times it is practised.

Prāṇa is not just the breath, and the *prāṇāyāma* exercises that you do are not intended to 'fill you with *prāṇa*'. If we can practise these *prāṇāyāma* exercises with inner awareness of what happens, perhaps they will be more meaningful.

The breath can be held at different parts of the body—at the tip of the nose, in the throat or at the root of the tongue, in the middle of the chest, in the solar plexus or even below that. You can actually feel it. All these have their own different effects.

The suspension of breath or breathing may be external or internal. The **Yoga Vāsiṣṭha** mentions specifically that the inhaled breath does not start at the tip of your nose. Twelve finger breadths from your body there is a magnetic field. The *prāṇa* starts from there, so when you exhale your breath it is held twelve inches away from your body. If you are serious about this, please try it. When you exhale and hold your breath (as we do sometimes) fix the mind there. You will be a lot more relaxed (if nothing else). Because you are not holding the breath at the tip of your nose, your concentration or your attention is outside you, so it is much easier to hold the breath. That is, your lungs are empty, your life force is empty (as it were) and held outside your body, as it were. At first it is 'as it were', but the yogi assure us that sometime it will really be so.

Then you draw the *prāṇa* in and hold it in your heart. That is internal retention or suspension of breath. It is impossible to do this mechanically. It is impossible for you not to become aware of everything when you are doing this—your whole body is tingling. The effort of holding the breath itself keeps you awake and alert.

The yogi deliberately introduces all these regulations—maybe for other reasons—but definitely to make you understand what is meant by thought and will interference. So what was automatic, mechanical breathing is first brought into the field of observation, and in that field of observation you try to manipulate it so that that observation (which is still observing the breathing) becomes familiar with this phenomenon of mind or thought interference. Then you let the whole thing go, and only the observation remains. There is no control, restraint or regulation, just this pure observation. This observation prevents (if one may use that expression) thought- or will-interference. The breathing goes on smoothly, straight on from the intelligence within you. That happens already in *prāṇāyāma*; and therefore Patanjali said that it will lead you straight on to concentration (*dhāraṇa*). [In the case of other sense functions, it may be useful if one cultivates this power of internal observation which does not interfere in the sense function.]

Prāṇāyāma can be used for all these purposes, but essentially it is meant to discover the activity of the self. *Prāṇāyāma* knocks the mind completely down, and by becoming aware of it, one with it, tasting it, it is possible to continue that state of mind. That way you can almost reach the source of the self. It is with the help of *prāṇa* that the self plays its games.

II. 51 bāhyā 'bhyantara viṣayā 'kṣepi caturthaḥ

There is a fourth type which is the spontaneous suspension of breath, while minutely observing something external or internal.'

The fourth type of *prāṇāyāma* does not involve holding your nostrils, inhaling, exhaling, retention, etc., but the spontaneous, total suspension of breathing without any effort, while you are keenly contemplating something either within you or outside of you. Any keen, total, one-pointed observation is accompanied by slowing down or even suspension of breath.

II. 52 tataḥ kṣīyate prakāśā 'varaṇaṁ

Then, the veil of psychic impurity and spiritual ignorance that covers the inner light is thinned and rent asunder

Prāṇāyāma is meant only to remove the veil of ignorance that covers the inner light or reality. It is because the inner light is covered over by a veil that the self arises and plays. When you practise *prāṇāyāma* in this manner the veil disappears, and the inner light that had been veiled is revealed, so there is clarity of perception and understanding. The mind and the intelligence become clear. If through *prāṇāyāma* that veil is removed, then in the inner light one sees that there is no self. At the same time the faculty is aroused which enables one to meditate deeply.

While you go on practising this *prāṇāyāma* the whole attention is concentrated and focussed within you, and therefore you must become aware of the thought processes also. If that inner veil is not lifted, and if there is no self awareness (or awareness of the rise and fall of thoughts within you), then you are not practising *prāṇāyāma*.

II. 53 dhāraṇāsu ca yogyatā manasaḥ

And, the mind attains the ability to concentrate, to focus its attention.

By the practice of *prāṇāyāma* you become eligible for the practice of *dhāraṇa* or concentration. With the help of what appears to be a purely physiological process—breathing—the yogi leads us on to direct observation of the mind and immediate concentration of the life force and the mind. That already makes it no-mind.

You are not told here that if you practise *prāṇāyāma* your lungs will expand, your asthma will go or you will start flying in the air, but the faculty is aroused which enables one to concentrate deeply. It aids contemplation and removes distractions, so it becomes easy to meditate. Again the same thing! Throughout the Yoga Sūtras the simplest message is,"*Practise yoga in order that these obstacles may be removed.*" When the obstacles are removed you see your self (which may mean the non-existence of a self) and life becomes enlightened. That is all! There are no gimmicks, it's an extremely simple, sane and beautiful definition of yoga: "*When your inner obstacles are removed, contemplation becomes easy.*" When we have learned the art of turning the mind and the senses inwards upon the mind itself, then we begin this inner work.

Once we have reached this stage we learn how to concentrate and how to meditate, how to be able to look within; how to shut out background music and how to be able to listen to the music and not to the speaker! There are innumerable exercises for concentration or introversion of the mind.

This suggests the skipping of the next limb, *pratyāhāra*, which is the gathering in of the rays of one's attention. There is a definite suggestion in the Yoga Sūtras that though *pratyāhāra* is mentioned (for the sake of scientific description of the total structure of yoga), the effective practice of *prāṇāyāma* itself achieves that, because *pratyāhāra* happens when you practise *prāṇāyāma*.

II. 54 sva viṣayāsaṁprayoge citta svarūpānukāra ive 'ndriyāṇāṁ pratyāhāraḥ

There is psychological freedom when the senses function spontaneously in complete harmony with the inherent intelligence (without thought- or will-interference) without being drawn into contact with their objects by cravings or false evaluations. This freedom is the fountain-source of energy since in it there is effortless (and therefore non-) movement of the energy.

Normally, the attention is extroverted. You are conscious of another, not of yourself. You are thinking in terms of external objects, not in terms of the perceiving subject. As you practise *prāṇāyāma,* this attention turns inward. This is *pratyāhāra.*

I do not know if it is possible to accept the usual translation of *pratyāhāra* as 'abstraction of the senses or the mind'. We don't know what that means. It has also been rather simply translated as withdrawal of the senses from their objects. What does it mean? When you open the eyes they see. What must you do now to withdraw the sense of sight from seeing? You cannot stop the eyes from seeing!

Pratyāhāra is not terribly difficult, nor is it a strange mystic practice that one is unfamiliar with. It happens to us very often, but because we pay no attention it seems to be strange or difficult when it is described to us. For instance, it happens when you are eating something and at the same time you are listening to some music in which you are keenly interested. You are so deeply absorbed in the music that the food is beineaten without your awareness. (However, if a pebble goes into the mouth with the food, it is spat out!) During that period your mind is not interfering with the business of eating, which happens without desire or ego interference. In other words the senses, being linked to the subconscious mind (whatever it is) or to the inner intelligence, function in their own pure, natural state. That intelligence flows, unhampered by value judgements or intellectual perversion. The intelligence functions purely, simply, absolutely beautifully. We all experience it every day without being aware of it.

The eyes are endowed with the faculty of seeing, the nose is endowed with the faculty of smelling, the ears of hearing. The whole thing is the intelligence. It is the intelligence that operates through the eyes, etc. Can you become aware of that without making unreal distinctions (e.g. that is beautiful, this is ugly etc.)? When the vision and the hearing etc. become pure and non-discriminating, without introducing divisions which do not exist, the senses do not recognise good and evil, beauty and ugliness, etc. If the division between the mind and the senses disappears, if they function as one unit, that is *pratyāhāra*. You can't will yourself into this or practise it, but you *can* practise the following:

Look at a cushion, for instance, and decide whether it is beautiful or ugly. Allow other thoughts regarding it to come into your mind. Then you realise that in all that, judgement is involved. Something is accepted and something is rejected. In this thing called acceptance and rejection a lot of energy is wasted. So the yogi says, "Now that you discover the operation of this perversion, go to the other extreme. Look at that without even thinking of what it is." If you can look at that cushion and refuse to let the word 'cushion' arise in your mind, your attention is not focussed on whatever it is in front of you, but on the mind, where the idea of cushion arises. Therefore, since the attention is totally focussed within yourself, you won't see the cushion. When you do that it is possible for a few moments completely to forget to see the cushion. This has come to be known as *pratyāhāra* in orthodox yoga circles.

However, if the yogi is a person who functions in this world, it is hardly fair to expect him to sit and live in a world of abstraction. Here awareness is aware merely of the source of the action or the experience. A natural change takes place. The senses function as if they are in total alignment and complete harmony with the *citta*—the undivided, indivisible intelligence. This can only refer to the fundamental principal of yoga. Do not divide the world or your own intelligence into good, bad, this, that, pleasant, unpleasant. It does not mean suppressing the *citta* or intelligence, it means that there is no mind or ego interference. When that happens, of course the ego reveals its nature. The awakened intelligence sees the thousand ways in which the ego tries to step in and pollute actions and experiences. There is psychological freedom and abundant energy.

II. 55 tataḥ paramā vaśyate 'ndriyāṇāṃ

With such an abundance of energy it follows that there is complete mastery (in the sense of ever-vigilant understanding) over the senses, as all psychological conflicts and confused movements of thought and energy cease, and the senses function intelligently without disorder and disharmony, inhibitions and excitation.

Then the senses function naturally, and that natural function brings about natural order and a natural control. (Let us use the word 'order' in preference to control.) in an orderly manner, there is no disorder or conflict within oneself. *Vaśyate* means 'to win'—it does not mean control or conquer, which have an aggressive tone. You are not fighting at all with any of these *indriya,* but you have won them over. The inner intelligence has won over the senses and the body, so that it doesn't want to function in a disorderly way. There is pleasure and delight in co-operation, in harmony. When you become aware of this delight, the mind and the senses do not want to interfere with that harmony.

First become aware of the disorder; when you do, already there is some kind of interference with what goes on within. This is what is mostly misunderstood. So the yogi says become aware of it, see what disorder feels like. In order to become aware of disorder you have to jump into it and experience it. Then when this observation becomes pure, in that light the disorder is cleared by itself. You don't want it, your attention is not there anymore and there is pure observation. This pure observation merely loves inner order and harmony and that love wins over your whole personality. So no part of your being wants to create or sustain disharmony any more.

CHAPTER THREE

III. 1 deśa bandhaś cittasya dhāraṇā

When the attention of the mind stuff is directed in a single stream to a chosen field, without being dissipated and thus distracted—that is concentration.

Now we are ready to enter into the inner chamber of yoga. The sixth step or limb is *dhāraṇā,* which is focusing the mind. If you hold a magnifying glass above a piece of paper and move it up and down, you will see that when it is either very close to the paper or very far away, it becomes transparent—which means it behaves like ordinary glass and the light which passes through that glass is spread out. In our case the mind functions like that. The attention is dissipated, spread out. But when you hold the magnifying glass in such a way that the light is concentrated and there is a pinpoint of light on the paper under the glass, you find that there is tremendous light at one point, and all around it is dark. That is what Patanjali refers to as *dhāraṇā*. The space around is completely dark—which means that the attention is not dissipated.

This is something with which we are familiar. For instance, if in a lecture you pay complete attention to what the speaker is saying, you probably won't hear the sound of the traffic; when you hear that, what the speaker is saying

The mind will hardly remain steady for a few minutes! It has its own subtle ways of slipping from your grip. A positive help in holding the mind is to fix it on an image of God. Even here, for the purpose of concentration, the mind should not be allowed to think various thoughts even concerning the image of God. That can come later, after you have learnt the technique of concentration. Here, again, a *mantra* is invaluable. Repeat the *mantra* and visualise the image of God in your heart or between the eyebrows; fix the mind there.

Evolve your own method to effect a conditional reflex with which to train the mind. Take a few deep breaths, look at a holy picture, sing a hymn, recite a *mantra* (first audibly and then mentally); all or any one of these must be done and persistently associated with the concentration practice so that once the signal is given the mind begins to get into the meditative mood.

Watching the breath or listening to your own breathing is one of the most powerful ways of steadying the mind. Start with this: first, watch the flow of the breath in and out. Mentally follow the breath right from the tip of the nose to the edge of the lungs. Become one with the breath, as it were. Then detach yourself from it and stand as a witness of this flow. Listen to the sound of soundless breathing. Slip the *mantra* into the breath now, and let the mind repeat the *mantra* along with the breath, rhythmically. One part of the mind repeats the *mantra* and the other listens to it. The sound must be clearly heard within. Now visualise the image of God or some such focal point within. Let this be radiant. Try to fix the mind there. If it wants to run away, do not encourage it or resist it. "*Gently and firmly bring it back to the object of meditation,*" says Kṛṣṇa in the Bhagavad

Gita. Wrestling with the mind will only succeed in driving it farther away. Go on with watching or listening to the breath and visualising the focal point. How long will the mind wander? It will eventually come under your control.

There is need for intense concentration. In order to bring about that concentration there is need for tremendous energy. Where there is such energy there is also concentration. These two—concentration and energy—feed upon one another. Intense attention is not possible if the rays of the mind and the inner energy are dissipated. Let us go back to the analogy of holding a magnifying glass in the sun. When the solar energy is concentrated it becomes powerful, the energy is released and the paper is burnt. When the mind is concentrating on something very seriously, the energy that is functioning through the other sense organs is temporarily withdrawn from them, so that the whole of the energy may be available to that one faculty which deals with the particular problem of the moment. By the practice of *prāṇāyāma, āsana*, etc., the attention is focused and dissipation of energy is prevented.

Once again you see that concentration applies to *yama, niyama, āsana, prāṇāyāma, pratyāhāra*; in fact to everything. It is not as though it is something which has to be practised after *prāṇāyāma*. It is necessary right throughout our whole practice.

If the yoga *āsanas* are performed with tremendous attention to what is happening—where some pain or discomfort is—then the *āsana* becomes efficient. In the same way, if you concentrate on *prāṇāyāma* as you do it, this *prāṇāyāma* becomes something cosmic. You are no longer concerned about the little wind pipe and the two small lungs, but it is as if the whole universe is inhaling and exhaling.

But one mysterious element is really needed in this practice, and that is interest, affection, love. Probably the ancient yogi introduced the element of God into it in order to inspire that love. If that love and affection is not there, the focusing of one's attention may not be so easy. You can violently coerce your attention to be focused on something, but then it is rearing to jump off at a tangent.

When you practise *dhāraṇā* you will understand others. When you realise God you will understand Him also. You will not want to play miracles, because you will understand why God wills that these things should happen. You will do nothing which is not God's will.

Dhāraṇā is the preliminary for *dhyāna,* meditation. Though we can practise concentration, meditation cannot be practised, it has to *happen.* If we prevent the distractions from arising we have created the atmosphere or field conducive to meditation, and in that favourable atmosphere it is possible that it *can* happen. (*See Appendix for more on concentration.)

III. 2 tatra pratyayai 'katānatā dhyānaṁ

When the cognition is entirely concentrated in that field thus becoming its own field of observation—that is, when the observer is observe—it is meditation.

Dhyāna or meditation is the most discussed topic among spiritual aspirants. It is often made to sound extremely simple. People believe, without the least reservation, that they 'enjoyed a good meditation this morning'. They seldom realise what true meditation is and how rare it is in the life of the average spiritual aspirant. (I do not say this to discourage, but to prevent self-deception.) Yet, meditation *is* possible. By the grace of God and *guru,* all of us might one day enjoy real, deep meditation. It is through that door that all of us have to pass from earthly body-consciousness—sooner or later! It is the goal of all yoga, whatever be the actual path chosen.

Meditation is indescribable. The risk in description is that the description becomes a reality; then, either you get frustrated because it doesn't become your experience, or—which is a greater danger—you *imagine* that you are experiencing it. Where there is no sincerity there is always misunderstanding.

One question can be disposed of here. Is meditation like self-hypnosis? The yogi says no. In this ocean of one cosmic being, the wave has already hypnotised itself into an independent entity. You are the cosmic being, but you have hypnotised yourself already into a self-limited personality. Therefore the yoga of meditation is not self-hypnotisation, but self-*de*hypnotisation.

Men of great achievement in any walk of life have experienced moments of deep meditation. Scientists, artists, mystics, devotees and others have 'lost themselves in their ideal'. It is like the tranquillity of a baby playing with an interesting new toy. The yogi wants to achieve this mind-control and tranquillity by a deliberate and conscious effort and direction.

Meditation will happen if the ground is ready and the distractions do not arise. In the initial stages you are battling with these distractions all the time. At one point you realise that the battling *itself* keeps the distractions going! Then you abandon your attention to these distractions, and focus it on the *mantra* or the object of meditation. That is all you can do. The rest of it has to happen by God's grace.

The moment you introduce an aim or a goal to meditation, meditation does not happen; and yet without introducing that, there is no trigger! The problem with the idea of a goal is that we are concentrating on *that,* rather than on what we are supposed to be concentrating on. For instance, if our goal is to be more relaxed, we are sitting tensely, waiting for relaxation to happen. It doesn't!

There is a very simple way to illustrate this: laughing means that the face assumes a certain shape, but if I want to make you laugh I don't pull your cheeks, but tickle your foot. Freedom from tension is not achieved by trying to work on the tension itself—you will become more tense; concentration of mind is not achieved by concentrating the mind but by doing something completely different. This seems to be the fundamental secret to meditation; and that is what the great masters of yoga suggested when they said to sit down and repeat your *mantra.* While you pay attention to the *mantra*—which is totally unrelated and unconnected with the problem—the problem gets dissolved.

The most important thing in meditation is not to try to solve the outside problem, but to taste the present mood of peace, joy and happiness that is flowing inside you.

The mind is one substance which seems to assume several successively different disguises. At any one time the mind can only be in a certain mood, it cannot be in two moods together. The master, by suggesting that you sit down and repeat your *mantra,* has made you temporarily forget your problem. A problem that is forgotten does not exist. Suddenly you discover that the unhappiness is not there any more. You realise that something in you is totally independent of the happiness or unhappiness that the environment imposes upon you. That is beautiful.

So meditation is a very simple way of getting rid of the problems that we create for ourselves. It is not as if the problems that face us every day can ever be removed, but the inner attitude can be radically and instantly changed. Meditation makes that possible by turning the attention to something completely different (which happens to be the source of all our problems), not by dealing with the problem head on.

Can you live in such a way that it does not create any problems for you or for anybody else? That is possible by the constant and diligent cultivation of this awareness. In the beginning it looks as though it takes a lot of effort; for every step you go forward, you seem to slip two behind. But practised with intelligence even the failures become successes. There is no failure, and no obstacles to the yogi, because if he falls asleep in meditation or reacts if he is insulted, he is going to contemplate that. That also becomes a starting point for meditation. So whatever happens in life becomes a starting point for meditation. In fact, therefore, there are no obstacles to real yoga practice. Whatever happens, pleasurable or painful, the self-awareness continues. The only failure is failure to be aware of this.

In meditation or outside meditation, in life or outside life, there is no attempt to 'get rid' of thought. Getting rid of thought is like sweeping all the waves away from the ocean.

Half the problem connected with meditation springs from thinking about it. Meditation is not the thoughts that one may have *about* meditation. It is possible to think about it, it is possible to talk about it and it is even possible to 'do' it, but none of these is *meditation*. Like sleep, it is something that has to happen. One does not know when it is happening, but in retrospect one realises that *something* has happened. For instance, when you sleep you do not know you are sleeping; if you know, you are not sleeping! On waking up the next morning you realise that you must have been sleeping. Even then you don't *know* you were sleeping, you only think you must have been.

What is it that puts an end to meditation? Strangely enough, the desire to experience meditation. It is just like what puts an end to sleep. In sleep one is at peace within oneself, there is great inner calm, happiness and joy. Somehow there is a desire to experience that joy, and peace—and that is when you wake up.

We are trapped in a strange and delightful problem. You need to meditate, but you cannot will yourself into meditation. Meditation is vitally important—not only to those of you who might be what you call 'spiritual seekers', but to those who want to become more alert in mind and intellect. Meditation is probably very important even to people who pursue what they call material goals. If meditation is a state in which there is no mental confusion, but inner harmony and peace, then it is of vital importance to everybody. Whatever be your aspirations—spiritual, intellectual, mental or material—one who knows what it is to meditate (or what it is to surrender oneself to meditation) realises that the key to any achievement lies there. But fortunately (or unfortunately) it is not possible to *do* it.

To begin with, it is extremely fortunate that this thing cannot be made to happen, for the simple reason that, if it could, it would be liable to be marketed (as we have already seen it being done) and what is worse, it could be misused and abused. It is unfortunate that though we aspire for this state called meditation it seems to elude us, and we are groping all the time.

Patanjali gives us complete freedom of choice of the object of meditation.

It is usual for the yogi to use a *mantra,* and many recommend the *mantra sōhaṃ. Sōhaṃ* is not a thing you repeat with your mind, but if you listen to your breathing you hear it repeating *sōhaṃ* already. Here I would like to introduce one thought: it is not that the mind or the attention is constantly repeating *sōhaṃ,* but you are listening to the breath saying *sōhaṃ*—'*s ō*' when you inhale, and '*haṃ*' when you exhale. *Japa* (repetition of a *mantra*) itself will lead you to meditation. It brings God's grace down upon you. Without His grace, no meditation is possible.

Before meditation can happen, the mind has to be concentrated. In the beginning the attention needs to be brought within the body. It is possible while sitting on a chair to wonder if the chair is soft or hard. The moment you think this, you find your attention sinking into your bottom. You suddenly begin to feel—for the first time perhaps—that there is a bottom on which you sit, and the bottom sits on something else. Immediately you find the attention gathering itself within you. (Why should we do that? Why not think of the other side of the moon, for example? For the simple reason that if the attention is focused on a small area it may be more manageable. It is as simple as that.) The attention is brought within the body and once that attention is narrowed down, you realise that only one thing is happening—you are breathing.

Then, sitting very comfortably you become aware of the body, of the seat and the cushion, of the sensation of the hands on the knees (or the lap). When you do that the attention returns to the body. That is the first step.

Now that the body has been taken care of, what does the mind do? There is a simple basic technique. The first and most intriguing discovery that you make when you sit down for your meditation is that the body is here, but the mind is elsewhere. How do we bring the attention back to where we are, here and now? (The body can only be here and now, it cannot be elsewhere.) How does one gather the attention and bring it into a certain field where it can be attentive?

Second step, you are breathing. Can you become more aware of it? In order to do this you must literally follow the breath from the time it touches the nostrils and enters into the lungs, until it flows out again. You can also visualise the lungs getting filled and getting emptied. Then the attention becomes even more sharply focused within yourself.

As you go on listening to the breath, if you have a *mantra*, like OM, you hear that sound within yourself. Become more and more deeply aware of this sound. Listen to it with all your heart, with all your attention. As you do so, if there are other thoughts intruding you can almost see them. Ignore them, continue paying attention to the *mantra*. Even here you will find that if there is an intruding thought you cannot fight it! So carry on with the *mantra* and the intruding thought will go.

You are watching the breath, listening to it with wonder. The spirit of wonder is the very essence of mysticism. The mind which says 'I know' is far away from all this—the arrogance of knowledge is the complete block to mysticism. The mind that begins to wonder can graduate from wonder to surrender, and reach somewhere.

As the yogi listens to the breathing with wonder, he

merely hears a *mantra*, a word. Now, there is a very serious problem. Sound is always produced by two things coming into contact, even if it is the air and something else—air and the vocal cords or the surface of a pipe. That is what sound means! When you hear a *mantra* within you, what is that sound made of?

If you are not interested in yoga theories, even when you are talking to yourself mentally, there is a sound. You hear those words. What is that sound made of? You can have your theories, but theories are not knowledge. The only honest answer to this question is 'I don't know.'

The yogi merely suggests that you don't try any more. Surrender yourself to that sound in total wonderment. At that moment the mental chattering comes to an end in wonderment and total surrender, and meditation happens.

Meditation is not thinking or contemplation, but enabling awareness to function within the object of concentration. It is the flow of the mind-stuff towards the object of meditation. You know the popular expression: 'Meditate upon a rose.' You can sit upon a rose if you are a bee, but you can't *meditate* upon a rose. Such expressions *are* used, however. What Patanjali demands is that you should meditate yourself *into* a rose. There is no effort or exercise of the individual will, but complete and total surrender to the Divine. Meditation is offering oneself to the Divine: *samādhi* is His gift, the fruit of His grace.

It is important to surrender, neither to conceptualise this thing called meditation nor to make it into a state or a dualistic experience. You hear the *mantra*. If you are repeating the *mantra* mentally, how is it that you are able to listen to it? Is there a split personality? How can you listen to something that you are saying yourself? When you are speaking aloud, the sound vibrations come out of your mouth and enter into the ears, but when the whole thing is happening within you, how is there a space or division within you?

Once again, one thinks of sleep. In sleep, no one says, "I am sleeping." No one experiences sleep in a dualistic way. It is when that dualistic experience is abandoned—or drops away—that this homogeneous experience of sleep takes place. That must happen in meditation. Whether you are using a *mantra* or merely listening to the breathing, whatever be the method you use, the division between the experiencer and the experience must completely disappear. When that happens there is meditation. At that point even the seeker must disappear, must surrender himself to that which is being sought. Hence the tremendous insistence upon surrender. (See also Sūtras II. 1 and II. 32)

He who learns this simple lesson from any type of practice of meditation, learns also that such surrender is the essence of peace, harmony, joy, happiness, efficiency and bliss, in life itself. Once this has happened it is possible that this spirit of meditation continues throughout the day, and the whole life becomes meditation. This means that while you are sitting and practising this as an exercise, the *mantra* (or the form of God) is the object of meditation. When you come out of your meditation room, whatever you do at the moment becomes the object of your meditation. Even what you and I may practise while being seated is meant as a help.

While talking, one should observe the arising of the 'I'. While eating and seeing, where does the feeling or thought, 'I am seeing him, I am talking here', arise? This is supposed to be done continually. We are assured by masters (again this can be a danger) that if you continually observe the arising of the 'I' during the waking hours—whatever you are doing—then it is possible to extend this consciousness through dreams. I am dreaming: to whom is the dream occurring? Who is dreaming? And then it is possible to extend this consciousness eventually even through sleep. That continuous self-consciousness is called *samādhi.*

So meditation is not to be confined to a certain time of the day or to a certain part of the house, but that is where you learnt the simple art of how to live totally. That spirit continues throughout the day. Later you will be able to meditate while talking and even then the intensity of concentration will be experienced, so that the attention is completely and totally focused upon your meditation subject. The attention may shift from one object to another, but every time there is total attention to that particular thing. Then one leads a divine life.

Useful Hints

It is possible to give a few hints which can leave the door open for meditation to come in, but even these are like preparing the bed as an invitation to sleep. You cannot 'go to sleep'. It is an expression—inadequate and erroneous—as all expressions are. Sleep has to come. You can only go to bed.

It is very necessary to have good posture—an upright posture, but not as 'stiff as a ramrod'. The yogi wants you to keep the back straight. All sorts of interesting reasons have been given, and one might be of interest to you. If the small of the back is held in, your back is naturally straighter than before, and it seems to promote alertness of the mind. The moment you slouch, the small of the back shoots backward, the spine curves forward and your alertness is gone. As long as the small of the back is moving forward, your mind is alert, whether you are sitting or standing. The small of the back holds the key, and therefore the yogi says to sit erect. Always try to meditate at the same time of day, at the same place and wearing the same clothes, so that the mind quickly enters into the meditative mood.

There are innumerable techniques, hints and suggestions. These are all necessary because each person has a different outlook and problem. What I say may be irrelevant to you, and you may have to evolve your own technique, knowing that these are all just techniques.

(*See Appendix for more meditation techniques.)

III. 3 tad evā 'rthamātranirbhāsaṁ svarūpa śūnyamiva samādhiḥ

When the field of observation and the observing intelligence merge as if their own form is abolished and the total intelligence shines as the sole substance or reality, there is pure choiceless awareness without the divided identity of the observer and the observe—that is illumination.

Concentration (*dhāraṇā*) is described as narrowness—it is a tying of the mind to a limited field. Meditation (*dhyāna*) is getting into it, becoming saturated with it, ensuring that only one thought, concept (or just this 'I' feeling) prevails in that small area. In *samādhi* or super-consciousness this narrowness, or limitation, is suddenly destroyed.

Here are three illustrations which show the difference between concentration, meditation and *samādhi*.

1. A king who is drunk (and so has forgotten that he is the king) stands in front of his palace, not knowing what it is. Admiration compels his attention and he gazes fixedly at

it. This is concentration where he forgets himself and everything else. Then he enters the palace and roams about within it. This can be compared to meditation. (Note the difference between this and thinking: the meditator is *within* the object of meditation, as it were, and not standing outside thinking about it.) He goes into the throne room. By now the effect of the alcohol is finished. Suddenly he remembers 'Oh, I am the king', and realises that he himself is the owner of the palace. This can be compared to *samādhi* or superconscious experience of the reality.

2. Suppose a man is standing in front of his burning house. He will be looking at it with intense concentration. No distracting thought will be in his mind. This is concentration. Then he remembers that something important is in the house, so he runs into the fire. Now he is surrounded by the fire and is intensely conscious of the fire; he is not only thinking *of* the fire, but he is thinking *in* the fire. This is like meditation. Finally, his clothes catch on fire, his body is burning and becomes part of the fire. It *is* fire! This is like *samādhi*.

3. When you are looking at that which you call a tape recorder, when your consciousness or attention is focused entirely upon that, its field is restricted to the tape recorder and nothing else. There is concentration. When there is movement of consciousness within it, when your whole mind or *citta* takes the shape of that tape recorder, there is meditation. When even the 'I' has disappeared and only the tape recorder exists, that does not call itself a tape recorder. You are the tape recorder, everyone is the tape recorder, everything is the tape recorder; then the tape recorder*ness* of the tape recorder is gone. When 'I' does not exist, where is identification? *Svarūpa śūnyam iva*—as if the 'I' doesn't

exist; where what was earlier on regarded as an object *alone* exists. That is, where you don't exist and I don't exist, your identity is gone and my identity is gone, there is *samādhi*.

It is not as though the object alone exists. Objects cannot exist without a subject! What was earlier on regarded as an object alone exists. Therefore even the object*ness* of the object has gone—it doesn't have its own form and its own identity; I don't have my form and my identity. 'I' is no longer I, and 'you' is no longer you. The two ends of the same handkerchief are seen to be nothing more than handkerchief. When there is neither this end nor that end, only the handkerchief, then there is *samādhi*.

Samādhi has been variously translated as contemplation, deep meditation, super-consciousness, enlightenment, trance, ecstasy, imperturbableness, total calmness, the peace that passeth understanding, or where movement of thought completely ceases. It is where consciousness (we don't call it the mind at all) becomes directly aware of the mind (*citta*) which merely receives these impressions. And therefore, the knowledge is pure, undiluted, unpolluted, undistorted. That *samādhi* looks carefully at what makes this impression or impact on the *citta* and there is instantaneous knowledge; because when there is no movement or thought within, whatever impression is brought into the mind by the senses is looked at and is understood directly, without the intervention of memory, prejudice or value judgement.

There is intelligence in every cell of your body, and in every cell of your brain. Intelligence fills your whole being (body, mind and soul) and is capable of looking after the body, the mind and the world and all its affairs—from moment to moment, from day to day—without all these calculations, worries, anxieties and fears. But now we are not aware of this intelligence. We are only aware of what is called egotism—'I'. 'I' can do this. The 'I' depends upon the memory bank and the *buddhi* or adjudicator. When the latter is dispensed with there is instinctive, blind action which leads to endless regret and remorse. If all these things are seen for what they are, then they come to an end. The inner intelligence or *ātmā* (or whatever you wish to call it) shines within itself without any interference by the *citta* or the ego; from moment to moment it acts spontaneously, and such action is pure, beautiful, wonderful, loving.

Usually that is called the purest form of love. If you have ever experienced such pure love, perhaps as an afterthought you realised that for those moments neither 'I' nor the other person existed, there was only love. We have all experienced this, only we have passed through all these experiences without becoming aware of them. The yogi merely asks us to become aware of them. When you are aware of this, the one thing that created endless problems in your life—the ego-sense, 'I', 'mine—disappears, but nothing else disappears. That is the end of the yogi's practice.

A funny story is told. (It is pure fantasy, but it has a lesson.) A young village boy went to a great yogi, who was meditating. The boy sat in front of him and thought, "What peace and joy radiates from this man's face. I must also have that peace."

When the yogi opened his eyes the boy took hold of his feet and said, "I won't let you go until you teach me how to meditate."

The yogi agreed and took the young man into a room, where he taught him the *mantra:*

Ōṃ namo bhagavate Vāsudevaya.

The boy sat down and started to repeat the *mantra*. After

a few minutes he asked, "Then what must I do?"

"Mentally visualise Kṛṣṇa as you repeat the *mantra*."

An hour later the yogi called, "What are you doing there?"

"I can't concentrate."

"When you close your eyes, repeat a *mantra* and think of Kṛṣṇa, what happens to you?"

"I am a cow herd. We have a buffalo at home, with lovely horns. I grew up with it, and whenever I close my eyes it is all I can think about."

"Very good. Now repeat the *mantra* and meditate on the buffalo."

In a split second this boy entered into *samādhi,* because the buffalo was the form that his entire being loved. "*Thou shalt love the Lord with all thy heart, with all thy mind and with all thy being.*" That happened in his relationship with the buffalo.

The father came and said that the boy was needed to do work in the cow shed, so the yogi called the boy; but there was no response at all, because the boy had gone into a deep trance. Then the yogi disturbed this by some kind of trick, and told him to come out.

The boy said, "Sorry master, the door is too narrow and my horns are so large. How can I come out?"

The moral of this story is that he had lost his individuality or personality, as it were—*svarūpa śūnyam iva.*

Samādhi may or may not need one to sit with closed eyes in a dark room, because it is supposed to be practised throughout one's daily life, whatever one is doing. It is possible that the mind functions, the senses still continue to receive impressions, the *citta* is calm and still (so it doesn't interfere at all), and the innermost consciousness becomes immediately aware of every experience—the truth as it is—independent of previous experience, prejudice and bias. (It is simple if one approaches the whole thing without getting bamboozled and dazzled by the word *samādhi*.)

When *samādhi* is perpetual it keeps you constant company all the time, so that whatever happens you begin to see the truth—not opinions concerning it. For instance, you repeat a *mantra*; you hear the sound. *You* hear the sound? You are repeating the *mantra* and you are hearing the sound—it's absurd! The 'I' has gone; the *mantra* alone remains. You are in *samādhi*. Again, as you read a Scripture the words enter your brain and suddenly you discover that you are interpreting that Scripture in your own way, in terms of past memory. You smile at it, you laugh at it—and in a moment you are back in *samādhi* again.

So, in that intensity of attention only that exists which you have chosen to observe, as if even 'I' does not exist. When the object alone exists, it is obviously the subject, isn't it? What do we mean by 'the object alone exists'? It is like the example of the handkerchief again: that end is you, this end is me. When that end is gone and this end alone exists, what exists in reality is the middle, the handkerchief. The 'I' is assimilated in 'you', and 'you' is absorbed in 'me'. (Sorry for the grammar!) What remains is what is–and that is *samāḍhi*.

What happens now? The 'object of meditation' shines, independent of the subject-object relationship. In other words, the distorting media of desire, fear, hatred and delusion are removed, and there is 'knowledge' of *That*. Knowledge is rather an inefficient word to use here, because in our mind knowledge signifies a bridge that links the knower with the object of knowledge. In *samādhi* only one exists. You are welcome to assert that the subject has merged with the object (of meditation) or that the object has become one with the subject, or that both the subject and the object have been dissolved into knowledge or (as the philosopher designates it) Consciousness.

All superimposition of percepts and concepts on what *is* are removed; and *That* alone exists. Even the word 'knowledge' or its philosophical term 'consciousness' is used only to prevent sleep being mistaken for *samādhi*. In sleep there is absence of any knowledge. In *samādhi* there is consciousness alone, free from all limiting perceptual or conceptual thinking.

III. 4 trayam ekatra saṁyamaḥ

When these three happen together there is perfect inner discipline. This can happen during what is commonly known as the practice of meditation, and during any other form of physical or mental activity.

Concentration of mind is the indispensable preliminary to meditation. Concentration and meditation together form the steps leading to the ultimate in yoga—*samādhi* or superconscious state of awareness. These three are really not three different stages (for example, as *āsana* and *prāṇāyāma* are, completely different and independent), but three parts of one whole. It is true that one can concentrate without proceeding to meditation; but meditation is not possible without concentration. Similarly, it is possible to stop with meditation without ever reaching *samādhi*; but the latter is not possible without meditation.

These three—concentration, meditation and *samādhi*—together are called *saṁyama*. *Saṁyama* means 'thoroughly restrained'. We saw in Chapter Two that *yama* is self-discipline. The prefix '*saṁ*' invariably means something that is well done, that is proper and perfect. So here *saṁyama* means that the *yama* becomes 'well done', proper and perfect.

The spiritual aspirant, who commenced his spiritual journey with a zealous attempt at self-control, reaches perfection in that control when he practises *saṁyama*. Lord Kṛṣṇa decares in the Bhagavad Gita: "*The objects of the world do not worry the man who has starved the senses; but the taste of enjoyment remains. This taste is destroyed only after experience of the vision of the Supreme.*" So long as the taste remains, so long the control is not complete or perfect. Only in *saṁyama* is the control complete.

III. 5 taj jayāt prajñā lokaḥ

When such inner discipline is mastered, there arises the vision that is wisdom.

When concentration, meditation and *samādhi* are practised simultaneously, there is illumination, inner awareness, inner enlightenment. Knowledge being one, it is always gained where there is total oneness.

Meditation does not necessarily mean closing one's eyes and sitting up straight. It is the cultivation of an inner awareness every moment of your existence. If from moment to moment, whatever you are doing, this light of self-awareness shines in you—revealing to you what your mind is doing, how your emotions are disturbing your attitude to life and to your neighbours, etc.—then you are in a perpetual state of meditation; and yours is an enlightened life. The enlightened life will be characterised by all the virtues that are described in the yoga texts. Such a life is truly blessed.

III. 6 tasya bhūmiṣu viniyogaḥ

This vision, (or the eye of intuition, or the eye of wisdom, or the inner light) can be directed to many fields of observation.

Once you have acquired this mastery over *saṁyama,* and the whole matter of attention has been thoroughly disciplined, then that disciplined attention can be directed (not so much applied) to any branch of knowledge. Through that you can gain all kinds of insights.

Saṁyama can be directed to anything you like, and will produce results. If you are practising this, since your attention is focused in one direction on one particular object, and since your whole consciousness is filled with this object to such an extent that *you* don't exist—the object alone exists—you will know that object intimately, immediately, in its very essence.

(As a matter of scientific interest, later in the Third Chapter Patanjali details a few such fields in which such a disciplined attention can be used. Two or three—what Hatha Yoga describes as 'psychic centres'—are mentioned.)

III. 7 trayaṁ antaraṅgaṁ pūrvebhyaḥ

These three are inner spiritual practices compared to the other five already described viz., discipline, observances, posture, exercise of the life force and introversion of attention.

With *saṁyama* we enter into the inner chamber of yoga. These three practices are not external as are the other five: moral disciplines (*yama*), ethics (*niyama*), postures (*āsana*), control of breath (*prāṇāyāma*) and sense-control (*pratyāhāra*). All these greatly help concentration, (*dhāraṇā*) though practices like *āsana* and *prāṇāyāma* are not always indispensable.

III. 8 **tad api bahiraṅgaṁ nirbījasya**

But even these three are external to that enlightenment in which the very seed of duality ceases to exist.

III. 9 **vyutthāna nirodha saṁskārayor abhibhava prādurbhāvau nirodha kṣaṇa cittānvayo nirodhapariṇāmaḥ**

Here, again, it is possible to conceive of three stages, though such sequence is not inevitable. At first there is the effortless, though not mechanical, habit of shutting out an undesirable or disturbing thought. This ability rises when there is direct awareness of the moment of the rise of the movement of restraint and the cessation of the movement of thought, and thus there is the understanding of the dynamics of thought. This understanding itself is the formation of the faculty of restraint of undesired thoughts.

The method suggested is this: the noise of the traffic outside is annoying you. That it is annoying you means that it is a *saṁskāra*. (Compare I. 18) A *saṁskāra* is something that is part of your nature. It is not a revived memory or a thought which you can observe, it is built into you. You begin to see it, and then it slowly fades away. It faded away because you began to observe it!

The yogis realised that you cannot possibly get rid of all *saṁskāras*, so they said, "Create the opposite *saṁskāra*. Train yourself to be watchful." You have created the impression of annoyance which has now become aggressiveness. By repeatedly trying, acquire the *saṁskāra* of being peaceful, cheerful and loving, so that every time this aggressive *saṁskāra* comes up, the other one begins to work.

III. 10 **tasya praśāntavāhitā saṁskārāt**

Though at first this may seem to involve effort, struggle and striving, when the habit of restraint is formed, there is effortless, tranquil and spontaneous flow of the movement of restraint, and the prevention of the undesired movement of thought.

If you think of a see-saw you might discover the meaning of this Sūtra. It is like a see-saw. As the aggressive *saṁskāra* comes up, the love *saṁskāra* goes down; the love *saṁskāra* comes up, the aggressive *saṁskāra* goes down. You have created these two *saṁskāras* and you are playing with them. You still have no control over them, otherwise you would remain with love on top all the time! That is not possible, because the other one comes up when you are non-vigilant. (Tragedy strikes one's life when one least expects it, and one gets involved in accidents when one least expects them. If you are expecting accidents, and therefore driving carefully and vigilantly all the time, you will probably never get involved in an accident; when one is non-vigilant there is tragedy.)

As these two ends of the see-saw move slowly up and down, can you see that moment when both of these are on an equal footing? No. But, if you are extremely cautious and vigilant you can detect the moment at which one end goes up and the other comes down. That is all you can do. When you have learned to observe the *saṁskāra* of aggression and the *saṁskāra* which restrains this aggression, and are able to detect the precise moment when the latter comes up, you have taken the first step towards dealing with the *saṁskāra* (though not controlling it).

Now, for the moment you have cultivated this vigilance, and that vigilance in itself is very calm and peaceful—the observer is extremely calm and peaceful. This is not part of your *saṁskāra*, it is a different intelligence—it is neither the love that observes the aggressiveness nor the aggressiveness that observes the love. It is completely aloof from all this: therefore when those two *saṁskāras* keep playing like cat and mouse, there is a sense of tranquillity.

Again if your love *saṁskāra* is stronger it is able to keep the aggressive *saṁskāra* in abeyance, and therefore there is inner peace. You think you have mastered the technique. If you are very vigilant you may even keep it down for some time, but the mind is still scattered with so many distractions; and when the mind is distracted the aggressiveess suddenly jumps up again.

III. 11 sarvārthatai 'kāgratayoḥ kṣayo 'dayau cittasya samādhi pariṇāmaḥ

The second stage is the non-arising of distractions on account of the weakening of the numerous distracting thoughts, and the effortless and natural unidirectional flow of the mind-stuff. At this stage, the mind-stuff is favourably disposed towards illumination as the obstacles to such illumination are rendered inoperative.

You must learn the difference between scattered thinking and one-pointed attention, because only when the mind is one-pointed and concentrated can you learn to observe the *saṁskāra* itself—not merely take a fling, blindly hoping to hit it. Raising the love *saṁskāra* to counteract the *saṁskāra* of aggression is blind flinging, a 'hoping to hit it'. You have still not come to grips with the *saṁskāra* itself. In order to do this you must know how to concentrate the mind, how to prevent it from being distracted. Watch very carefully—when is the mind scattered, and when are all its energies one pointed? Then you learn what it is to contemplate.

To me the word 'contemplate' sounds very much like being in a temple: con-templ-ate. You must build this temple of contemplation and get into it—not stand outside and look at it. There you are whole, and the whole of your being is in this observation of the *saṁskāra.*

This process is nearly endless, whatever you do, because you have not come face to face with the *saṁskāra* itself. You are only dealing with its different manifestations, with the superficial impressions. How does one clean the mindstuff so that there is no conditioning, no *saṁskāra* at all?

III. 12 tataḥ punaḥ śānto 'ditau tulya pratyayau cittasyai 'kāgratā pariṇāmaḥ

When the two movements of thought-arising and thought-subsiding, the movements of distraction and restraint, are of equal force, the mind-stuff is in a perfectly balanced state, which is one of non-division or no-polarity. There is neither (volitional) thinking nor suppression of thought, and the intelligence has its natural, effortless unidirectional movement which is in fact no-movement.

That door is open to you when you are able to observe and discover for yourself the moment at which these two *saṁskāras* come to exactly the same level, when they are of exactly the same strength, perfectly balanced. Then the mind is neither distracted by the *saṁskāra* of aggression (the active *saṁskāra*), nor the counter *saṁskāra,* but it is in an absolutely quiet, peaceful state and there is total vigilance—not only concerning the *saṁskāra* which you wish to avoid or overcome, but in regard to even the *saṁskāra* you had planted deliberately to deal with the other one.

You are free. The criminal and the policeman are both thrown out of your house! When you have a thief in your house and you call the police you are not going to suggest that the policeman should kick the thief out and make himself at home in the house. You have the thief with you; get the policeman also and very carefully shove both of them out at the same time—not one after the other. Then you are free.

It is an interesting technique. If you create a mental picture of it and work with that mental picture it is no more valid than any other piece of memory. It is junk, useless!

Is it possible to change what you have accepted as your nature – i.e. violence, aggression or intolerance, easily being offended or easily offending others? Can you observe this? As soon as you observe it stirring within you, can you plant a restraining power, a restraining habit?

If you are intolerant and aggressive, it is often very difficult for you to deal with this straight away. But again, if you watch your behaviour fairly closely you might discover that intolerance also shows in some petty mannerisms – like biting your fingernails, for instance. So, in order to develop this habit of vigilance, tell yourself, "I'm not going to bite my fingernails any more." You may think that it is easy, but it is not. First, you will not know when you are doing it, but remind yourself after the event; and then gradually, by constantly reminding yourself after the event, it should be possible to remind yourself during the event, perhaps; and then (after sometime) just before.

When you learn to restrain it by habitually repeating this method of restraint, you become friendly with restraint and therefore there is greater peace of mind. You become less and less intolerant, less and less critical, less and less offensive, and therefore more peaceful. But that is nothing, because the *saṁskāra* is still there! So you learn to not let your mind be distracted and to keep a rigorous watch on this *saṁskāra.* Then you get into the state of *samādhi*; *samādhi* in the waking state, *samādhi* in life. you watch and see that there is this pendulum swinging all the time. You have brought about a complete change in your nature.

III. 13 etena bhūte 'ndriyeṣu dharma lakṣaṇā 'vasthā pariṇāmā vyākhyātāḥ

Thus (that is, by explaining the dynamics of thought) the nature, characteristics and changes in the states relating to all the cognitive faculties and their objects have been explained: for they are closely related to and are essentially non-different from the movement of thought in the mind-stuff.

III. 14 śānto 'ditā 'vyapadeśya dharmā 'nupātī dharmī

For a substance itself is put together and recognised as such by, and is non-different from, a particular characteristic which may be in a dormant state, in an emerging state or in an uncertain or potential state.

III. 15 kramānyatvaṁ pariṇāmānyatve hetuḥ

Surely, it is because of the existence of such a clear distinction of character of substances and of the order in the sequence of the changes, that there is predictability of the transformation.

III. 16 pariṇāma traya saṁyamād atītā 'nāgata jñānaṁ

Therefore, knowledge of the past and of the future (and such knowledge as not already possessed) follows the practice of threefold inner discipline (concentration, meditation, and illumination together) in relation to the fundamental principle of the three stages of the movement of thought—the movement of restraint, the non-arising of distractions, and the perfectly balanced state.

III. 17 śabdā 'rtha pratyayānām itare 'tarā 'dhyāsāt saṁkaras tat pravibhāga saṁyamāt sarva bhūta ruta jñānaṁ

Language, meaning and conceptualisation are always superimposed on one another, causing habit-patterns in communication. By the practice of the threefold inner discipline on their differences there arises an understanding of the sounds uttered by all beings.

III. 18 saṁskāra sākṣātkaraṇāt pūrva jāti jñānaṁ

By the practice of the threefold discipline on the inherent tendencies, and by the direct perception of such tendencies, knowledge of previous existence arises.

III. 19 pratyayasya para citta jñānaṁ

In an intimate knowledge of the ground of the Mind, there is what at first sight appears to be a supernatural knowledge of 'other' minds, too, because in fact the intelligence that is misunderstood as the mind is invisible.

When the *citta* is made calm and peaceful and the *prāṇa* is concentrated, the *prāṇa* acts upon the *citta* and you get subtle vision. If you practise *prāṇāyāma* and meditation every day you will get this very soon. If you watch yourself when you talk to other people, your *citta* will be clean and crystal-like and also extremely subtle. Because it is like a crystal it will reflect whatever object comes near it. You may develop powers of thought-reading, because when someone comes near you, you may reflect his thoughts. (Therefore, because the mind is like crystal, at that stage it is very necessary that you select your company. The thoughts and desires and motives of your friends will be reflected in your own mind.)

You will spontaneously be able to love and to understand everybody. Understanding is looking at the other man as he looks at himself. The result is that you will always be peaceful, you will not be upset by anybody. If a man comes and scolds you, you know why he does it. You look at it not as someone else looks at it, but as he looks at it himself. Only the yogi who has reached the stage of true *dhāraṇā* will be able to understand everybody and love everybody. That is what we are all interested in, though Patanjali extends it to other objects.

Any power that you get or use will take you away from God. Therefore, turn the whole practice towards God.

III. 20 na ca tat sā 'laṁbanaṁ tasya 'viṣayībhūtatvāt

This, however, does not imply particularised knowledge of the other personalities–e.g. the motivations, the conditioning or the background of the 'other' minds—for knowledge of the 'other' mind is impersonal and devoid of images and details.

III. 21 kāya rūpa saṁyamāt tad grāhya śakti staṁbhe cakṣuḥ prakāśā 'saṁprayoge 'ntardhānaṁ

By the practice of the threefold inner discipline on the form and the substantiality of the body, one can comprehend directly the energy that makes it possible to 'grasp' it with the eyes and so forth (for the flow of lightwaves is the form): and when this energy function is suspended, the dynamics of perception is made inoperative, the link between the perceiving eye and light is severed as it were and invisibility occurs.

(Some editions have an additional Sūtra here, suggesting similar phenomenon with the sense of hearing.)

III. 22 sopakramaṁ nirupakramaṁ ca karma tat saṁyamād aparānta jñānaṁ ariṣṭebhyo vā

Action performed here yields results either immediately (if the action is of great intensity) or in course of time (if it lacks intensity). By the practice of the threefold inner discipline on the intensity or on the chain of action-reaction or the law of cause and effect, there comes knowledge of death (though not knowledge of the ultimate extinction of the ego-sense or liberation). This knowledge can also be gained by such discipline directed towards omens and portents.

III. 23 maitryādiṣu balāni

By the practice of the threefold discipline on qualities like friendship one becomes an embodiment of such qualities naturally, and thus one gains great moral, psychic and spiritual strength.

III. 24 baleṣu hasti balādīni

By the practice of the threefold discipline on various kinds of strength (physical, mental, moral, psychic and spiritual) one grows to be as strong as, say an elephant.

III. 25 pravṛtty āloka nyāsāt sūkṣma vyavahita viprakṛṣṭa jñānaṁ

By correctly directing and focussing the light of perception in which the senses and their objects (the whole of nature) function, knowledge can be gained of the subtle, the hidden, and even the remote objects or phenomena.

III. 26 bhuvana jñānaṁ sūrye saṁyamāt

By the practice of the threefold discipline on the sun a knowledge of the physical universe is gained.

When this *saṁyama* is directed towards the sun, one's consciousness becomes one with the sun; and the universe and the composition of the solar system—and therefore the entire universe—is known. For instance, if you direct your meditation at the tape recorder you will know exactly how this tape recorder works, how it is assembled. Now, here comes the mischief. Patanjali himself says, "Please don't do this. I have described it to you in order to be truthful and scientific, but these are distractions."

III. 27 candre tārā vyūha jñānaṁ

By the practice of the threefold discipline on the moon, there arises a knowlege of the stellar system.

III. 28 dhruve tad gati jñānaṁ

By the practice of the threefold discipline on the pole star, there comes a knowlege of its movement (or the movement of the stars).

III. 29 nābhi cakre kāya vyūha jñānaṁ

By the practice of the threefold inner discipline at the psychic centre at the navel (the Manipura cakra) the knowlege of the physiology of the body is gained.

III. 30 kaṇṭhakūpe kṣut pipāsā nivṛttiḥ

By the practice of the threefold discipline at the pit of the throat (or, the psychic centre known as the Visuddha cakra) freedom from hunger and thirst is gained.

III. 31 kūrma nāḍyāṁ sthairyaṁ

By the practice of the threefold discipline on the kurma-nadi, steadiness of the body and the mind is gained.

III. 32 mūrdha jyotiṣi siddha darśanaṁ

By the practice of the threefold discipline on the light that appears in the crown of the head during meditation, one has the vision of sages who have attained perfection.

When you are proficient in *saṁyama* and direct this to the light in the crown of the head (which means after the *kuṇḍalini* has awakened and is taken *cakra* by *cakra* to the *sahasrāra*—the topmost centre of your consciousness) then you will have a vision of the *siddhas*, sages, enlightened ones. You can see Jesus Christ, Buddha, Kṛṣṇa or whoever you want. You can also have a vision of the object of your meditation. This can be a guide, a lamp unto your feet.

This one Sūtra in this section dealing with psychic accomplishments is sensible. But, in a way, Patanjali regards even that as a sort of distraction.

The accomplishments listed in the other Sūtras can happen spontaneously, but if you are going to struggle hard to attain perfection in concentration, meditation and *samādhi,* why must you waste all that talent to get knowledge of the stellar system, for example, or the ability to read other's thoughts? What for?

III. 33 pratibhād vā sarvaṁ

All these can also be gained by direct intuitive perception. (Or, by the practice of the threefold discipline on the inner light, all knowlege is gained.)

III. 34 hṛdaye citta saṁvit

By the practice of the threefold discipline on the spiritual heart (or the psychic heartcentre Anahata) there arises knowledge concerning the mind-stuff or the undivided intelligence.

III. 35 sattva puruṣayor atyantā 'saṁkīrṇayoḥ pratyayā 'viśeṣo bhogaḥ parārthatvāt svārtha saṁyamāt puruṣa jnānaṁ

The external object is totally distinct and different from what the experiencing personality thinks it is. When, in a state of ignorance, the personality forgets this, and as the object is imagined to be external for the enjoyment of another (which is the enjoyer), he experiences pain and pleasure. When the threefold discipline is directed towards the substance of this self or personality (or, towards the selfishness), there arises the knowledge of the indwelling intelligence, with its conditioning which is the ignorance.

III. 36 tataḥ prātibha śrāvaṇa vedanā 'darśā 'svāda vārtā jāyante

Thereupon (since knowledge of ignorance is the dispelling of ignorance, and the intelligence that comprehends the mental conditioning is unconditioned) there come into being enlightened hearing, feeling, seeing, tasting and smelling—free from the perversions, limitations and distortions born of ignorance.

III. 37 te samādhāv upasargā vyutthāne siddhayaḥ

But even such excellent sensations and feelings and the psychic powers described thus far, which on the surface appear to be desirable and encouraging aspects of perfection, are in fact impediments to enlightenment as they, too, distract and externalise the attention.

Distractions are lovely! There was an extraordinary incident in the ashram in Rishikesh when my master, Swami Sivananda, was alive. One day a young man approached him and said, "Swami, in the legends and myths of India there are stories of great men who meditated for a thousand years. It is described in these legends that even the gods were worried about this, so they wanted to disturb their meditation. They sent a beautiful, young celestial nymph there to disturb their meditation. Does it happen even now?"

The master very lovingly turned towards him and asked, "Why are you asking the question?"

The young man said, "If that is true, I would also like to meditate."

Those great yogis meditated on God, and the celestial nymphs came as obstacles; but this man wanted to meditate in order to *get* the obstacles! The obstacles themselves seem to be so tempting that we are satisfied with the obstacles.

The famous prayer, "Lead me not into temptation," means, "I am so fond of being tempted, that only You can prevent me from being tempted. If You leave me alone I am tempted all the time." (I am not making fun of this.) Also, there is a hidden meaning in it—that the next time you are tempted you will blame God. "I prayed, 'Lead me not into temptation,' and now You have led me into temptation. It is Your fault."!

Because these results are promised for a serious practice of meditation, we get caught in the snare of result-hunting. Why is it so? There is a basic insincerity. If this basic insincerity is not there, then the whole of yoga is easy; and if the basic insincerity *is* there, then the life of that person is full of obstacles.

III. 38 bandha kāraṇa śaithilyāt pracāra saṁvedanāc ca cittasya para śarīrā 'veśaḥ

When there is loosening of the bondage of the consciousness to the body, as also an understanding of the proper channel of the consciousness's entry into and its withdrawal from the body, the mind acquires the ability to enter another body.

III. 39 udāna jayāj jala paṇka kaṇṭakādiṣv asaṅga utkrāntiś ca

When the anti-gravitational vital force that has an ascending flow is directly understood, there follow powers of levitation, and passage over water, mud, thorny bush, etc., without coming into contact with them.

III. 40 samāna jayāj jvalanaṁ

When the vital force which maintains equilibrium and which fills the entire body with light, life and power, is directly perceived and understood, there is effulgence and radiance of one's

personality.

III. 41 śrotrā 'kāśayoḥ saṁbandha saṁyamād divyaṁ srotraṁ

By the practice of threefold discipline on the relation between space, as the medium of sounds, and the sense of hearing, supernatural hearing is gained (since the flow of sound-waves is identical with ether or space).

III. 42 kāyā 'kāśayoḥ saṁbandha saṁyamāl laghu tūla samāpatteś cā 'kāśa gamanaṁ

When the threefold inner discipline is directed towards the relationship between the body and the space in which it moves, and when there is contemplation of the weightlessness of cotton, the body acquires the quality of weightlessness and moves in space with ease.

III. 43 bahir akalpitā vṛttir mahā videhā tataḥ prakāśā 'varaṇa kṣayaḥ

Beyond all these is the state of consciousness which is not the product of thought: and that is the cosmic intelligence which is independent of the body (or bodies—physical, astral and causal). By the practice of the threefold discipline upon that, the veil that covers that light of cosmic intelligence is removed.

III. 44 sthūla svarūpa sūkṣmā 'nvayārthavattva saṁyamād bhūta jayaḥ

By the practice of the threefold discipline on the gross (tangible, with form) and the subtle (intangible, formless), and their conjunction, and the direct perception of their apparently substantial nature, there arises the perfect understanding of the elements that constitute that existence.

**III. 45 tato 'ṇimādi prādur bhāvaḥ kāya
saṁpat tad dharmā 'nabhighātaś ca**

Thence follow psychic powers like the ability to reduce the body to the size of an atom, etc., and perfection of body and immunity from the ravages of the elements of nature.

**III. 46 rūpa lāvaṇya bala vajrasaṁhananatvāni
kāya saṁpat**

What constitutes perfection of the body? Beauty, grace, strength, and adamantine firmness.

**III. 47 grahaṇa svarūpā 'smitā 'nvayārthavattva
saṁyamād indriya jayaḥ**

By the practice of the threefold discipline on the sense-functions (their action, their characteristics, their fragmentary nature, their mutual relationship, and their substance or their meaningfulness in relation to the indwelling intelligence on account of which alone they are able to function) comes their total understanding and true mastery over them.

The basic problem of yoga is *indriya,* the senses. *Indriya* are the senses, not the organs of sense (the eyes, ears, tongue, and so on) or the organs of action. Someone explained it very beautifully and I think I cannot improve upon it: "The senses are not just the gross organs, either of action or cognition, but are those organs with which you function when you are dreaming." With closed eyes, when you dream, you see! With what do you see? With the *indriya.* That is the *sense* of sight, the *indriya.* The eye is the fleshy, gross physical organ. Similarly, when you hear someone you dream about talking to you in your dream, that is the *sense* of hearing.

The problem that the yogi faces is psychological distraction and psychological distress. These two disturb the mental equilibrium and keep you from self-knowledge. How do you deal with it? Shall you suppress? Suppress what? It is no use closing your eyes when you don't want to see someone. You can still see—better perhaps. The distraction is *there,* not in the person standing in front of you. If you poke your eyes out you will still dream about what you saw years ago. If you puncture your eardrums you will still hear some kind of noise in your brain. If you are a compulsive alcoholic you can tie your legs to the bed, because you know you walk in your sleep and you might go into the pub! But you may become more alcoholic in your bed, thinking and dreaming of alcohol, craving for it. Or if you think that you just need one glass and then the craving will go, you will find that not only does it not go, but it is strengthened and comes back a little later. So neither suppression nor expression work.

So yoga is neither a science of suppression nor of expression; neither a puritanical thing nor license—neither/nor. There is a third thing, *jaya. Jaya* is victory. This Sūtra suggests that you can achieve victory in the sense of understanding. *Jaya* could mean winning over, not merely gaining victory. The feeling 'I am a victor' is not there—but you can come to terms with the *indriya*, the senses. So *indriya jaya* means to come to terms with the senses and sense organs, so that they neither form a distraction or disturbance, nor create psychological distress.

The yogi says, "Why don't you try to understand what is happening to you?" When the senses are unruly they distract and disturb you, they leap to some kind of psychological distress. This is the active part of it. When it comes to the receiving end, once again there is pain and suffering. As you try to push this pain away, to suppress and overcome this suffering, you only aggravate it. Pain becomes more and more painful as you push it away. It is a vicious circle. For instance if someone pokes a needle towards you and you hit it back, that is when it punctures. In pain and in panic when you push it away from you, it is then that it hurts. Rejection is pain—pain is rejection.

So both what is called sin and what is called suffering are based upon the senses—not just a physical part of the sense organ, but the inner senses, *indriya*. That is the source of all one's troubles and difficulties, of sin and suffering.

Grahaṇa is action. What is the function or the action of the senses—not the sense organs? What is their essential nature—*svarūpa*? What *is* the sense? What *is* sight, what *is* hearing, what *is* the sense of touch? And what are their functions? We have never asked these questions.

How is it that when sight sees, there is a feeling 'I' see—*asmitā*? How is it that when the sense of hearing hears, there is a feeling 'I' hear? Therefore, at what stage and on account of what does the ego sense—*asmitā*—arise? We think that at least we know all the other senses, but what is this ego sense? How does *that* come up?

There is a strange paradox related to the sense organs: from one point of view it looks as though *they* perceive objects outside; on the other hand, they themselves seem to be an object. For instance, with your ears you are listening to these words; or, the ears are listening to these words. You are not even aware that there is a thing called 'ear' which enables you to hear!

If something goes wrong with your eardrum, then you hear the ear *itself*. People who have a punctured eardrum hear all sorts of things. Now the ears are not hearing the external objects, the eardrum *itself* has become the object of hearing. If you ask a professor of physiology to explain all this to you, will you really know that way? No! So the yogi tries to find an answer to these questions: "What is the nature of these senses, what is their function? How does the ego sense arise, and how does it play a dual role of being both subject and object?"

When *saṁyama* is directed towards the senses (not only their function, their knowledge and how this stupid confusion that what the senses do, 'I' do, arises) it is not possible for the answer to these questions to be transferred from one to the other. You have to find them for yourself. Therefore only the questions, "What are the senses, what is their function, what is this ego sense that seems to link itself with these senses and what is the meaning of sense experience? How is it that the senses regard the outside world as their objects and they themselves become the objects of my understanding?" are asked. The answers are not given.

When you hear somebody provide an answer to these questions you may think you know, but it is not right to say then, "I think I know". The correct way to put it is, "I think *he* knows," because you are merely listening to him–you know nothing.

The word *saṁyama* (*dhāraṇā, dhyāna* and *samādhi*— concentration, meditation and knowledge) can be looked at in a different way in this context. When you are listening to somebody else, at that stage you can only say, "I think he knows." So you are still ignorant. When you practise concentration you realise, "I think I know." When you enter into the state of meditation it is, "I know I think." Then when you are in the third stage of knowledge, of *samāḍhi* it is, "I know."

When the answer to these questions is found, then there is *indriya jaya*—mastery in the sense of understanding.

III. 48 tato manojavitvaṁ vikaraṇa bhāvaḥ pradhāna jayaś ca

When such understanding has been gained, the senses function with the speed of the mind, and there is direct perception without the need of intermediary instruments (even the sense organs) and the realisation of oneness with the entire cosmic nature.

If you understand your own senses you understand the whole universe. If your own senses are under your control, the whole universe is under your control. Then the senses function with lightning speed spontaneously and without suppression, craving, or value judgement. That is what is called 'God's will', which is without any personal motivation whatsoever: *tato manojavitvaṁ vikaraṇa bhāvaḥ*

Then they are absolutely perfect, uncorrupted instruments: *pradhāna jayaś ca.*

The whole world is conquered, or won over; the whole universe is understood. It is said in the Yoga Vāsiṣṭha: "*To one whose feet are shod, the whole world is covered with leather.*" You don't have to go on covering the whole world. If you cover your own feet with shoes, you can walk wherever you like. That is the yogi's attitude.

III. 49 sattvapuruṣā 'nyatā khyātimātrasya sarva bhāvā 'dhiṣṭhātṛtvaṁ sarva jñātṛtvaṁ ca

The direct realisation of the independence of the indwelling intelligence from the mind, that is from the conditions to which the psychic and the physical nature is subject, brings with it superintendence over all states of being, and omniscience.

This is the stage of "I know." The yogi knows the senses,

senses, the answers bo these questions of what the senses are, what their functions are, how the ego-sense arises, what the world is. There is also the feeling at that point that therefore one is neither dependent upon, nor a slave to, the outside world, and need not suffer or behave foolishly as ignorant people behave. One is the master of one's mind and destiny, because the body, mind etc. are all under one's perfect control – which implies a division within oneself – a dualism.

It is one of the extraordinary features of yoga philosophy that even the dualism of, "I know" ('I' as the subject and all the rest as the object) is not frowned upon or ridiculed. If one is at the stage where he has the answer to all these questions we have just asked, it merely means that he knows all the factors concerning himself – how his mind and organs function, all his tendencies (*saṃskāras*), past impressions, and so on. He knows everything concerning himself; and, by extension, he also knows how an enlightened person, a stupid fool, a yogi and an aspirant function, and what the possible difficulties and problems of others are – not because he is able to read other's minds, but because he knows how the mind *itself* functions. He has the key – *sarva bhāvā 'dhiṣṭhātṛtvaṁ.*

One of the characteristics of a yogi is that he is the master of his own thoughts, feelings and emotions. To be a master of one's emotions does not mean that he is totally free from all emotions. Emotions come when he invites them, and they leave when he lets them go. The switch is in his hand, not in somebody else's. He is able to know all. (To 'know all' does not mean fortune reading or where to find a lost key, etc. and all that sort of thing. That is a ridiculous pastime in which the true yogi does not indulge. See I. 25)

Here there is clear knowledge or understanding of the distracting influences, of the sources of psychological distress. The yogi knows how the latent tendencies function, and how craving arise within himself; and he knows these things happen in others. Then there is clear perception that this is how the senses function, how the ego-sense arises, how the mind functions – throwing up cravings and desires, good desires, bad desires, etc. He begins to feel that these are all functions of the sense, the ego-sense and the mind – not me. 'I' am free from all of this.

'I' – the observer (not the ego-sense) the undivided intelligence which is able to observe this – temporarily frees itself from all these distracting influences, and says, "I am not involved in all this. I am independent and I am free".

Here it is freedom from. (Let us go back to the example of the river.) It is like the man who, when he realises he is drowning, wants to free himself from this drowning, and so swims out of the river.. The intelligence isolates itself – that is also a form of independece, of freedom (if you are satisfied with it).

It is possible for a person at that stage of development to say as he is drowning, "Well it's only the body that dies – I am independent of the body." But still the individuality continues it is possible for a being – who has achieved independence or freedom in that way – to be caught once again. Just as, having saved yourself from drowning and reached the shore, on finding your friend in difficulty you go back into the river again.

III. 50 tad vairāgyād api doṣa bīja kṣaye kaivalyaṁ

When there is no craving or attraction even fro such supremacy and for such omniscience, all of which suggest a division in consciousness, and when the sense of duality which is the seed for imperfection, impurity, or conditioned existence ceases, there is total freedom and a direct realisation of the indivisibility and hence the independence of intelligence.

Vairagya is dispassion or disinterestedness. The yogi has now arrived at the point where he is neither distracted nor subject to psychological distress because he has the feeling (or realisation) that he is beyond their reach. He is therefore able to know all these things and superintend all these situations. He suddenly realises, "I am aware of this, I am alert and therefore I think I am free from all that. If that is so, if this is freedom, how did I lose it in the first place? As long as this dualism exists the possibility of my falling into this trap also exists, but as long as I am alert I am alright. If I lose that for one minute, I'm going to be lost."

He enters into another state in which he sees the danger of the two vital statements contained in the previous Sūtra: I must be the master of my mind and the senses," and, "I must know all about myself." Even that division—I know myself—is dangerous, because that is the cause of the chain reaction of mischief. Even the desire to experience self-knowledge as if it were outside of yourself—an object of your own knowledge and understanding—is risky. So he says, "I don't want even the feeling that I am the master of my mind and senses, or that I know myself. I don't want that experience as a divided experience." Then once again the great surrender happens.

The word *vairagya* here means 'I'm not interested in this. I'm not even interested in being a great yogi.' But the yogi says this at *that* point; not where we are. Most people are not interested in becoming a great yogi, so this feeling should not arise at our stage. It arises only at that stage where one is able to say, "Everything is under my control, and I know everything." At that point, even the seed of defect is destroyed. *Doṣa bīja kṣaye. Doṣa* is defect, *bīja* is the seed, *kṣaye* is destruction.

You don't say, "I've given up all my bad habits." You may have given up your bad habits, but the seed is still there and therefore it can sprout again and come up. The seed of defect is the craving for what is called a divine experience—mastery of one's own mind and senses, the craving for the experience 'I know all about my mind and senses', and all that stuff and nonsense. Even that is gone. Then there is *kaivalya*, freedom. Total freedom, but not *from* anything. Freedom, period!

There is freedom, and the freedom *is.* That is very much like (back to the Swan River again) when the man who is drowning suddenly feels 'I am not drowning at all. I am the river, I am the body, I am the all.'

There are two ways of asserting that you are not drowning. One is to say, "I am the spirit, I am not the body. I am not drowning, the body drowns and I will go up to heaven." That is one way. That was the state described in the previous Sūtra.

The other way is to say, "I am the river, I am the body. If I am the river and I am also this body, who is drowning where?" You don't say that the whale is drowning in the ocean. It is there, it is part of the ocean, it *is* the ocean. So when you become both the Swan River *and* this drowning body, there is no drowning at all. You are free. You are not free *from* anything, just free.

In that freedom life goes on and all actions continue. The actions are spontaneous, without the interference of ego sense, motivation, sense craving or repulsion. The senses function spontaneously. Such actions are pure; such actions are called God's will. There is complete understanding and coming to terms with the mind and feelings. Since they are also freed from motivation, feelings, emotions, attraction and repulsion, etc., such feelings are pure. We may call it pure love. (Why must we call it pure love? Because we call something else love.)

Such a person's feelings are always love, his actions are always pure and divine. Such a life *itself* is divine.

III. 51 sthāny upanimantraṇe saṅga smayā 'karaṇaṁ punar aniṣṭa prasaṅgāt

Invitations that involve the demonstration of such powers or of the characteristics of enlightenment, even when extended by those in authority whether on earth or in heaven are summarily rejected without being swayed by attachment or even curiosity. Otherwise, undesirable consequences may arise again, by the revival of duality, superiority, hope and despair, etc.

III. 52 kṣaṇa tat kramayoḥ saṁyamād vivekajaṁ jñānaṁ

Undistracted by these, one should proceed to transcend time. By the practice of the threefold discipline in relation to the truth of the moment, without the interference of thought which creates the false sequence of time, there arises understanding which is born of the faculty to perceive the false as false and hence truth as truth.

III. 53 jāti lakṣaṇa deśair anyatā 'navacchedāt tulyayos tataḥ pratipattiḥ

From such understanding flows knowledge or the natural ability to distinguish between reality and appearance, even where they do not have other obvious distinguishing marks related to their species, characteristics and location and hence seem to be similar. The possibility of confusion is thus completely overcome.

III. 54 tārakaṁ sarva viṣayaṁ sarvathā viṣayaṁ akramaṁ ce 'ti vivekajaṁ jñānaṁ

Such wisdom born of intuitive and immediate understanding is the sole redeemer. It is everything. It has everything. It encompasses everything. It is the unconditioned and undivided intelligence spontaneously functioning from moment to moment in the eternal now, without sequential relationship.

III. 55 sattva puruṣayoḥ śuddhisāṁye kaivalyaṁ

When thus there is pure equilibrium which is non-division between the indwelling consciousness and all (objective) existence, between the non-moving intelligence and the ever-moving phenomena, between the unconditioned awareness and the rise and fall of 'The thousand thoughts'—there is freedom and independence of the infinite.

CHAPTER FOUR

IV. 1 janmau 'ṣadhi mantra tapaḥ samādhijāḥ siddhayaḥ

The attainments listed in the previous section are not only the fruits of the threefold inner discipline, but they are congenital in some, and in others they may follow the right and intelligent use of certain medicinal herbs or of certain mantras (mystic formulae or advice) or they may follow the kindling of the psychic fire.

Perfection or right understanding seems to be related to one or the other of these factors—*janmau* (birth itself), *aṣadhi* (which literally means drugs), the use of *mantra*s (not just one *mantra*), *tapas* (austerity—various forms of penance) and *samādhi*.

Some people are enlightened or are close to enlightenment at birth. One example with which we are all familiar is Ramana Maharṣi. In his childhood he had some experiences, and from then on it was one long, unending, uninterrupted self-realisation. Drugs are another means of dealing with the distractions of the mind, but you must know what those drugs are, and how to use them. In the same way there are special *mantra*s for calming the mind and enabling insight to develop. Even *tapas* (austerity—standing upside down, hanging by the feet tied to a tree, and so on) has been used. Meditation, concentration and *samādhi* have all been utilised as means for attaining perfection or self-realisation (not only psychic powers).

With the help of these, a certain altered state of consciousness can be brought about in which the reality is realised. When reality becomes clear, error ceases—because error is not something that exists. For instance, a mirage exists and water exists, but water in the mirage does not exist, has never existed. That it is a mirage is true, that water is water is true, but the seeing of the water in the mirage is error. When you begin to see the mirage *as* a mirage, nothing goes away—but something has gone! This is a puzzle that each one has to work out. Nothing has happened, the mirage remains a mirage. There is still the appearance of water there; but the erroneous feeling that there *is* water has gone. That is all that goes—nothing else need go. When the truth is realised, the error disappears without making any change anywhere. But there is a big change; you don't go to a mirage to have a drink of water! That is the beauty which one has to grasp, by God's grace.

There is no visible external difference between the enlightened man and the non-enlightened or ignorant man, because both of them see the mirage; but in the enlightened man, craving is totally absent. If you find craving in a man who talks as if he is enlightened, he only *talks* as if he is enlightened.

Samādhi itself can lead to perfection. If it does not lead to perfection now, in this life span, what happens? That is suggested in the next Sūtra:

IV. 2 jāty antara pariṇāmaḥ prakṛtyā 'pūrāt

However, congenital endowments are not accidental, as the incidence of birth is determined by the character or quality with which one's whole being is saturated.

When this body is dropped, that which dwelt in it continues to exist. It takes on another birth, as it were, because the ignorance is not completely gone.

There is a vague idea of what the truth is, but it is still more or less an idea. You are still practising, struggling; you have not reached perfection in *samādhi*. Probably in a meditational experience you have a glimpse of the truth; but when you open your eyes there is a doubt. If at that point the body drops, your nature is saturated to some extent, and the next birth takes on from there.

People like Ramana Maharṣi, who right from birth, as it were, have a spiritual inclination or tendency, inevitably walk the spiritual path, so it looks as though perfection is very close to them.

In Rāja Yoga the practice of *samādhi* is an ongoing process, ending only in enlightenment. This *samādhi*, though it is interrupted by all sorts of things, is really not affected by what happens *with* the body, or *to* the body, in this birth or in the next birth, because the truth is there always.

IV. 3 nimittaṁ aprayojakaṁ prakṛtīnāṁ varaṇa bhedas tu tataḥ kṣetrikavat

To be so saturated does not involve acquiring or adding some new quality; for the transmutation of one's nature is not effected by the introduction of a new cause but by the removal of that which obstructs the realisation of that nature. The new practice is a catalyst and is otherwise useless: and people of different natures make different choices. As in agriculture: there is fertility in the seed and the soil, and effort is directed at the removal of the weeds and the pests.

This Sūtra is introduced here in order that you may not cling to the rungs of the ladder instead of ascending it, in order that you may not fall in love with the boat and forget to cross the river. All your struggle and your *sādhana* is merely an instrumental cause, not a direct cause; it is not as though that without it the truth will disappear and the self become unreal. Don't think that all the *sādhana* that you are doing is of great importance. If you do, you are stuck in that *sādhana.*

Don't think that *sādhana* is going to bring you enlightenment; enlightenment is already there. In accordance with the assets and liabilities that you have brought forward from a previous life span, you choose your path. There seem to be all sorts of distinctions and differences. One person does something, a second does something else and a third does yet something else, all of them proceeding in the same direction towards enlightenment, self-realisation. All these are really and truly of no consequence whatsoever, though they are necessary.

Here we are caught. You cannot attain enlightenment without these, yet they do not lead you to enlightenment. You hold in front of you a beautiful mirror covered with an inch of dust. You want to look into the mirror, but nothing is seen. When you take a piece of cloth and wipe it, you see your beautiful face. You realise that it was not the wiping that created the reflection—the capacity to reflect is there in the mirror, not within the cloth with which you wiped it—but if you had not wiped it, you could not have seen your face. Wiping is only incidental to it. That is what is called *nimittaṁ.*

We meditate, chant and study, etc. These are not going to bring about self-realisation, but without them no self-realisation is possible. You must give them their due importance without exaggerating and making them the goal, the vital essence. When you see that each person will choose a path that is in conformity with the assets and liabilities brought forward, you develop a tremendous understanding. You don't go about hitting people on their heads, you leave them alone. They're all going towards the same destination.

The practice of yoga is like a gardener putting forth tremendous effort in order to cultivate and make plants grow, but whatever he does is merely an effort to remove the obstructions. The soil contains fertility, the seed contains the plant. He brings these two together, and when the plant is about to germinate he probably removes some weeds, indirectly helping the plant to grow. He can neither grow the plant, nor produce it. The plant is in the seed already. He has no ability to germinate, only the earth has that ability. All that he does is to bring about the right conditions in which what already exists is realised.

Nimittaṁ is an instrument. When you write a letter with your pen, the pen is an instrument in your hands. The pen did not write the letter, but you could not have written a letter without a writing instrument. There again is a very puzzling, paradoxical situation. Without it *you* cannot and without you *it* cannot. So from one point of view the pen is useless for writing a letter. You have to be there, but you must pick up that pen and write the letter. The pen could lie for eternity on the table and it would not write the letter, and you could struggle for eternity and not be able to write the letter until you pick up the pen. So both these extreme views must be avoided by the intelligence.

It's quite possible that you were born a saint, but that will evaporate if something is not done to further it. Just because you were born a saint (or at least you think so) you are not absolved from further effort. Of course if it is really true that you were born a yogi, naturally you will engage yourself further in the yogic path, as long as there is life in the body. What is it that makes one feel that because one performed some miracle as a child that one is supreme? That was only an instrument's game, and the moment you put the instrument down on the table, the letter ceased to be written.

In the same way the *mantra* and even drugs are all instruments. People have been discussing this problem *ad infinitum* because a great man called Aldous Huxley in a book entitled 'Doors of Perception' has mentioned a drug experience as having been 'up there', 'out there'. Is that true? Can the drug itself give you the experience? It is one of the aids perhaps, and it has to be used intelligently; for instance, if you pick up a pen and start rubbing it with its bottom, no letter could be written.

While you are using an instrument you must know how to use it. There must be full understanding of the advantages, disadvantages, limitations and ability. Some people may question Aldous Huxley's declaration that LSD is of great use in attaining heightened states of consciousness, but I don't know first hand. I have never experienced any of these; but vaguely in my own mind I can compare the effect of these drugs to a cup of coffee, for instance. Even in the ashram in Rishikesh if I wanted to get up and meditate early in the morning or late at night and the mind was dull due to various causes and circumstances, I would take a cup of coffee and sit and meditate. The coffee drives the drowsiness away and you can meditate. If you don't want to take coffee, do some *śīrṣāsana* or vigorous *bhastrīka prāṇāyāma*. (Coffee is a drug, shouting *kīrtan* is a *mantra*, and *śīrṣāsana* and *bhastrīka prāṇāyāma* are *tapas*. All these things are aids, that's all. But after having done all this, what you are going to do with the effect only you know.) You get up at four o'clock, have a cup of coffee, then you are wide awake. But the coffee and LSD or whatever it is, is not going to put you into meditation.

Perfection is not brought about by these, nor is perfection possible without some kind of effort and practice. Here you are caught. Perfection is not the end result of any process, nor is it independent of any of these. Both are necessary—not in a causal relationship, but in a relationship of the essential and the incidental (the essential being the perfection which is already there and the incidental being the aids, the help.) So perfection is neither brought about nor created, but the end result.

If something comes into being now, it has to cease a little later; but perfection or enlightenment is a fact of existence, it is not something that you and I are creating. It is like the reflection in the mirror, it exists at all times. Because of the dust covering it you are unable to see it; wipe it and you can see the reflection in the mirror. Why is it that all this effort that we have put into our meditation and our spiritual practice is considered to be *aprayojakaṁ* —useless, except as an aid?

IV. 4 nirmāṇa cittāny asmitā mātrāt

Any attempt to introduce a new transforming influence can only erect one more barrier—as such a construction of the mind-stuff (as the new influence or image is) is obviously and only the product of the ego-sense.

Whatever you put together with the help of your mind is related to your own ego. Please remember that earlier on Patanjali had said, "Whatever be the concept of self that you may have, it is all put together by the mind and the ego (which is the mind)."

In life itself, everything that happens to us and everything that we do is made possible and inevitable because of this image formation. It is because you have a certain image of yourself that you crave for something. If you don't have an image of yourself as a man, there is no craving for companionship of a woman. If there is no image in oneself of being a woman, there is no craving for a child.

It is of these images that cravings and aspirations are born. For instance, it is because you have an image of yourself as a weak person that you conceive of God as a strong personality. God is omnipotent. Why? Because you are impotent. That is the image you have in your mind. You are unable to achieve what you desire to achieve, and therefore you feel that you are weak. So having built the image of weakness of the self you then build another image called omnipotence of God, and you worship God. I am not saying that this worship is good or bad, but it is good to understand it without any prejudice whatsoever.

The mind is constantly restless. This restlessness is also an image that is formed in you. How do you know the mind is restless? Because you think it is restless. Because you have no peace of mind you form an image that you are restless, and it is that image that clamours and aspires for a God who is all peace. You have an image of what a peaceful mind should be. Since you cannot look at the being that you are, you think a completely peaceful mind must be 'like this'. That is already an image! And in comparison to that image, you are restless. But comparisons are unavoidable. You see a man sitting peacefully, but you don't know what he is doing within himself. You look at him and think, "If only I could sit quietly like that." You have built an image in your mind of what a peaceful state is, or must be. That is what creates restlessness. You become aware of restlessness and so you say, "Oh my God, I am restless, I have no peace of mind." And you create an image of God that is absolute peace. I'm not saying that the expression 'God is Peace' is not true, but as an image it is deadly. Clinging to one of these images is as good or as bad as clinging to some other image.

Why does the mind build an image at all? The mind builds an image of God to suit its own image of itself, and that is the basic problem throughout our life. Even your day-to-day affairs are guided by this. Instead of beating about the bush, Patanjali says, "Why don't you look within and see where the image is born." This looking within is meditation. Then suddenly you discover that in meditation you are building another image. Perhaps that is the only time when the fact that there is a self-image becomes clear, otherwise it is not clear. For instance, even the feeling 'I am a man', is an image. You are not aware of this because you have become reconciled to it. What we call a fact in our waking state is nothing but an image put together by the foolish ignorant mind, and repeatedly affirmed each day. That is how it becomes a reality.

Substituting one image for another image is not going to help us either, because the image is still an image. Changing the hair style doesn't make a woman a man, or a man a woman; it only leads to a certain amount of confusion! Instead, Rāja Yoga suggests, "Look within and try to see where the image is made. Look at this phenomenon of image building *itself*." When you learn to look at it you are meditating, whether you are sitting quietly with closed eyes, or running around with open eyes. Incidentally, that was Buddha's realisation, too. On the day of enlightenment he is reported to have said, "You builder of images, you will not build any more images—neither an image of enlightenment nor an image of liberation or salvation." Even an image of *mokṣa* or liberation is a trap. Can we free ourselves completely and totally from all self images?

IV. 5 pravṛtti bhede prayojakaṁ cittam ekam anekeṣāṁ

However many such images one may build within oneself, all these are projected by a single ego-sense in the mind-stuff, though the operations of the diverse successive images may vary, giving the false feeling of methodical and rapid spiritual progress.

The *citta* (the mind) is only one, but on account of *prayojakaṁ* (one's nature, one's practice) the same thing appears to be a different experience in different people. One person meditates and sees the Virgin Mary or Jesus Christ. Wonderful, there's no harm in it. Someone else sees Kṛṣṇa dancing around. That's also wonderful. There is no harm in it. The same *citta* plays different tricks in different people.

Whatever be your thought, whether it is virtuous or vicious, it's all the play of the mind. One kind of mental activity gives you inner happiness or peace of mind and so this is considered to be better. Some good thoughts are constructive and therefore are encouraged because they compel you to promote the welfare of society. If you are thinking positively, thinking of the good of others, you would surely do something about it, so those good thoughts are exalted. If you go on entertaining vicious thoughts, it is inevitable that those vicious thoughts must be translated into vicious actions, destructive of society, and so they are said to be a bad thing. What is the difference between good and evil here?

From the point of view of a seeker who wants to reach perfection, there is only one simple difference—the spelling. One is g-o-o-d, the other is e-v-i-l. Without totally abandoning evil thoughts, (which is a necessary preliminary step) you are getting nowhere. You have not even put your foot on the first rung of the ladder of yoga. But this is said in order to caution you against resting on the fifth rung of the ladder. "I have got there, all my evil thinking has been abandoned, now I think God-thoughts only—not only good thoughts." But thoughts are thoughts, whether they are God thoughts, good thoughts or evil thoughts.

Because you are of a certain nature, your thoughts share that nature. All the thoughts of a man who is a drunkard, a debaucher and a vicious scoundrel, are evil. He is honestly and faithfully manifesting his nature; and a swami, a holy man, is honestly and faithfully manifesting *his* nature. What is the difference? Fire is hot, ice is cold. You don't expect fire to be cool. It is the nature of fire to be hot; it is the nature of ice to be cold. It is the nature of that man to behave in that way; it is the nature of this man to behave in this way.

What do we, as students of yoga who have learned to abandon evil even right from the early yoga practice, learn from this? We learn not to consider ourselves very superior and not to condemn others. That man is merely manifesting his own nature. We should not hold him responsible for that. If you have been walking this path—not only in this birth, but maybe in several previous births—it is natural for you not to think those evil thoughts. So there is no glory here. Because of different inner equipment, predispositions and natures (if one may call it so) each one thinks differently and has different experiences, but the mind is the same.

IV. 6 tatra dhyānajam anāśayaṁ

Hence, the no-image that is born of meditation is the best—because it does not create a receptacle for itself, entrench itself as a real image and colour the mind.

So instead of hanging on to these experiences produced, put together and created by the mind, the yogi bent on reaching perfection engages himself in this enquiry. The enquiry itself becomes *jñāna*. And, knowing that all constructions are bound to be destroyed—even psychological constructions called doctrines, dogmas, faith and belief—the yogi steers clear of all those things. If he sees a brilliant vision he recognises it as one kind of construction which is not going to last, because all that is put together by the mind must eventually be destroyed. So without resting in it or on it, the yogi's intelligence moves on.

If the mind comes to a rest thinking that *this* is the truth, and *that* is not, there the mind is creating a concept of truth, and it is going to rest there. To say, "I have attained enlightenment," is stupid nonsense. Your meditation should have no support at all. When the mind feels like resting somewhere, keep going, this is not the goal. The mind is still functioning, still building an image called perfection, enlightenment, God or the self. The understanding of this simple truth enables you to go on. You become aware of those experiences, of heightened states of consciousness, but you go on.

Meditation is meditation only if it leads to the self, but as the self is not an object, one cannot determine 'This is it'. When there is such determination of the self, that 'This is it,' there is an image, and you are trapped there.

There should be observation without an observer, there should be meditation without a goal of meditation. There is a constant seeking without an object to be sought; there is love without an object to love or to be loved. That is what Rāja Yoga is all about.

IV. 7 karmā 'śuklā 'kṛṣṇaṁ yoginas trividhamitareṣāṁ

The yogis' actions, springing from such no-image, are therefore neither pure nor impure whereas in the case of others, actions are of three classes, kinds or types—viz., pure, impure and mixed.

In the case of such a yogi, whatever actions take place in his life are colourless and untainted, though in the eyes of the observer such actions appear to be done by him. I am deliberately avoiding the use of the word 'pure'. It is better to phrase it negatively, and say his actions are untainted and without any colour, white or black, because there is no self-image and therefore there is no aspiration, craving or desire. There is no goal other than life itself, truth itself, consciousness itself.

When the self-image of the yogi has been destroyed, or there is no image, from where do these actions flow? In our case the actions flow from the image that we have of ourselves, and they are naturally directed towards a goal, an achievement. The achievement is the complement to what we are. We lack something, there is something wanting in us, and we want to fulfill that want or craving, and therefore we strive. When these things are not there, there is no ego-motivation or image-motivation.

Then, from where do the yogi's actions arise, and what is their destination? That is totally unpredictable. They arise in that power, that consciousness, that energy which gave rise to this whole universe, where the creation of the universe took place. (Call it God if you wish.) So only the yogi, in the eyes of others, is a channel for divine will. He does not say, "I am performing the will of God," for then there is an image; nor does he say that he is an instrument in the hands of God. He might use the formula, but he doesn't mean it, because then there is an image. He might or might not use the word 'I'. (There were some great yogis who refused to use the word 'I', but that doesn't mean that they were enlightened!)

So the yogi is one in whom there is no self-image. He is also alive, he is also functioning here in the eyes of others, but his actions are totally uncoloured by likes and dislikes. There is no image to form a relationship with others and, uncoloured by likes and dislikes, there is therefore neither a definition of goodness nor condemnation of evil. You may look at him and say, "Look what a vicious thing he has done," or, "What a great thing he has done," but so far as he is concerned, these things don't exist. Good and evil do not exist in his case, and therefore he does not incur *karma*. In our case our actions (*karma*) are not only black and white, but also a lot in between. Some actions are diabolical, some very divine, some are human and some are half animal.

IV. 8 tatas tad vipākā 'nuguṇānāṁ evā 'bhivyaktir vāsanānāṁ

The images that are built in the mind—and the actions that flow from them—colour the mind creating tendencies which manifest when conditions are favourable.

When these actions arise in the self-image, they confirm that image. You cannot work this image formation out, because every time the image is allowed to act in the manner in which it is bound to act, it is being confirmed; and what originally was merely imagination becomes almost real. What was a vague curiosity in the beginning becomes an action and then becomes confirmed as a tendency. Take smoking or drinking, for instance. You might smoke just out of curiosity, then an image is formed that all important people smoke. This image then craves for a cigarette, which then makes you feel happy or elated. By starting as a curiosity and then being indulged in repeatedly, it becomes a tendency. You cannot avoid this tendency being formed by fighting it. If you are ashamed of your own drinking habits, you will organise a cocktail party!

This tendency cannot be overcome, either by satisfying it or by suppressing it. It is not possible to deal with it unless the whole dynamics of action and reaction is understood. You are compelled to do this, because there is something that says you need it. Something said that this is desirable. Because there was a desire, the object became desirable—it is not the other way around. A thing is not desirable unless you desire it. There is nothing in the world that everyone desires. (This refers only to an object, not abstract qualities.) It only becomes desirable because you desire it, and you desire it because there is an awareness, a feeling that you lack something. That is the image. Since this self-image is dented, it is looking for a fulfilling complement. If you still cling to the idea that the self-image *is* dented, imperfect, you try to repair it, make it whole, and that leads to other complications.

Why is there this image at all? Who builds these images, and what is their content and character? Since this enquiry—*vicāra*—is a quest without a goal, and since meditation is an observation without creating the image of an observer, it has nothing whatsoever to hang on to. People get frightened of this. Perhaps for a few minutes you feel that you are falling into nothing. Then you realise that if you are dropping into nothing there is no harm, there is no 'fall'. So although there may be an initial fear or a frightening experience, that passes away.

This same self-image that we have creates an image called the other. It is not as though the other exists and I create an image of it. If the self-image is not there, the other is not there. And even in the absence of the other, the self-image creates what is *called* the other. (In a dream a self-image is created. The dream creates within me another thing called me, experienced as the me during the period of the dream; and that dream image creates another one within itself. If that self-image is not there, the 'other' is not there.) So it is this self-image that creates the other and then establishes a so-called relationship. All actions originate in this funny fictitious relationship. This fact is seen in meditation. Because of the recurrent arising of this phenomenon of the self-image and the other image in meditation, one becomes aware of one's tendencies.

A tendency is a groove, and it is formed by this chain reaction. I don't know if we dream the same dream again and again, but in this thing called the waking state we tend to cut the same groove again and again. We are looking for the same phenomenon, because in-so-far as the waking state experience is concerned, the self-image is dug in, confirmed. "I am So and so, I am a man, etc." By repeated confirmation, this is taken as a fact. Even one's own defects and deficiencies are dug in, and since they are rooted, the factors that compose the self-image are also rooted.

You also project the self-image onto what is called the

'other' in the same fashion. A tendency is formed, the same actions are repeated, the same experiences are experienced. When this action is repeatedly performed by the self-image, it is coloured by the self-image and becomes black, white or grey. Unless the actions arise from a 'no image' consciousness, the actions themselves are coloured in various ways. It is the self-image that projects this coloured action towards an assumed relationship, and when this bears fruit it becomes a tendency.

The fruition of past action—coloured action, action based on the self-image that has matured into a tendency—does not come to an end. This wretched thing keeps on repeating itself, in spite of and unbeknown to you. The tendency takes you unawares. When the condition is ripe it arises and manifests itself. If you are really and truly aware of this chain reaction you are able to see that this is not something natural—not an action that arises from the 'no image' state—but something which arises because of a tendency formed by previous actions committed in a state of ignorance. When you are aware of this it does not arise, it just bubbles within and doesn't really become an action; but when you are unaware and the circumstances are favourable, you are taken for a ride.

These tendencies are called *vāsanās*. *Vāsanā* is a mental conditioning, and in common language it also refers to aromas, scents, smells. If you handle garlic, for instance, the smell remains on your hands for a long time after you've washed them. You try to mask it with some perfume and for a little while it seems as if the garlic smell has gone and the perfume has come. But the perfume wears out and the garlic comes again. Similarly, when circumstances are favourable, the tendency that is hidden within you comes up again.

The yogi is not concerned so much about the reaction of the action that is performed by him in the form of good luck, bad luck, happiness, unhappiness, pain or pleasure, but he is seriously concerned with this inner tendency that the action of the self-image generates within himself, because that is what keeps the whole thing going.

IV. 9 jāti deśa kāla vyavahitānāṁ apy ānantaryaṁ smṛti saṁskārayor eka rūpatvāt

The relation between the actions, the tendencies they create, and the manifestation of these tendencies in behaviour may be vague: especially when the behaviour and its antecedents are separate in time, place, and embodiment—yet the latent impressions (tendencies) and memory are identical in nature.

It is possible that a tendency does not get a favourable opportunity to spring into action for a long time. For example, say you haven't smoked a cigarette for years and you feel that you have completely eradicated the habit. That is what you think! This Sutra goes so far as to suggest that you may think you have beaten the habit, but you have not.

Do you remember having smoked a cigarette about thirty years ago? If you are able to remember, the tendency is still there. The memory itself is the tendency. There is no real difference, the difference is merely verbal. We make a verbal distinction, "I remember that I was a fool, but I have completely discarded that foolishness and now I am a wise person." Be careful, because as long as you remember that, the devil is still there. The converse is not true. You may say that because you don't remember, it has gone, but the tendency is still there. You have merely forgotten the past experience. When a favourable opportunity presents itself, the memory will arise, and the *saṁskāra* (the scar or tendency) will also arise.

Such a dreadful situation exists as long as there is a self-image, and the self-image is born of ignorance. The self-image creates the 'other' on account of this ignorance. Since the self-image and the action and reaction—which is the experience—are based upon the tendency, all these things lead to the experience of what is called pleasure and what is called pain. First there is ignorance and this ignorance gives rise to a self-image. The self-image creates all sorts of other images and enters into relationships, and the feed-back is experienced as pleasure and pain, happiness and unhappiness. When these experiences arise there is hope, fear and frustration.

IV. 10 tāsāṁ anāditvaṁ cā 'śiṣo nityatvāt*
IV. 11 hetu phalā 'śrayā 'laṁbanaiḥ saṁgṛhītatvād eṣām 'bhāve tad abhāvaḥ**

**However, it is difficult to determine their exact operation, and it is futile to analyse them. These memories and these tendencies are beginningless—for hope or desire-to-live is permanent.*

***Yet, since these tendencies have a cause-and-effect relationship with ignorance (that is, they are the result of ignorance and also the cause of its perpetuation) they disappear when the cause (ignorance of the spiritual truth) is dispelled, and vice versa: they support and promote each other and are bound to each other.*

All these, including this chain reaction, are beginningless in time, so don't try to trace them to their beginning to find out when they commenced. That is one remarkable and wasteful pastime we indulge in when we psychoanalyse ourselves. We try to isolate this tendency and race its origin back to childhood. It is a useless game, because there you are assuming that this tendency has a specific origin in time.

Ignorance and self-image are ageless. From one point of view one may say that the child is innocent and that all the other bits and pieces of conditioning are infused into the child right from birth; or, from another point of view, before birth there was a self-image which gave rise to this birth. It's another form of self-image. The infant is not aware of its own self-image for the time being, just as in sleep you are not aware of this self-image. It does not mean that it has gone. It has not, because it wakes up. It is the self-image that wakes you up from sleep and it is the self-image that gives rise to birth, to the conception itself! It is the self-image that is floating around looking for a vehicle in which to embody itself. So when we try to analyse the present problem and take it to its origin in time, we are frustrated.

Ignorance is beginningless, the self-image is beginningless and the relationship that the self-image creates is also beginningless. The experience of pain and pleasure is beginningless, and therefore desire, craving and hope are also beginningless. But there is a beginning in another sense, i.e. one is able to understand the origin of this chain reaction—which is ignorance—not in time, but in truth. One is able to look at this chain reaction, see and understand the links in the chain, and arrive at the origin of this whole scheme.

One depends upon the other. Why does the self-image arise? Because of ignorance, because you don't know what you are, or who you are. Can you go back on those links—not in time, but immediately? If you can, you see the whole pattern; immediately you see that there is constant hope, craving and desire, and that desire arises because of the experience of pleasure and pain. The desire is for prolonging that pleasure and avoiding this pain.

The experience of pleasure and pain arises on account of the relationship that you have with the 'other', whether the other is an object, another human being or psychological experience (all these constitute the 'other'). Because there is this contact with the other and some experience arose from that contact, the experience is divided. So what is the cause of experience?

The immediate cause of experience is the relationship, and the cause of this relationship is the creation of the other, the experience of the 'me' This 'me' creates the other, and the rest of the other things follow. What is the self-image? You don't know, and because you don't know who you are or what you are, the whole wretched thing started from there.

This you can become aware of immediately, without linking it with time, without saying either, "I'll do it the day after tomorrow," or, "All these arose twenty-five million years ago". Whereas in time these things are beginningless, in truth they have a beginning; and that is the root of the whole thing—ignorance. When the ignorance is dispelled the self-image is dispelled, contact is dispelled, and experience, hope and frustration all come to an end. That is liberation.

IV. 12 atītā 'nāgataṁ svarūpato 'sty adhva bhedād dharmāṇāṁ

But that does not imply that the past (the memory and the tendencies) is false, and that the future is abolished (by their disappearance). The past and the future exist in reality, in their own form—because the characteristics and the natural differences of countless beings follow different paths.

The past and the future exist—*svarūpato*—in their own form. The past exists as past, the future exists as future. When you plant a seed, a tree grows out of that; the tree was in the seed only potentially. In relation to the plant that you see now, the seed was the past and the full-grown tree is the future. In the young child there is the potential adult; the adult has the potential of old age and death. There is the past in reality—in its own form. When you say the past *is,* it is not as if it is present physically now, but the past is the present now as a memory. It is not present as it was present when it was present, but the past is present as a memory. You cannot object to that, you cannot sweep it away or pretend it doesn't exist. (It's a very clever and beautiful argument.)

The future also exists in the present as a potentiality. How do you know? You see that some seeds look alike; some seeds even look like cockroach droppings. You don't know which is a seed and which is something else. When you throw them into the soil the cockroach droppings don't grow but the others do, because the potentiality of germination was in the seeds and not in the cockroach droppings. *Anāgataṁ*—the future, *svarūpato*—in its own form. Don't look for the tree in the seed. It is not there, but it is *potentially* present.

One cannot deny the existence of the past and future, because when one observes nature one sees that there is growth. Growth implies change and change implies moving from one state to the other. In that which has grown there are the growth symptoms and there are the signs of growth. This was a child, this was a young person. You're able to see that. The symptoms of having grown up are seen in the adult, and the symptoms of the future are there in that person, as potentiality.

How do we know that the future is present as a potential and the past is present as memory? All things do not grow in the same way. As you go on contemplating this statement, meditating upon it, it grows more and more beautiful."All things do not grow in the same way. This is how he grows, this is how she grows, this is how this grows." When this is truly seen, all your prejudices disappear in an instant. So by observing the different patterns of growth, one realises that there is something called the past and something called the future.

The nature of one leads in one direction and the nature of another one leads in another direction. Is this direction good and that direction bad? Patanjali says, "Leave it alone. Simply recognise that since these distinctions do exist, they point to the simple truth and fact that the past and the future exist in their own form." It is possible that potentially you are supposed to be a holy man; if you are, then you will become a holy man. It's possible that potentially you must become a violent aggressive person. There's no problem there. If you realise that this is what was potentially there and this is what has become manifest, there is neither glory in it nor a fault in it. Society may applaud you or punish you; that has nothing to do with you. The potentiality having manifested, 'I' has nothing to do with it. You go out into the garden, plant the seeds and do all sorts of fantastic things and then a cyclone comes and pulls them down, or some vandals come, pick all the fruits and take them away. Why should you be worried? There was the potentiality of action in your arms and that potentiality has been made manifest. What you had to do, what you could potentially do, has been done.

IV. 13 te vyakta sūkṣmāḥ guṇātmānaḥ

These differences are of the quality of the beings, not of the being itself. And, they may be either subtle or obvious.

These inherent distinctions could be apparent, gross, very easily detected and perceived, or they could be subtle. The differences exist only in their qualities; there is a slight distinction here, but not in the essential being. Fundamentally we are all one, there is no problem about that. As living beings we are all one, but as human beings we differ from animals and plants. As plants, all are equal, but in certain qualities each plant differs from the other. As human beings we are one, but as 'you' and 'I' there is some difference and some distinction; and these distinctions belong not to our fundamental essence as human beings, but to something else, to the individual. Not your nature, but your quality is different from mine. I am a human being, you are also a human being. There is no difference there, but in our qualities we are slightly different. You have a certain quality, I have a certain quality. Neither that quality, nor this quality is necessarily good or evil, but in relation to something else it may be considered good or evil. Our essential nature is not tainted by these qualities.

IV. 14 pariṇāmai 'katvād vastu tattvaṁ

Surely, the material world exists: though it is seen that it constantly undergoes change, there is some substance which thus undergoes change.

You exist as an individual. Even that is not denied. You and I are very similar at a certain level and very dissimilar at a certain other level; it is not as though you and I are completely one. This is the beauty of the Yoga Sūtras in contradistinction to the other Vedantic texts, which say that individualities are nonsense.

Patanjali says, "You exist as an individual." How do you know? Because I grow into something other than you, something which is not you. The individuality is there, and it is that individuality which continues to undergo change. For instance, one individuality blossoms as a teacher or a doctor, and another individuality becomes an artisan. Just as you are an individual, so the other person is also an individual. Here *your* quality flourishes, there the *other* quality flourishes.

Accept the truth, but don't blindly extend it to cover whatever you want to cover. You'll recognise the reality of what it is, but rigorously train and discipline yourself not to go beyond that. One individuality goes that way, the other individuality goes this way. Although they are apparently different, fundamentally they are one and the same.

IV. 15 vastu sāṁye citta bhedāt tayor vibhaktaḥ panthāḥ

The world of matter is entirely neutral and homogeneous. Differences (like good and evil, beauty and ugliness) are perceived because such differences are created by viewpoints oriented to different directions or goals.

The world outside exists, but it does not come and hit you. The objects of the world do not proclaim anything. Scientifically it is possible to declare that a carpet is definitely different from a table fan; but the carpet does not say, "I am a carpet," and the table fan does not say, "I am a table fan". When you extend it a little further, no object in the world says, "I am good," and definitely no object says, "I am bad". A lion lies there as quietly and as beautifully as a cow lies somewhere else. Nature has not written on the forehead of the lion, "This is a vicious animal, don't go anywhere near," nor written on the forehead of the cow, "This is beautiful, worship it." They are neutral, and silent. Both these objects (which are real and diverse, one very different from the other) are *sāmye* —neutral.

They are what they are—*citta bhedāt*—but the distinction arises in your mind. In the original form in which the word *citta* was used, it seems to refer to undivided consciousness. Here this *citta* is used in the broad sense of 'mind' a mind that has all the conditioning in it, that is polluted—*citta bhedāt.* Your mind is different from my mind, and therefore the object is seen, not only differently, but from a different point of view—*vibhaktaḥ panthāḥ.*

Now we have two things. First of all, there is an external objective distinction: a leaf is different from a carpet. Secondly, there is an internal, subjective division. Whereas objectively two carpets are the same—Kashmiri prayer mats, for instance—the conditioned mind thinks that one is better than the other, more elegant than the other. The subjective distinction is based upon *citta bhedāt* ñ my mind is different from yours.

Why is my mind different from yours? My mind is conditioned in a different way; my background is different, my upbringing is different and my scale of values is different. The culture in which I have been brought up is different from yours, and therefore my culture has conditioned my mind to look upon *this* as civilisation and *that* as barbarism. My upbringing, training and education say that this is bad and that is good. In Western culture, a glass of whisky is an insignia of civilisation, and smoking *gānjā* is terrible. One is accepted socially and the other is not. In other cultures whisky is considered a greater evil than *gānjā*!

So your point of view distorts the perception of the object still further. Then why don't we say that it is the perceiving mind alone that determines the existence of the object? Just as one says that 'this is beautiful', 'that is ugly', it is possible for one to say that this is a carpet only because one recognises it as a carpet. "If the mind did not recognise that as a carpet, it would cease to be a carpet," says the objector. This is another extreme argument.

In answer to that Patanjali says:

IV. 16 nacai 'ka cittatantraṁ vastu tad apramāṇakaṁ tadā kiṁ syāt

An object or a substance in this world is not dependent for its existence on one mind. Else, would it not cease to be if that mind does not cognise it?

The object does not depend upon one mind. Supposing your mind is deranged and you become completely mad. Will this carpet cease to be a carpet at that time, or not? You can go on taking this to the other absurd extreme. If you become raving mad and start cutting the carpet and eating it, does it suddenly become food and not carpet? Supposing you embrace a statue, does it become a friend and cease to be a statue? Thus the mind may become temporarily insane, but the object remains what it is.

There is of course the famous question: "If a tree fell in the Himalayas two hundred miles away from all human habitation, did it make any sound at all?" Patanjali says, "Yes." Independent of your viewpoint, the object exists, and independent of your hearing ability, that which exists, exists. (Vāsiṣṭha might come in and say that that's because the cosmic consciousness recognises it.) Here Patanjali says that things exist in themselves whether or not you, the individual, comprehend them. That is, even before the TB virus was seen or detected by the scientists, it already existed; it always existed. Even before the laws of nature were discovered by the scientists, the laws themselves were there as a reality. Nobody could question that.

So the existence of the object does not depend upon one mind comprehending the object.

IV. 17 tad uparāgā 'pekṣitvāc cittasya vastu jñātā 'jñātaṁ

However, a particular object or substance is comprehended or ignored in accordance with whether the mind is or is not coloured by that object, and is therefore attracted or repelled by that substance. Hence the quality or the description of the substance is dependent on the mind: whereas its existence is independent of it.

Why do we become aware of some objects and remain ignorant of other objects? The objects exist, our diverse minds exist and the different points of view also exist. (When we say different minds, it only means different points of view.) Objects become known to you or remain unknown to you. They are not dependent upon your mind, but their qualities are dependent upon your perception. They become known to you when you establish a relationship with them; they remain unknown to you when you do not establish such a relationship, when you remain indifferent.

There are billions of people on earth whom you do not know. Their existence is of no consequence to you and therefore you do not know of them. Once their existence (or the existence of these diverse objects) means something to you, once you begin to like them and depend upon them, then you will know them. This is a fairly scientific and realistic appraisal of the world and the objects, as well as an appraisal of the subjective mind and its modifications, points of view and conditioning. Patanjali points out that these two constantly interact one on the other.

IV. 18 sadā jñātāś citta vṛttayas tat prabhoḥ puruṣasyā 'pariṇāmitvāt

All such changes, colourings and modifications of the mind are always known to the lord of the mind, the indwelling intelligence, since the intelligence is changeless.

Objects keep on changing. First there is the seed, then the little sapling and then the big tree. That goes on in what is called the external world, and internally also all sorts of changes take place. What you ignored at one point, you recognise now; what you liked at one point, you dislike now; what you disliked at one point, you like now. It seems to be a totally disorderly situation, and yet the mind or the intelligence within the mind (or beyond the mind) cannot function in a state of confusion.

There cannot be orderly, predictable growth; and yet all that we have been discussing so far implies an orderly predictable growth. Even in the earlier chapters, change was discussed as predictable because it follows a certain pattern—a certain growth pattern for a tree, a certain growth pattern for a man or a woman. All these potentialities are inherent, and the manifestation of the potential demands orderly growth, otherwise there is no sense or order in creation. Every day the sun rises in the east and sets in the west. There is an order in this universe, in spite of the fact that the world keeps changing and the mind keeps changing. Yet all this does not lead to perpetual confusion, because all these changes or modifications in the mind, in the *citta,* are forever known to some intelligence. These *citta vṛtti* are your own mental modifications or moods. [*Citta vṛtti* can also be translated into 'the mind's effort at measuring the external world'. A concept is something with which the mind measures what it sees. See (I. 2)]

First of all there is an acceptance of the ignorance of the external world. What the world is, we do not know. The mind measures the world in terms of its needs. If you are a botanist, when you look at that tree you are looking at it for the botanical names, the properties and so on. When a dietician looks at that, she says, "Ah, there are plenty of avocados, that's good protein." Nobody is seeing the tree for what it is.

Now, by whom are all these games that go on in the mind known? They are known by *prabhoḥ puruṣa*. What is *puruṣa*? That which is behind the ego, that intelligence that says, "I am Swami Venkatesananda," that which rests in this body, is *prabhoḥ puruṣa*. That *puruṣa* is not deceived by the mind and its thoughts, its measurements, its *vṛtti* or its moods. That lord—*puruṣa*, soul or intelligence within—observes and knows all these goings-on in the mind, because he doesn't change. So here the master says that these *citta vṛtti* (mental modifications or thoughts and notions which arise and fall in the *citta)* are known to the *puruṣa*, or the spirit—whichever you wish to call it—from moment to moment. The intelligence within that shines without undergoing any change and is absolutely steady—whether you are awake, asleep, dreaming, building castles in the air, thinking that you are thinking, or thinking that you are meditating—is absolutely steady.

Prabhu is like water in the ocean. *Citta vṛtti*, being like the waves, are rising and falling all the time. It is not possible for one wave to observe another wave because by the time it is collapsing the next one is rising, but to the water all these waves are known. Imagine that the water has tremendous intelligence and powers of observation. Water knows from moment to moment how many waves there are, how these waves rise, exist and fall. Though waves rise and fall, water does not undergo any change at all. What water is in relation to the waves in the ocean, this intelligence is in relation to all these modes and moods and thoughts that arise and fall in the mind.

IV. 19 na tat svābhāsaṁ dṛśyatvāt

Surely, it cannot be said that the mind is self-luminous and can know itself; it (its changes and modifications) is perceived only by the inner light or the indwelling intelligence.

It looks as though it is the mind that knows, that thinks, that has knowledge. But the master says that it shines because of an intelligence within, that it is that intelligence that really knows all this. Why? Does the mind not have the power to know? Patanjali says, "No." The mind itself is known by the intelligence within, so that you are able to observe what goes on in the mind. As long as you are thinking, the observer is also the mind—or one thought observes another thought, one wave observes another wave. By the time the observer wave is rising, the observed wave is collapsing. So the observer wave says, "Oh, I looked into myself, all is quiet now." Why? Now instead of the observed wave you have replaced it with an observer wave. If you are angry and you try to observe that thought, because you have created a new wave in the mind called the observer, the observing wave seems to have collapsed—though it is still there.

Thinking about thought, observing the mind itself with the mind, is of no use. The mind itself is an object of observation to this inner intelligence. The mind is like a mirror, it seems to shine, to reflect, but in itself it has no power at all. It shines only in the light borrowed from this inner intelligence.

IV. 20 ekasamaye co 'bhayā 'navadhāraṇaṁ

Nor can it be said that the mind is simultaneously both the perceiver and the perceived, the observer and the observed. For, then there would not be rational comprehension.

Is it possible, asks someone, for this inner intelligence to know the mind, and the mind to know the object? Here Patanjali says that is not possible, it is terribly silly. Who is the observer now? Are there a string of observers? If the mind observed the external object and the intelligence observed the mind, the mind could cheat the observer, the intelligence could cheat the mind. There would be confusion and chaos—whereas we see that there is no such chaos in life. Life goes on smoothly, there is order in the functioning of the intelligence.

This means that there is only one real observer and that is the intelligence, the witness. It is that intelligence which is the witness of the mind and of the world, which is not involved in the mental modifications (the change that the mind undergoes) and which does not undergo the change that the world undergoes. It is this intelligence that links the mind with the object. In other words, that intelligence is one and indivisible and, like the waves arising in the one mass of water called the ocean, the thought arises *here*, the object arises *there*.

Thus the world and the mind are not two eternally separate entities, but two aspects of one cosmic totality, very much like what goes on in dream. In dream you create yourself and also others, and that 'yourself' in the dream talks to and plays with the others whom you have created, treats some as enemies and some as friends. That is what is suggested here. There is this inner intelligence which is undivided. At one point it is the mind which thinks, which observes, which sees the objects outside and which measures. Because it is ignorant of their real nature, it creates notions and concepts about them. All this happens in this undivided inner intelligence, which is uninvolved in both the changes that take place in the mind and in the external world of objects. That is cosmic intelligence and it is what it is, forever and ever.

If the mind itself is considered the source of knowledge and understanding, if you think that there is nothing other than the mind, then there is no comprehension. If you consider that it is the mind that knows the world and itself, there is no understanding. This Sūtra merely says that if the mind is both the perceiver and the perceived, the observer and the observed, there is no comprehension, only hallucination. If it is possible for one to analyse or to understand the mind with the mind, it is like water being diluted by water. Nothing happens and yet there is a tremendous illusion of a comprehension.

This Sūtra is also a serious blow to most of the techniques that people adopt—meditation, science of the mind and self-understanding, etc. One can see this in one's spiritual or religious practice. It is the mind that conjures up an image called God, chews it, experiences it, sees it and pats its own back, saying, "I have seen God". Much of what goes by the name of religious experience (as well as hallucination) falls into this category. The mind thinks that it is able to know, to understand. As a matter of fact even our normal emotional experiences fall into this category. One must understand that what is a painful experience is nothing other than what the mind itself regards as a painful experience, and then suffers from. Who is it that created it, that named it a painful experience, that has converted an experience into a painful experience? The mind.

We discussed in a previous Sūtra that the world in itself is a neutral object. It is the moods of the mind that determine whether these experiences or objects are painful or pleasant, happy or unhappy. That applies even to your own psychological experiences. What are they, except what the mind has decided to create within itself? For instance, you dislike this experience, you hate it, and it becomes painful from your point of view; since you are involved in it, it hurts you. If the mind decides that another is a pleasant experience, then it becomes a pleasant experience, otherwise it does not. The same mind says: "I am experiencing pain or pleasure." It's a vicious circle, and therefore there is no comprehension of the reality. You are experiencing, chewing your own ideas; you are a cannibal. The thing itself is not experienced. One doesn't know what it is.

It is possible for observation to take place without creating an observer in the mind. The mind being a mere reflecting medium—something that receives an impression of the image or the object—it reflects the world. There is no observer here. The mind goes on changing its moods, the object goes on changing its shape and there is an observer of the whole lot. That observing intelligence is supreme; it is a mysterious connecting link, the substratum for both the object as well as the mind. It is like the sun that shines on the mirror that is reflected on the wall. The light belongs to the sun, there is only one light; the mirror is a reflector, not the source of light.

IV. 21 cittā 'ntara dṛśye buddhi buddher atiprasaṅgaḥ smṛti saṁkaraś ca

If it is assumed that there are two minds—the observer and the observe—this would result in logical absurdity (since both are based on the same intelligence, who designates the distinction?) and also confusion of memory or universal schizophrenia, which is not found to be the case.

If you think you have two completely different minds, one overseeing the other, one controlling the other, one directing the other, then there may be such a terrible confusion that there would be universal schizophrenia. *Smṛti saṁkaraś ca* is 'a confusion of memory'. Which mind is going to receive what kind of impression? But we are unable to function intelligently or sanely in such a condition, because it is not the real condition.

It is the experience of everyone that this inner intelligence is undivided and indivisible and therefore in it there is observation without an observer. The mind is an observed object. Just as you are able to see another, even so the moods of the mind are also observed. One is able to say, "My mind is disturbed, dull, confused or clear," so the mind itself becomes an object of observation.

IV. 22 citer apratisaṁkramāyās tad ākārā 'pattau sva buddhi saṁvedanaṁ

The undivided intelligence or homogeneous consciousness in which there is no movement of thought is aware of its own enlightened or awakened nature on account of its awareness of the apparent movement of thought. There is paradoxical movement in non-movement, which is the total intelligence.

Suddenly Patanjali uses another word. One who studies these Sūtras has to take note of the special Sūtra where a new word or concept is introduced. *Citta* can be (and has been) used both in terms of the substratum for the mind or the undivided intelligence, and also for the ordinary mind or the individualised consciousness. Now suddenly Patanjali uses the word '*citer*'. This *citi,* in contra-distinction to *citta,* is intelligence. One has to understand these words and, suited to the context, one has to study and meditate deeply upon these Sūtras and then arrive at a proper understanding.

Citi is consciousness, undivided and indivisible intelligence. Thus it encompasses, synthesises and links the object with the mind. Let us go back to the mirror. The sun shines on the mirror, the mirror directs a beam of light onto the wall, and the light links all these three. What are the three? The three are one; the same light is reflected in the mirror and projected onto the wall. Somehow there seems to be a link, but the link is also light. It is not as though there is one light there, another light in the mirror here and a projected light in between. The light is in effect one, single and indivisible. If you obstruct that light the mirror becomes dead, useless, and the object is not illumined.

In this indivisible intelligence the mind seems to shine as if independent, and it seems to have the power of comprehension. It seems to be an apparent reality, but that is not so. When it faces this inner light it seems to have a luminosity of its own, and in that luminosity the external object is seen.

All these are dependent upon this one, single, undivided and indivisible inner intelligence. In this inner intelligence there seems to arise an entity called the mind, which is not an entity totally independent of this inner intelligence. It reflects this inner intelligence in such a way that it seems as though that mind itself is intelligence. That intelligence comprehends a thing called an external object, projects its own ideas, its own notions and its own definitions upon it, and then says, "I know this to be So-and-so." What sees? It is this inner intelligence that really sees. That, being consciousness, is always conscious, ever aware.

Whether the mirror is turned towards the sun or away from the sun, the sun always shines. Whether the mind functions—thinking, feeling or experiencing—or whether it goes fast asleep, that intelligence is always there. If you and I are conversing with each other, you are listening and I am talking, and the mind is very active. In that state, obviously this mind-mirror is facing this inner light, this intelligence. Therefore the intelligence is reflected in the mind, enabling it to function—even to feel that it is an independent entity capable of knowing and under-standing an object. Then later we fall asleep; the mind covers itself with a veil and goes to sleep, but that inner intelligence is awake even then. The sun never sets; it is the earth that turns around. Even so, this inner intelligence is forever awake, forever alert, forever intelligent, forever conscious. It is always aware, it is *awareness*. Why does it shine? It shines because it *is* awareness.

How can that which is one be experienced at all? It cannot be experienced as an experience. Only because it is of the nature of awareness can it be aware of itself. Since the very nature of the reality is awareness, there is aware*ness*. In the state of enlightenment (if it can be called so) the awareness is not aware of itself as an object, but there is awareness. If at night you want to see something you light a candle or a light, and in that light you see the object. If your child has dropped a candle on a bundle of clothes in the next room and you realise that there is a fire, do you take a candle to go and look at that? Without the use of another light the burning bundle of clothes announces, "I am here." All that you do is merely follow the light to its source. That is *dhyāna,* meditation.

Meditation is not making that an object. The self (or this pure awareness) shines by its own light, and the attention merely follows that, and there it is. It is not seen as an object, it is seen as that which *is.* In that light you imagine that itself to be an object. You are the light, that is the light, between both is the light; and yet you thought it was something else. That light is the truth or the reality which absorbs the 'you' and the 'me', the subject and the object. 'Absorb' is the wrong word. To go back to the example of the handkerchief, the cloth does not absorb the two ends; but if you see these two ends as two ends, and suddenly look into the middle, these two ends seem to have got into the cloth!

What exists is what existed and what will exist. What is now gone is that which never was. There is only one cloth, but you saw two ends in it. When you realise that there was only one cloth, what happened to the two ends? They are still there, not as ends of the cloth but as the cloth.

IV. 23 draṣṭṛ dṛśyo 'paraktaṁ cittaṁ sarvārthaṁ

The same mind takes on the role of the observer and the very same mind then observes the colouring of the mind which becomes the observed—the subject and the object: it is indeed everything. Hence, the self is but an idea.

Now comes the final thing. Enlightenment is not the result of what you do, but it does not happen without you doing what you are doing. I do not know how the Christians interpret this saying of Jesus, which is exactly the same, "Knock and it shall be opened." The door does not open if you don't knock, and the door does not open because you knock. Don't think that when you knock that somebody else *must* open it. The same thing can be said of grace; grace by its very definition does not depend upon your deservedness. If you deserve his affection and he gives it to you, that is business exchange; but when you don't deserve and still he is affectionate towards you, that is grace. This was also said by Jesus in the Sermon on the Mount. But that should not lead you to feel that God's grace *will* come. It may not! So you have to knock. You have to practise yoga, meditation and all the rest of it.

Enlightenment is there already, because it is the subject which has no object. There is another beautiful description of this consciousness as neither subject nor object. (Back to the example of the handkerchief again.) Here is a piece of cloth. This is one end of the cloth and this is another end. I am holding one end with my left hand and one end with my right hand. Can you see the two ends? Apparently this end is the subject and the other end is the object. Of course when *this* becomes the subject *that* becomes the object, but there is no end at all, it is just cloth.

Now Vāsiṣṭha says that what is the reality is something between the subject and the object; but it is not something *between* the subject and the object, because if you say it is between here and between there then you are able to take it out. This is not possible, because that is also included in it. The subject and the object are also included in consciousness. These two ends are also included in this cloth. It is not as though the end is there and then cloth starts from somewhere else. So between the subject and the object is the reality; and in the reality there is no subject and no object.

In that reality, all these experiences arise and fall. When an experience arises in this, that experience is accompanied by its opposite. When there is an experience of pleasure there is at the same time an experience of pain. If you drop a big rock in a swimming pool a wave is created, and right next to it there is a hole. When you build a brick or mud house, you are digging a hole somewhere. So any of these dualistic notions carries the opposite with it, and therefore there is no opposite.

Here is a piece of paper; this side is facing me, that is the opposite side. All our life we are trying to have one side, not the other. You cannot do that. If I want this side, that side also comes with it. You can even do something very clever. There are two sides; if you take half of these two, it will be one! But if you take a sharp knife and cut it in half you have four sides now! This is what we do when we try to solve our problems. When you are looking for a thing called pleasure, pain comes with it; and you don't want that pain. So you cut that into half and create four more—for the simple reason that this unity, that combines or links all this, is the truth.

IV. 24 tad asaṁkhyeya vāsanābhiś citram api parārthaṁ saṁhatyakāritvāt

Though the mind is motivated in its actions by numerous and diverse tendencies, in reality it exists and functions for another, because it is able to function in conjunction with the undivided indwelling intelligence. The mind does not exist apart from that intelligence and the diverse tendencies.

IV. 25 viśeṣa darśina ātmabhāva bhāvanā vinivṛttiḥ

One who sees this completely and clearly is freed from the false and imaginary notion of self.

IV. 26 tadā hi vivekanimnaṁ kaivalya prāgbhāraṁ cittaṁ

Then the whole mind flows towards wisdom and the realisation of complete freedom or liberation.

IV. 27 tac chidreṣu pratyayā 'ntarāṇi saṁskārebhyaḥ

It is possible during such periods when this awareness of this freedom is interrupted there arise other thoughts on account of the mind's past habits of thinking.

IV. 28 hānam eṣāṁ kleśavad uktaṁ

These habit-moulds are also to be treated as sources of psychic distress or disturbance and got rid of in the same manner described already.

IV. 29 prasaṁkhyāne 'py akusīdasya sarvathā viveka khyāter dharma meghaḥ samādhiḥ

Where there is no interest in or attraction whatsoever even for the highest kind of intellectual knowledge and experience and where there is uninterrupted self-awareness there comes a state of enlightenment which is like a cloud that showers virtue or order.

IV. 30 tataḥ kleśa karma nivṛttiḥ

When thus order is restored in the mind and therefore in behaviour, all actions that favour psychic distress are effortlessly avoided.

IV. 31 tadā sarvā 'varaṇa malāpetasya jñānasyā 'nantyāj jñeyam alpaṁ

Then, since all the veils have been removed and all the impurities have been destroyed, there is infinite knowledge—little remains to be known or experienced (or, the objects of knowledge or experience are seen to be conditioned, finite and worthless.)

IV. 32 tataḥ kṛtārthānāṁ pariṇāmakrama samāptir guṇānāṁ

Thus, they who have realised this have fulfilled their mission in life. And the beginningless succession of changes of the qualities or characteristics, that was falsely assumed to be related to the self—which itself was the final notion—comes to an end. (Or, the succession of changes of qualities that have reached the fulfillment of their purpose, comes to an end.)

IV. 33 kṣaṇa pratiyogī pariṇāmā 'parānta nirgrāhyaḥ kramaḥ

What is regarded as continuous succession is only a series of individual and independent moments. When the last moment is not apprehended as being part of a continuum, the false notion of succession and therefore of time comes to an end.

There is no sequence in time. Sequence in time is a misnomer, illusion; and by contemplating the non-sequentiality in time you see that each moment is an independent moment, totally unrelated to the past and the future.

There are two completely different approaches to a problem. One is to solve it—you may *have* to solve it—but there are other situations in which it is not possible to solve it; but it *is* possible to dissolve it, to see exactly what it is. When the problem is dissolved there are no psychological or emotional hang-ups resulting from that; then our relationships will be smooth. To dissolve it is to deflate it—in other words, it is not invested with importance. So in other words, both of us independently decide that it is unimportant.

First of all, the problem becomes important when the memory stores it. The events themselves are not stored. Each act is an independent act, unrelated to the previous one, but the memory starts piling these up. It is then that it becomes heavy. For instance, the hunger that we experienced just before lunch is just one day's hunger. We have experienced hunger every day for the past years, but that does not add up to a cumulative effect of hunger today. So the body intelligence is capable of dealing only with one problem, the problem that is right in front of it now.

The body intelligence is only capable of spontaneous action. It is not capable of dealing with an accumulated effect.

IV. 34 puruṣārthaśūnyānāṁ guṇānāṁ prati prasavaḥ kaivalyaṁ svarūpa pratiṣṭhā vā citiśakter iti

The qualities and the characteristics of a person have no goal or motivation any more. They return to their cause, ignorance! There emerges creative independence. The undivided cosmic intelligence, which is omnipotent, regains as it were its own identity.

OM TAT SAT

APPENDIX

VṚTTIS

Vṛttis or modifications of the mind are the only basis for the changes that your mind undergoes. They are successive. You do not know of a state or mood other than these, because as long as you are awake you are a slave to these thoughts. You don't even know if there is an 'I' apart from the moods of the mind. You are merely studying them, because you feel you are trapped in these changing moods of the mind and it doesn't feel good. It is possible that during these changes the change also brings along a little bit of pleasure, but that pleasure is not appreciated and doesn't seem to be very pleasant, because while you are enjoying it you are also conscious that it is going to come to an end. There is going to be a reaction to it, you are going to lose it. It is much easier for you not to have enjoyed this pleasure in the first place, than to have it and then lose it. If you didn't have it at all you wouldn't be unhappy at the loss!

Can you manoeuvre this so that only one kind of experience is had by you? That is absurd. Once you have seen that things keep revolving from one to the other—day and night, day and night—it is absurd for you even to think of a condition in which only day or night will prevail. Looking at this, can you accept that life is miserable? It is not possible, because there is something which rebels against this condition. Can you live in the hope that one day you will be free from this? No, this hope doesn't solve the present problem. When somebody is ready to jump on your throat, you can say "One day I will be strong and fight you." He will floor you now! So a future hope doesn't solve the present problem, however much we may pretend it does.

There is no possibility of getting away from this, nor can you ever hope to get reconciled to it. It is then that you are intensely and immediately conscious. You are caught up in this problem which is with you until it is finally solved. You cannot rebel against it because it is with you.

In the Buddha's last sermon he said "Live in this world as if you are living in the room with a cobra." There is no sense in teasing a poisonous snake that is under your bed. It will strike you. You don't get reconciled to it and you don't accept it. It may not accept *you*! You can't reject it, you can't revolt against it and you are locked in this room alone with the cobra. Then you live with such tremendous alertness and care—not in the sense of worry, but in the sense of "I am looking at it, I don't let it go out of my inner vision for a single moment." That is called *nirodha,* control.

Control is not suppression of these *vṛttis,* because you cannot suppress them. When they are controlled it means that you are living with such intense alertness and care that in all these changes you are really unaffected.

Suddenly, like a flash of lightning, you begin to understand that these changes happen, but there is an unchanging witness to all this. That which is aware of these changing moods is itself not changing. The whole thing takes place in one substance—intelligence—that in its unmodified state is able to watch all the modifications that take place on its own surface. The whole thing is *citta*—just as the waves, streams, currents, and moving substratum is ocean. Ocean is not the name for just one part of this structure; the whole thing is the ocean, the whole thing is the *citta.*

The movements take place only in relation to an observer. The river flows only in relation to a person standing on the bank of the river, but if you *are* the river, there is no movement, no motion, no change. Today the hair on your head has grown perhaps 1/50th of an inch. You don't even know it grew, because it is part of you. You are that, you are the whole thing, you are the totality.

It is only when you separate yourself from any one of these experiences that it is seen as a movement. When you are the total existence, total intelligence, there *is* no movement. When 'I am' the total consciousness, all changes that take place in that total consciousness are part of the total consciousness; just as in one body, for instance, tremendous activity is going on all the time—venous blood is being pumped into the heart and the heart is pumping out arterial blood—but as you are sitting in meditation you seem to be completely immobile, steady and firm. When you look at small fragments of your own physical body, you find tremendous activity going on in every department, but when you view the whole thing it is one—stable, steady and peaceful. There are no changes at all. That is *citta vṛtti nirodha*.

I don't think that there are simple words in which this simple phenomenon can be explained, or the Sūtra quickly translated. One has to understand the whole concept of *vṛttis*. Only as long as you isolate one little *vṛtti* and look at it does it seem to be painful or pleasant. When the whole intelligence is seen as one, realised as one, there are no problems and no suffering.

GOD'S WILL

If you are able to get rid of all the notions that arise concerning a certain relationship, then the natural relationship remains. In short, when the *vṛttis* are gone, life goes on; and to what happens *then* people have used the expression 'God's will is done'. It is not as though this person *knows* what God's will is; it only means that this did not happen on account of his individual will. There is a section in the **Yoga Vāsiṣṭha** which describes this very beautifully:

" The desire that arises in the course of one's own natural functions devoid of craving, is that of a liberated sage. But that desire which is bound up with craving for external objects, is conducive to bondage. When all ego-based notions have ceased in one's heart, the attention that is directed naturally is also the nature of the liberated sage.

"That which is afflicted by contact with external objects is the craving conducive to bondage. The non-volitional desire which is unaffected by any object is liberation.

"That desire which existed even before contact with the objects, exists even now and for ever. It is natural, therefore sorrowless and free from impurity. Such a desire is regarded by the wise as free from bondage. 'I want this'—when such a craving arises in one's heart, it gives rise to impurity. Such a craving should be abandoned by a wise person by all means and at all times. Give up the desire that tends to bondage and the desire for liberation, too. Remain still like the ocean, knowing that the self is free from old age and death. Let not these disturb your mind. When the whole universe is

realised as illusory, craving loses its meaning."

EXPRESSION AND EXPERIENCE

The movement of energy in consciousness is experience from one end and expression from the other only in relation to the personality. Consciousness has this energy inherent in it and therefore there is no duality there. The energy is constantly in motion. (That is what energy means!) In relation to that energy *itself* there is no motion. In relation to consciousness there is no energy at all—it is inherent in it, just as you are a living being. (A living being means you are alive! You don't have to say, "I am a living being who is alive". There is no living being who is dead!) Energy is motion, and therefore there is no motion as far as the energy is concerned. It is only when it is compared, or related, to something else that one could say that there is motion, there is a duality. That motion itself is undivided.

The individuality or personality seems to exist from a certain point of view (or plane of understanding.) It is that individuality which interprets that movement of energy in consciousness as experience here, and expression there.

The personality is dependent upon its own conditioning (predisposition), and its own mood—two things are involved here. Sweet is not sweet to all beings; and even in the case of those beings to whom sweet is sweet, it is not *always* sweet. So the characterisation of the experience as pleasant and unpleasant is dependent on these two things.

It is the personality that receives this movement of energy, which first interprets it as experience. There *is* no experience, it is a mere vibration passing through; it would not bother you at all, if the 'I' were not there. Because the 'I' is set up as something independent, it bothers you, touches you. When it touches you, depending upon your previous predisposition and present mood, you call it pleasant or unpleasant.

The same movement of energy is seen as experience at one stage and expression at the other stage. Your expression is my experience, and my expression is your experience. This means that what is called expression at one point becomes experience at another point—the two points being two ends of the same object, the same substance. It is like road signs when there is construction on the road. On one side the caution is "Ten miles per hour zone begins." On the other side it is written "Ten miles per hour ends." If you are going from this side it begins, if you are coming from that side, the same thing is the end. The end is the beginning! You think that there are two ends, but there are two beginnings, too. If that is to be the end, this is the beginning and if that is to be the beginning, that is to be the end. So if it is to be an expression there, it is an experience here—and *vice versa*. It is the same thing.

All these are clearly, but confusingly, interrelated. Clearly if you can see it clearly, and confusingly if it is confusing to you. From me it is expression and in you it is experience. If that experience is interpreted by you as good, the expression that proceeds from here is supposed to be good action. (Isn't that what is meant by 'the happiness of all beings'?) So if you are happy, what he is doing is good, if you are unhappy whatever he is doing is evil, never mind what he calls it. Do you see the point? It is quite simple. Expression and experience being the two ends of the same stick, you cannot say 'I know you are made miserable by what I am doing, but what I am doing is very good.' It is *not* good. Something is missing, something is wrong somewhere.

The characterisation of experience and the characterisation of expression are entirely dependent upon 'me'.

As long as the me is there the division will continue to be, the distinctions will continue to be and the struggle will continue to be.

CONCENTRATION

The world around us presents various experiences through the senses—the ears, eyes, nose, the tactile sense and the sense of taste. At least through the first four the world constantly pours into your mind; and yet what you do not pay attention to immediately, does not exist, (at least it is not perceived). In the same way, perhaps, the memories of all the events that have taken place since our birth are stored in the brain, but until the attention or selective perception is focused upon a particular memory, it is not revived. For instance, this morning when I was looking for a name, as soon as I looked at that person the attention was focused upon that particular bit of memory, and the name was remembered.

This happens to us all the time. It is concentrating our attention that makes us revive this memory and enables us to perceive the world. So concentration is not something that is only part of yoga practice, but something which we do nearly all the time—otherwise if all the memories that were stored in your brain suddenly made themselves manifest now, you would go crazy. For instance, when you go to the theatre or watch a Western movie film, all your attention is gripped there—you don't even know who is sitting next to you.

This gives you an indication that it is possible for you to focus your attention. The yogi wants to know *how* to make this happen. To deliberately and voluntarily focus the attention upon something, is concentration. If somebody watches your breathing while you are concentrating and entering into the meditative mood, he will see that the breath becomes very fine and smooth. In meditation the breathing becomes so fine that you almost do not notice it—there is no deep breathing at all, the breath is nearly suspended. The entire force of the mind, the beam of consciousness, seems to flow in one stream. Mind is a flowing thing, it is not static. You can't arrest it, or bottle it up. When you think you have stopped the functioning of the mind you only *think* you have stopped it.

To concentrate is to let the mind flow in a single direction and let this happen where and how you want. There is a restriction of the spatial dissipation of mental energies. For instance, at one time you can hear something, you see all sorts of things, you can smell cooking, you feel the chill wind, you are thinking partly of what you are going to do tomorrow—all the rays of the mind are dissipated. When all the rays are gathered together and beamed on a single object, this is *dhāraṇā* or concentration.

Though ultimately the distinction (or the division or distance) between the experiencer and the experience has also to be abolished, the yogis insist that you become aware of what you are doing at the moment—though that awareness is not meditation. For instance, while you are driving a car become totally aware of everything that you are doing—the feeling of the steering wheel in the hands, the feeling of the back resting on the seat—everything. Then you are there, you are driving and you know exactly what is happening. Why should you do this? Because if you don't your mind, your heart and soul is somewhere else, and the driving takes place automatically, mechanically, blindly.

In yoga we learn to focus and direct the beam of attention on itself, on the perceiving subject. You may look at the object in front of you, but its perception takes place within you. When the entire stream of consciousness pours within you on to that spot where this is perceived, the picture becomes clearer and clearer. Instead of seeing what is outside, see its reflection within. Then begin the questions "Which is the reflection of what? Is this the reality which is reflected within me, or is that the reality which is reflected there? Is that a tape recorder which is reflected in my mind as a tape recorder, or do I have the thought that that is a tape recorder and therefore it is seen as a tape recorder?" Which comes first? Does the idea arise in you that that is a tape recorder, or does it come and hit you on your head and say, "I am a tape recorder"? The two (if they are two at all) happen almost simultaneously. There is a confusion, and one doesn't know which is the substance and which the shadow; which the reality and which the reflection.

Once the attention is focused in a single beam, one end of the beam of attention is the idea that arises and the other end is considered the object. You don't know what the object is, but is it possible for you to watch the subject, the idea that arises, and hold it in sharp focus? Can this single idea be held intensely?

Intensely means without the interference of tense—past, future or even present tense. When you look at a girl, for instance, the idea arises "That is Miss So-and-so". That is past tense. You remember that she might go to Europe next year. That is future tense. You think she is a nice girl. That is present tense.

What creates these tenses—the present, past and future tense? Thought! So when you dismiss (or when the intense observation itself dismisses) these three tenses, then the attention has gone beyond tension (which is born of the tense) and gone beyond thought. That is where the reality is—beyond thought and beyond the tense. This does not mean that thoughts are bad or thoughts are to be abolished. If thoughts are abolished completely, then who knows what thought is? Keep the thought and look into it.

So first there is the focusing of attention, then the attention is focused on itself, intensely. When all these three tenses are removed, you are intensely watching her—or watching the reality of what is here, the idea of what that is. When this ideation which arises within becomes absolutely clear (for the simple reason that the attention is totally absorbed in it) that is meditation.

MEDITATION

Simple Method

Here is a simple procedure that in due course will enable you to enjoy deep meditation:

1. Sit preferably facing east (the sun rises in the east) or north (there is great power in the north pole) with a symbol of God or a lighted candle or lamp placed in front of you at eye level. The best posture is, of course, *padmāsana* or lotus posture. If you cannot do this, sit in any comfortable position with the spine erect. The best time is from 4 a.m. to 6 a.m., but if this is not possible, do it as soon as you wake up. It is good to have a quick bath, but if this is not possible without loss of the good morning hour, have a quick wash of hands, feet and face.

2. Chant a few hymns or offer your own prayer, audibly, to the Lord. This is like switching the radio on and tuning it. Raise the mind to a higher level. Imagine you are in the presence of God. This may appear to be self-hypnotism, but the results are astounding.

3. Chant OM deeply, concentrating on the solar plexus, feeling that the sound vibrations arise from there. Feel that these sound-vibrations travel upwards towards the crown of the head, through the vagus nerve. They actually will.

When they reach the throat region, close your lips and continue Ommmmmmmmmmmmm and let the sound 'fade out' at the crown of the head. Do this three or six times.

4. If the OM-chanting has not succeeded in completely turning the mind inwards, and especially if there is some external disturbance, do this: breathe deeply, but effortlessly, and at the same time close the glottis a little bit, so that the breath produces some sound. (It is not the vocal cords, but the glottis that helps to produce this sound—not unlike when you are suffering from a mild cold.) Let this sound also fade away and do not stop abruptly. You will find that your mind follows this sound and 'goes inwards'.

5. Breathe slowly now. Watch the breath. Now listen to it without producing any sound even with the throat.

6. Mentally repeat your *mantra* (any name of God or sacred formula or OM) now, as you breathe in and out, without straining the breath. Associate the *mantra* with the breath—this is the trick. Repeat it once while you breathe in and once while you breathe out. If the *mantra* is long, break it into two; repeat half while inhaling and half while exhaling.

7. Keep looking at the picture, symbol or flame in front of you. (That is what you have been doing all the time, at least from step 4.) But transfer that symbol to within yourself. Feel that the image is in your own heart. 'See' it there. Do not stare at the picture or flame in front of you—if you do your eyes will get tired and begin to smart—but let the symbol go out of focus. Do not worry. Your eyes will not blink, water or smart.

8. Now close your eyes, and visualise that image of God. Feel His presence within your heart. Let it be radiant and 'living'.

9. Gradually let that image expand till it occupies your whole body, the room in which you are sitting and eventually the whole world. Feel this. Feel that you yourself are just a little part of God, but one with Him.

This *must* lead to meditation. That which you visualise now will become real in due course.

10. Sit like this for a minimum period of 20 minutes. Gradually increase the period. If, by the grace of God and guru, you lose body-consciousness and enjoy sitting, carry on! The prescribed time is only the minimum.

11. After this, offer a prayer to the Lord for the health and long life of the sick (whom you can actually visualise in front of you) and peace and prosperity of those who are suffering. This is very, very important. This is the greatest service you can render to humanity. You feel your oneness with all—that is the spirit of No. 9 above. You can easily radiate health, happiness and joy.

12. Get up slowly. Do not immediately run away. Take a few minutes before you leave the meditation-room. Your mind and your nerves were extremely calm during this practice and if you suddenly jump out of that mood and rush into company, you might 'injure' the nerves. This is very important.

13. Do not sit for this practice within two hours after a meal. Do not wear tight clothing.

14. Do not eat anything for half an hour after this practice. And, do not take a bath immediately either.

15. If you wish to do a few rounds of *prāṇāyāma,* you may do so before you start this meditation-practice, or soon after step 2 above.

Meditation on the Self

Meditation is the direct and immediate observation of the arising of the 'I' with no mediator at all. No mediator is of any use to you here, because a mediator is another distraction. Even words and description of meditation may be another distraction.

Therefore yogis have given us very nice exercises, which again must lead us on nonstop to the discovery of the ego. Where does the ego sense arise? When one is able to observe where the ego sense arises, *that* is meditation. Here one immediately realises that this is the mischief maker, the villain who has brought about a division, who has disrupted the harmony that exists all the time and who has destroyed love.

Yoga can also be interpreted as the junction of the fracture and the healing agent. The darkness of ignorance and the light—that junction is also yoga. When these two come together, healing takes place. What is healing? Making it whole. Making it whole is just a phrase, it was whole already! Unlike the fracture of a bone, consciousness cannot be fractured. You and I are one for ever. Nothing can disrupt our unity, harmony and love, just as in our sleep we forget our identity and regain it when we wake up, and yet the identity has not been disrupted. You and I are one, there is this oneness and oneness alone, but there is some mysterious loss of memory. Meditation restores that knowledge, that understanding.

What is meant by 'meditation on the Self'? The Self is the meditator and the Self in meditation contemplates whatever it contemplates; and whatever it contemplates it becomes, because that contemplation and the Self are not two different things. That thing itself becomes you. 'You' becomes 'that', 'that' becomes 'you'. There is no distinction whatsoever. It's quite simple and beautiful. The Self is intelligence, the Self is the essence of the unconditioned mind, the pure mind; and in that there is an idea, a thought, a dream, a vision.

* * * * * * * *

Can you cultivate any quality—humility, for instance? How do you do that? What is the mind seeing at that time? If you say "I am a very humble man. If you don't recognise this, I'll fight you!" what kind of humbleness is that?

If you are a bully—rude in your behaviour, vicious in your thoughts—and you want to become suddenly non-violent, what do you do? Is it as simple as changing your shirt? You can pretend or think that you have dropped all violence, but at the least provocation it will come up. If you are ashamed of yourself, you can either pretend or rationalise it. For instance, there was a very violent Swami in India. One day we questioned him: "You get angry so easily. You scold people and are rough with them. Why?" His reply was: "Yes of course I am. We swamis are the ones who can, because we are here to correct all these people. Angry? Yes, definitely I can get angry." Why rationalise it?

Do you understand the difficulty? It is not possible for you to cultivate these good qualities. So, what *can* you do? You must grow in meditation, in self-awareness; and as you grow in this self-awareness, you *see* self-awareness. Meditation does not mean closing the eyes! Self-awareness means awareness throughout the day. There is self-awareness as I am sitting here talking to you. As you are sitting here listening, can you also watch yourself? Can you also watch what is happening to the mind all the time?

When you can do this you discover, firstly, that this bad-temper, falsehood, greed and so on are disturbances to the mind and therefore painful. Only when you realise, can you see directly for yourself that what you and I call evil, is painful—not because you see what someone else told you, but you see for *yourself* that it is painful.

Secondly—which is even more interesting—by this self-awareness you see that there is absolutely no difference at all between the emotion of hate and the emotion of affection. (I don't want to use the word love.) Both hating and affection involve the same charge of energy; though you see that affection is a very pleasant thing, while hate is unpleasant, painful. When you can see this for yourself, then you have won the battle.

Meditation on a Mantra

You cannot really focus your attention on things that are created by something or other from outside. If, for instance, you try to contemplate a feeling like aggression, there *is* no aggression or excitement. You realise that you were excited some time ago, but now you are not. Therefore a specific voluntary mental activity, which *can* be observed, is introduced in the form of a *mantra*. You are observing the mind or the *citta*, but only a specific field—the *mantra* sound that is heard. (If you have learned how to observe that *mantra* you have also learned how to observe every mood that arises in the mind—fear, worry, etc.)

Your eyes may be directed at the tip of your nose, your forehead or wherever you want to look, but you are not looking out at all. If you are serious in the practise of concentration it doesn't make the least difference if your eyes are open or closed. If you have resolved that you will not communicate with another it is easy to keep the eyes open in meditation. But when there is the possibility of communication, keeping the eyes open may be a distraction.

The eyes do not see what you think you see! What the eyes see, only the eyes know. *You* do not know! When the attention is directed to the *mantra* within, the eyes can do what they want to do. Even this we have experienced in our life, sometime or other. For instance, when you are enjoying yourself on the beach and suddenly you remember that you have left the washing machine on, then you are not seeing what you are looking at, you are looking at what goes on within you!

When it comes to the use of a *mantra* in *japa* make sure that your whole attention is listening to the *mantra*. The attention is focused on a specific field. The *mantra* should not be vague, but absolutely clear. When the observing intelligence is locked in with the object of its own observation—that is, only these two exist in the world—there is complete and total concentration. Only the observer and the observed exist.

For a moment you realise that even the observed is reflected in you, it is not outside of you. It becomes clear in the example of the *mantra.* When you think you are repeating the *mantra,* you hear the *mantra;* when you think you hear the *mantra,* you are repeating the *mantra.* They are two aspects of the same thing, they become interchangeable. When the whole mind becomes the *mantra,* there is meditation—nothing else bothers you. (That is what happens to two lovers. Their own personality is gone, the whole mind is occupied by the other person. If this has not happened to you, you don't know how to love!) You are aware of nothing other than this *mantra,* but you are aware of a division between the one who repeats the *mantra* and the one who listens to the *mantra.* There is a division there: 'I' hear the '*mantra*'.

Then comes the last stage.

You repeat the *mantra* and focus all your attention on it until that sound becomes uppermost. You have then avoided the distractions and there is clarity of vision. When this *mantra* is the only thought (or object) that occupies the mind, that is called meditation already. But it is not a rigid static affair, because the mind—being vibrating consciousness—is not still, in the sense of dead matter. (It is very much like the sunshine in which we sit. The sun's rays pour on us in the same way that you are focusing your attention on the meditation object.) There is a stream of consciousness flowing towards it, and in meditation the object becomes clearer and clearer. You are not meditating *on* the object, you are meditating *in* the object. It looks as though you are entering into it, looking at it from inside. Standing outside and looking at it is concentration, and entering into it is meditation.

That is when you begin to ask "Am I repeating the *mantra* or am I listening to it?" At that point you are entering *into* the *mantra*.

You ask yourself "If the *mantra* sound is mind, what am I? Am I inside of it or outside of it? If I am in it I am also the mind, 'I' is also the mind." The mind, which was spread out as the world, has come to be restricted to this *mantra*. The only problem that remains is "What is the relation between this mind and me?" There is no verbal answer to that question, but when it arises it is possible that the *mantra* sound is suddenly not heard. (When meditation becomes deeper and the *mantra* alone remains—which means that the listener gets dissolved, meditation happens and the 'I' is not there—you will know what that means.) Here the 'me' blends into consciousness and the *mantra* blends into consciousness. Then there is no hearing of the *mantra*, because 'I' doesn't exist. This is something that cannot be put into words.

The mind has to be extremely alert in order to enter into this meditation. Meditation cannot enter into you; you must enter into it. The whole of your mind, the whole of your self must enter into meditation—"As if 'I' does not exist." That is when *samādhi* happens.

(Something else may prevent you from hearing the

mantra—you may fall asleep and on waking may think that you have entered into deep meditation! It is important to recognise that this was sleep.)

One cannot really say when concentration ends and meditation begins, or when meditation ends and *samādhi* begins. One flows into the other, and therefore the three are regarded as one unit.

Spiritual Growth

The change that is brought about by meditation is drastic, and total. It is so subtle that you yourself will not know it. The change that you *know* has taken place in you is not a desirable or healthy change.

You look in the mirror every day. The face this morning was not different from the face you saw yesterday morning, and that wasn't different from the day before yesterday. You can go on and on and come to the absurd conclusion that the face you saw today is exactly the same as it was twenty years ago. It's not true at all! Can you tell me that on the 1st January 1959 your nose grew half an inch longer? It didn't. It was exactly the same as the previous day. And yet, it *has* grown. The whole body grows, but without making the change felt. That is real growth.

If you wake up one morning and look at your face in the mirror and see that it has grown overnight—there is a lump on your cheek, for instance—you will rush to the doctor and have it cut out. It is dangerous!

In exactly the same way, any growth you are intensely aware of isn't real growth. If you used to smoke like a chimney last year, and this year you go around all the time, telling everybody "I don't smoke, I don't smoke now," you are still smoking. It is smoke, smoke, smoke that is coming out of your mouth! You used to smoke visibly last year and now it is invisible smoking. At the least temptation or provocation you will go back to that, because the mind is still smoking.

Real and total change is something that one is not aware of, because the change has been brought about deep within. The whole consciousness has undergone change. The consciousness was filthy, and now it has become clean. You don't see the change within yourself. But it may be noticed by other people.

It is what others have noticed in a yogi that has been recorded and handed down as discipline. People have noticed that a yogi doesn't tell lies, doesn't harm others, has pure thoughts, is not greedy, is clean in clothes, surroundings and in mind, etc. and leads a very simple life. They have put all these things together and given them as commandments. (See II. 29)

Aspects of the Mind

In meditation the stream does not flow outward, but inward. In order to understand an object, you cannot possibly let the attention flow onto the external object; you must examine your own mind (or consciousness) which apprehends and sees an object. The 'I' cannot possibly know what it is, because the vibrations that are emanated by it enter the senses—eyes, ears, etc.—and they are gathered by that aspect of the mind which is called *manas* (the coordinating agent or the registrar of the mental university).

For instance, if you look at a tape-recorder, the eyes see something, the ears hear something and the hands feel something. All these sensations are gathered together and co-ordinated by the *manas*. With that information the mind approaches another department, the memory bank or *citta*. "Did you see anything like this before? It is black and has a handle sticking out, such and such dimensions and makes a noise all the time. What is it?" The memory bank says, "Tape recorder."

The whole thing is projected again on to what is called the *buddhi,* or awakened intelligence. *Buddhi* is not a dull, routine, mechanical intelligence, but awakened intelligence which can recommend and give valued judgement, e.g. "It's a good one," "It's not such a good one," "I can afford it," "I cannot afford it." Then the entire thing is again presented to what is known as *ahaṃkāra* (egotism) which issues orders:

"Right, I'll buy it." "I don't want it." "I'll steal it." "It may be dangerous," etc.

Some of the yoga Scriptures even have detailed locations for these aspects of the mind. The *manas* (the co-ordinating agent) is said to be in the mid-brain, and the *citta* (memory bank) is supposed to be in the heart. It is the *citta* that provides emotional energy. (Don't you say, "He touched my heart," etc.? These are all figures of speech, but they do mean something. Even though physiologically the heart may not be a thinking organ, it seems to play some part in evoking emotional equilibrium or emotional outburst.) The value judgement or the *buddhi* is supposed to be on top of the brain. (Therefore, when you are confused you put your hand to the brow, "What must I do?" You are squeezing your *buddhi* to see if something will come out of it!) The *ahaṃkāra* or egoism is in the region of the heart.

So *manas* or the co-ordinator is in the middle of the head; the *citta,* or mind stuff or emotional part of your being, is in the heart; the *buddhi* is on top of the brain and the *ahaṃkāra,* or egotism, is also in the region of the heart.

If something in our daily life has an extraordinary emotional impact we act foolishly, because the head doesn't play any part at all in this—the senses are not co-ordinated here, nor is the *buddhi* consulted.

Immediately your emotional being is touched, the ego jumps in and says "I must have it." Afterwards you sit and regret for your whole life-time! Therefore, whenever there is a strong emotional reaction, the reaction is immediate, unthinking and unintelligent.

SAMADHI

Do you have the right understanding to know what is happening when you meditate? When you don't know, you associate some kind of hallucination or a deep comatose state with meditation and *samādhi.*

In the yoga Scriptures or *Śastra* there are descriptions of two types of *samādhi—jaḍa samādhi* and *caitanya samādhi. Jaḍa samādhi* is a state of stupidity, which is very easily mistaken for *caitanya samādhi* or superconscious state.

Here are stories which illustrate this:

In 1946 in our ashram in Rishikesh, we had a visitor, a remarkable man between 30 and 40 years of age. We were all youngsters in our early twenties. This man used to meditate, sitting in the lotus posture on a block of stone on the bank of the Ganges. He became almost one with the block of stone. In those days the Master himself used to conduct a prayer class in the mornings, from 5 am to 7 am. That gentleman would sit there from 4 am without a movement. We youngsters were terribly impressed with him because we found it very difficult to sit for half an hour in the lotus posture without something hurting, whereas this man maintained a perfect posture for three hours.

Sometimes I used to escort Swami Sivananda to his room and he would look at this chap and say, "Hm! See!

Samādhi". We didn't know whether to take him seriously, or whether he was jesting.

One day we were standing around talking to him. At seven o'clock this gentleman got up from his rock seat and walked into the presence of the Master. "Ah, you are meditating. Very good, very good! How long do you meditate?"

This man thought that the Master was very pleased. "Three hours, Swamiji."

"In deep meditation?"

"Yes, Swamiji. I have been doing this for the past fifteen years. Regularly, every morning from 4 to 7. Deep meditation".

All the time we were thinking that the Master was full of admiration for this man, and he was going to appoint him Lord of Heaven!

"Hm." He paused and then he suddenly burst out, "Look at him. Drowsy, sleepy. What is meditation?"

(We were all stunned and the man didn't know what to do with himself.)

"You were sitting and sleeping. Do you know what *samādhi* means? It means touching the omnipresence, coming into contact with the omnipresent, omniscient, omnipotent Being. To be one with the Creator of this Universe, to be one with this Cosmic Power. If you do that for half a second you will have such energy, such power, that you would roll up the whole Earth and play with it like a tennis ball. Look at this dreamy fellow! Drop this business—go and do some hard work and wake yourself up."

Another time a *sādhu* was sitting in the lotus posture under a tree on the bank of the Ganges, steadily looking at the tip of his nose—I saw him at about 7 am one day, and he was still sitting there at 3 pm. It looked as if he was in *samādhi*. I was impressed!

Two or three nights later there was a terrible commotion in the temple where he was living. I asked the chief priest of the temple what had happened. He said that that *sādhu* was a scoundrel and had been causing trouble. He was able to sit still for so long because he had taken a special drug. Whatever you are doing at the time the drug takes effect, you will continue to do while under the influence of the drug. So if you start laughing when you take it, you will laugh for eight hours!

People do all manner of things. There are people in the Himalayas who occasionally keep vigil all night, singing. They also take some drugs in order to keep themselves awake. But will it lead to enlightenment? No. Hallucination? Yes.

Some of us are capable of hallucinating with wide open eyes, without taking any drugs. Most of us are being fooled already with what we see in this world.

If you look into your own mind you can see a million hallucinations. All you have to do to see a drama is to look within and see what is going on in the mind. All your fears, worries, anxieties, hopes and cravings are a funny drama. They are all hallucinations already! Why must you take a drug in order to get into another hallucination?

Hallucination is not *samādhi* because it has not

produced a complete and drastic change in you. *Samādhi means* that complete and drastic change. The change must be total, complete.

If this drastic change is not brought about, then whatever one is doing is only wishful thinking. Wishful thinking is a very mild form of hallucination.

GLOSSARY

abhiniveśa: clinging to life in this body.

abhyāsa: practice, right exertion.

ahaṃkāra: 'I am'-ness, self-consciousness.
ahiṃsā: non-injury in thought, word and deed.
ānanda: bliss.
aparigraha: non-covetousness.
artha: actual thing in itself.
āsana: posture.
asmitā: egoism, I-ness.
aṣṭaṅga: eight limbs.
asteya: non-stealing.
ātmā: the Self.
avidyā: ignorance of the Self.
aviśeṣa: a non-special experience.
Bhagavad Gītā:The Scripture of yoga. A dialogue between Lord Krishna and Arjuna; a small excerpt from the Indian Epic, The Mahabharata
bhastrīka: forceful bellows breathing (hatha yoga).
bhāva: : mental attitude, inner feeling, purity of thought.
*bhāvanaṁ:*mental attitude,contemplation.
bhoga: enjoyment.
brahmacarya: celibacy.
Brahman: the Supreme Reality.
bhrānti: delusion, false idea.
bhūte: gross physical elements that constitute the physical universe.
caitanya: absolute consciousness
cakra: psychic centre in the human body.
citta: sub-conscious mind, indivisible intelligence.

darśan: audience, lit. 'seeing'.
daurmanasya: despair.
dhāraṇa: concentration.
dhyāna: meditation.
draṣṭā: see-er.
dṛg: the see-er.
duḥkha: pain, misery , grief.
dveṣa: repulsion.

gānjā: marihuana.
guru: teacher, preceptor.

Hatha Yoga: physical yoga.
hiṃsā: violence.

indriya: the senses.
Īśvara: God.
iṣṭadevatā: one's chosen deity.

jaḍa; insentient, non-intelligent
japa: repetition of a mantra.
jaya: victory.
jīva: soul

jñāna: wisdom.

kālena: time.
karma: action.
karuṇā: compassion.
kleśa: affliction, pain.
Kṛṣṇa: Hindu God.
kriyā: dynamic activity
Kriyā Yoga: the yoga of action.
kṣetram: field.
kuṅḍalini: primordial cosmic energy located in the individual.
liṅgamātra: an experience with special characteristics.

mantra: Sacred syllable or word or set of words through the repetition of which one attains perfection or the realisation of the Self.
maitrī: friendliness.
mokśa: liberation from bondage.
mudita: complacency, joy.
mūla: root.
nidrā: sleep.
nimitta: instrument.
nirodha: control, understanding.
nirvāṇa: liberation.
nirvicāra: without logic and enquiry.
niyama: moral virtues.

pracchardana: hold the breath out.
prajñā: consciousness.
prakāśa: light of intelligence.
pramādāḥ: carelessness, guilt.
pramāṇa: proof.
prāṇa: life force.
praṇavaḥ: sacred symbol OM.
prāṇāyāma: control of prāna.
praṇidhāna: surrender.
prasādanaṁ: purifying, clearing;gra ce.

pratipakṣa: of the opposite.
pratyāhāra: sense control.
puṇya: merit, virtue.
puruṣa: the supreme Being.
rāga: attraction, liking.
Rāja Yoga: yoga based on Patanjali's Yoga Sūtras.
Ramana Maharṣi: South Indian sage.
Rāma: Hindu god.

sādhanā: spiritual practices.
sahasrāra: thousand-petalled lotus at the crown of the head.
śakti: spiritual or psychic power.
samādhi: super-conscious state.
saṁśaya: doubt, suspicion.
saṁskāra: tendency, impression.
saṁtoṣād: contentment.
saṃyama: dhāraṇa, dhyāna and sam ādhi.
santoṣa: contentment.
sārūpya: having the same form as God.
sarvangāsana: shoulder-stand.
sattva: purity.
satya: truth or truthfulness.
śauca: cleanliness.
savicāra: samādhi with reasoning and deliberation.
siddha: a perfected being.
siddhis: psychic powers.
śīrṣāsana: headstand.
Śiva: one of the Hindu trinity, the preserver.
smṛti: memory, code of law.
smṛtayaḥ: thinking of, calling to mind
soham: I am That.
śraddhā: faith
sthira: firm.

stithi: material existence.
sukha: happiness, joy.
sūkṣma: subtle, invisible.
Sūtra: aphorism.
svādhyāya: study.
svarūpa: essence, essential nature.
tapas: austerity or simplicity.
tat: That.

Upaniṣads: Ancient texts dealing with the ultimate truth and its realisation.

vairāgya : dispassion, uncolouredness.
vāsanā: subtle desire.
Vāsiṣṭha: Sage
vīrya: seminal energy, strength, power.
vicāra: enquiry.
videha: bodiless.
vikalpa: imagination.
vikṣepa: tossing of the mind.
viṣaya: object of perception or enjoyment.
viśeṣa: a special experience.
vitarka: logic, counter-argument.
vṛtti: thought wave.
vyādhi: disease.

yama: self-control or virtue; the God of Death.
yoga: union.
Yoga Vāsiṣṭha: An ancient Hindu scripture; Sage Vāsiṣṭha's teaching to Lord Rāma.
Yoga Sūtras: Patanjali's aphorisms; the basis of Raja Yoga.

INDEX OF SŪTRAS

na tat svābhāsāṁ dṛśyatvāt IV. 19
nimittaṁ aprayojakaṁ prakṛtīnāṁ varaṇa hedas tu tataḥ kṣetrikavat IV. 3
nirmāṇa cittāny asmitā mātrāt IV. 4
nirvicāra vaiśāradye 'dhyātma prasādaḥ I. 47
paramā 'ṇu parama mahattvānto 'sya vaśīkāraḥ I. 40
parārthatvāt svārtha saṁyamāt puruṣa jñānaṁ III. 35
pariṇāma tāpa saṁskāra duḥkhair guṇavṛtti virodhāc ca duḥkham eva sarva ṁ vivekinaḥ II. 15
pariṇāma traya saṁyamād atītā 'nāgata jñānaṁ III. 16
pariṇāmai 'katvād vastu tattvaṁ IV. 14
pracchardana vidhāraṇābhyāṁ vā prāṇasya I. 34
prakāśa kriyā stithi śilaṁ bhūte 'ndriyātmakaṁ bhogā 'pavargārthaṁ dṛśyaṁ I I. 18
pramāṇaviparyaya vikalpa nidrā smṛtayaḥ I. 6
prasaṁkhyāne 'py akusīdasya sarvathā viveka khyāter dharma meghaḥ samā dhiḥ IV. 29
pratibhād vā sarvaṁ III. 33
pratyakṣā 'numānā "gamāḥ pramāṇāni I. 7
pratyayasya para citta jñānaṁ III. 19
pravṛtti bhede prayojakaṁ cittam ekam anekeṣāṁ IV. 5
pravṛtty āloka nyāsāt sūkṣma vyavahita viprakṛṣṭa jñānaṁ III. 25
prayatna śaithilyā 'nanta samāpattibhyāṁ II. 47
puruṣārthaśūnyānāṁ guṇānāṁ prati prasavaḥ kaivalyaṁ svarūpa pratiṣṭhā vā citiśakter iti IV. 34
ṛtaṁbharā tatra prajñā I. 48
rūpa lāvaṇya bala vajrasaṁhananatvāni kāya saṁpat III. 46
śabda jñānā 'nupātī vastu-śūnyo vikalpaḥ I. 9
śabdā 'rtha pratyayānām itare 'tarā 'dhyāsāt saṁkaras tat pravibhāga saṁya māt sarva bhūta ruta jñānaṁ III. 17
sadā jñātāś citta vṛttayas tat prabhoḥ puruṣasyā 'pariṇāmitvāt IV. 18
samādhi bhāvanārthaḥ kleśa tanū karaṇārthaś ca II. 2
samādhi siddhir īśvara praṇidhānāt II. 45
samāna jayāj jvalanaṁ III. 40
saṁskāra sākṣātkaraṇāt pūrva jāti jñānaṁ III. 18
saṁtoṣād anuttamaḥ sukha lābhaḥ II. 42
śānto 'ditā 'vyapadeśya dharmā 'nupātī dharmī III. 14
śauca santoṣa tapaḥ svādhyāye 'svara praṇidhānāni niyamāḥ II. 32
śaucāt svā 'ṅga jugupsā parair asaṁsargaḥ II. 40
sa pūrveṣām api guruḥ kālenā 'navacchedāt I. 26
sa tu dīrgha kāla nairantarya satkārā "sevito dṛḍhabhūmiḥ I. 14
sarvārthatai 'kāgratayoḥ kṣayo 'dayau cittasya samādhi pariṇāmaḥ III. 11

tapaḥ svādhyāye 'śvara praṇidhānāni kriyā yogaḥ II. 1
tārakaṁ sarva viṣayaṁ sarvathā viṣayaṁ akramaṁ ce 'ti vivekajaṁ jñānaṁ I II. 54
tāsāṁ anāditvaṁ cā 'śiṣo nityatvāt IV. I0
tasmin sati śvāsa praśvāsayor gati vicchedaḥ prāṇāyāmaḥ II. 49
tasya bhūmiṣu viniyogaḥ III. 6
tasya hetur avidyā II. 24
tasyā 'pi nirodhe sarva nirodhān nirbījaḥ samādhiḥ I. 51
tasya praśāntavāhitā saṁskārāt III. 10
tasya saptadhā prānta bhūmiḥ prajñā II. 27
tasya vācakaḥ praṇavaḥ I. 27
tataḥ kleśa karma nivṛttiḥ IV. 30
tataḥ kṛtārthānāṁ pariṇāmakrama samāptir guṇānāṁ IV. 32
tataḥ kṣīyate prakāśā 'varaṇaṁ II. 52
tataḥ paramā vaśyate 'ndriyāṇāṃ II. 55
tataḥ prātibha śrāvaṇa vedanā 'darśā 'svāda vārtā jāyante III. 36
tataḥ pratyak cetanā 'dhigamo 'py antarāyā 'bhāvaś ca I. 29
tataḥ punaḥ śānto 'ditau tulya pratyayau cittasyai 'kāgratā pariṇāmaḥ III. 12
tat paraṁ puruṣakhyāter guṇa vaitṛṣṇyaṁ I. 16
tat pratiṣedhārtham ekatattvā 'bhyāsaḥ I. 32
tatas tad vipākā 'nuguṇānāṁ evā 'bhivyakttir vāsanānāṁ IV. 8
tato dvandvā 'nabhighātaḥ II. 48
tato ṇimādi prādur bhāvaḥ kāya saṁpat tad dharmā 'nabhighātaś ca III. 45
tato manojavitvaṁ vikaraṇa bhāvaḥ pradhāna jayaś ca III. 48
tatra dhyānajam anāśayaṁ IV. 6
tatra niratiśayaṁ sarvajña bījaṁ I. 25
tatra pratyayai 'katānatā dhyānaṁ III. 2
tatra śabdā 'rtha jñāna vikalpaiḥ saṁkīrṇā savitarkā samāpattiḥ I. 42
tatra sthitau yatno 'bhyāsaḥ I. 13
te hlāda paritāpa phalāḥ puṇyā 'puṇya hetutvāt II. 14
te pratiprasava heyāḥ sūkṣmāḥ II. 10
te samādhāv upasargā vyutthāne siddhayaḥ III. 37
te vyakta sūkṣmā guṇātmānaḥ IV. 13
tīvra saṁvegānām āsannaḥ I. 21
trayaṁ antaraṅgaṁ pūrvebhyaḥ III. 7
trayam ekatra saṁyamaḥ III. 4
udāna jayāj jala paṇka kaṇṭakādiṣv asaṅga utkrāntiś ca III. 39
vastu sāṁye citta bhedāt tayor vibhakttaḥ panthāḥ IV. 15
viṣayavatī vā pravṛttir utpannā manasaḥ stithi nibandhanī I. 35
viśeṣa darśina ātmabhāva bhāvanā vinivṛttiḥ IV. 25
viśeṣā 'viśeṣa liṅgamātrā 'liṅgāni guṇaparvāṇi II. 19